THE CIRC

THE CIRCUS ANIMALS

James Plunkett

ARROW BOOKS

Arrow Books Limited
20 Vauxhall Bridge Road, London SW1V 2SA

An imprint of the Random Century Group

London Melbourne Sydney Auckland Johannesburg
and agencies throughout the world

First published in Great Britain by Hutchinson 1990
Arrow edition 1991

© James Plunkett 1990

Printed and bound in Great Britain by
Cox & Wyman Ltd, Reading

ISBN 0 09 971150 8

To my daughter
Valerie
with love and gratitude

Aunt Amy was very excited but unsure that she wished to look at animals going through a repertoire of tricks because she had read that teaching these tricks sometimes involved an element of cruelty. On the other hand, as a child she had adored the circus clowns and felt she would enjoy their activities as much as ever.

'A Flask of Brandy'

And on my way I saw:
Item, a clown who was on stilts;
A bear saluting with a paw;
Two pairs of dancing dogs in kilts;
Eight midget ponies in a single file;
A very piccolo of ponies;
Then the princess far off in her smile;
And the seven beautiful distant ladies:
And then—

Padraic Fallon

Contents

Part One

Chapter 1

On Ascension Thursday, a Holy Day of Obligation, Lemuel Cox fulfilled his duty by attendance at the eleven-thirty Mass in the Church of Saint Kevin in the Parish of Edmundscourt. The journey of four miles or so was made as usual in Miley Langan's pony and trap. He enjoyed it even more this time. The sun shone warmly. The river, winding side by side with the long driveway from his house to the entrance gates, mirrored white wisps of cloud and yellow gorse. Beyond the gates the mountains lent their company to the public road for most of the journey and, crossing the bridge into the town itself, Lemuel and Miley were greeted by a loitering group of locals who waved as the pony and trap rattled past.

Edmundscourt, an estate town and an old market centre, retained its ordered look, though the estate that had brought it into being had surrendered long since to agitations, boycotts, outrages and various land reform acts. The big house itself was now a boarding school for Catholic young ladies of the more comfortable classes, run by the Sisters of Mercy. Their red blazers with the school crest were in evidence here and there along the footpaths. They would have a free day to mark the feast, Lemuel Cox knew. He could see no sign of the grey tunics and blue blouses of the young ladies from the Protestant boarding school, but for them, perhaps, free days were not invariably granted.

Later on, while kneeling at Mass and conscious of the packed congregation and the unusual hustle and bustle in the streets outside, Lemuel Cox began to feel a need for some closer contact with his fellow beings than was his custom. It was a desire which occasionally troubled him. It could be lonely to be restricted for too long to the company of his only sister and that of Mrs Holohan, their housekeeper.

When Mass was over and the mood persisted, he decided to do something about it by having lunch in the hotel. He despatched Miley Langan off on small errands and telephoned his sister to let her know. Then he ordered a glass of sherry. While sipping it at the window he decided to write the letter he had been contemplating for a week or more. Hotel notepaper lay already on the table in front of him. He uncapped his pen and wrote the name *Francis McDonagh* on the topmost sheet. Then, after a few seconds of thought, he began:

My dear Frank . . .

He was sealing the envelope when Miley returned.

'I got the eggs for Miss Stella,' Miley reported.

'Good,' Lemuel Cox said, handing Miley the letter. 'Take this and post it off. I have another short note to write while you're doing so. Then when you get back I'll have lunch sent to you in the bar.'

'I could wait until you have it done and post both of them,' Miley suggested.

'No,' Lemuel Cox told him. 'I'll post the second one myself.'

'You'll want a stamp for it then?'

'A stamp won't be necessary,' Lemuel replied.

Beyond the iron railings of St Stephen's Green, under a blue sky and a warm sun, the bell of the Catholic university church began to sound. The familiar tones brought him to a standstill. Frank McDonagh remembered the rope hanging down through the rafters of the main porchway and the indignity to be endured if, when it fell to his turn to operate it, he misjudged and heaved on the rope too vigorously. Its upstroke would hoist his schoolboy weight irresistibly until it dragged him first to his toes and then several inches clear of the ground. A couple of times he got stuck in mid-air and had to be retrieved physically. On such occasions the glass panels of the inner entrance door would mirror for him his adult rescuer and his own helplessly rotating figure in white surplice and purple soutane. His canonicals, his father used to call them. When not in use they hung with a line of others in the long press in the vestry, a card above the hook identifying them in his still unformed handwriting: *Francis McDonagh*. How long ago? Fifteen years? Seventeen years? Never mind. A long time.

The pathways, the plots, the fountains, the flowerbeds flaunting their colours, these were as familiar as the bell strokes. So too was the odour of humus under the tangle of branches at the edge of the pond. In the sunlight beyond the branches the ducks moved placidly, a rib of water widening behind each.

It was Ascension Thursday. The vestments, his missal told him, would be white. At the entrance to the Pro-Cathedral, intermittently visible through a forest of moving legs, a notice board propped against a holy water font announced to him in scarlet letters:

> Holy Year 1950
> Grand Pilgrimage to Rome.

He edged his way in. In the heat and the shimmering air, heads bowed, knees genuflected, the choir spun intricate webs of sixteenth century Italian polyphony. He glanced at his watch for no reason at all, then searched his missal for the Proper of the Time and marked it with a ribbon of green silk. That done, he addressed his by no means unwavering attention to the proceedings.

The red and white pole above the entrance belonged to the hairdresser who rented the ground floor. Frank, passing beneath it into a hall that was haunted by odours of lotions and shampoos, climbed the stairway to the second floor where a frosted door bore a nameplate:

> Kenny, Morrissey & Co.
> Publishing, Editing, Advertising Agents.
> Inquiries.

The door opposite proffered further information:

> Kenny, Morrissey & Co.
> Building Trade Journal; Field & Farm Gazette;
> Laughter Parade; Construction And Allied
> Workers' Union Bulletin; etc. etc.

He entered the door on the left, noting as he did so that Miss Downey was absent from her post behind the Inquiries panel. Jackson, who was reading his morning paper, glanced up briefly to say, 'Margaret phoned.'

'How long ago?'

'About half an hour. Nothing urgent she said. And Morrissey was looking for you. He's beyond in his office.'

'I'll phone Margaret first.'

But there was no response.

'She's probably at Mass,' he said, replacing the receiver.

'On Church holidays,' Jackson complained, 'this bloody city grinds to a halt.'

'We are a God-fearing people,' said Frank, smiling.

The room's one window was wide and overlooked the street. He sat under it at his desk on which a number of incomplete drawings lay scattered, and began to examine them one by one. After an interval Jackson looked up again and said, 'You ought to go across to Morrissey.'

'I'd forgotten,' Frank said, rising quickly.

He made his way back to the office across the landing where Morrissey was seated at his desk. Morrissey left his pen aside.

'How is Margaret?' he asked. 'It's getting close, isn't it?'

'Any day now.'

'Take a chair. I've an appointment down town so I'll be as brief as I can.'

Frank sat down.

'You were asking for a salary increase some time ago and I've been thinking over it. It seems reasonable – especially in the circumstances. The trouble is – Mr Kenny.'

'Have you spoken to him?'

'Not yet. But I intend to in a day or two, and I feel that if I were able to tell him you had offered to take on some extra responsibility, the chances might be greatly improved. For instance, if you took on editorial supervision for one or two of the magazines it would take some of the pressure off Kenny and myself.'

'I've no experience of that kind of work,' Frank said.

'There's nothing to it. The time-consuming part is looking after the layout and pastedown and I can show you that in a few hours. I'm certain Kenny would be glad to fork out an extra two or three pounds a week in return.'

'I'd jump at the chance.'

'Good. The other matter was those political cartoons of yours. I showed some of them to Con Andrews and he thinks he might be interested in them for the *Review*. I'll follow that up as soon as I can. Meanwhile I must go. I'm almost late as it is.'

Morrissey struggled painfully to his feet, bracing both hands on the desk top for leverage. He carried a hip injury from childhood. Frank handed him his walking stick from the corner and held open the door.

'I suppose the streets are packed,' Morrissey said.

'Choc-a-bloc,' Frank told him. 'Ascension Thursday.' Morrissey delayed to address the ceiling.

'Shite.'

6

Wielding his stick and lurching from side to side in his haste, he clattered his way down the stairs.

Lemuel Cox told Miley to drop him at the entrance gate. The walk, he said, would help his digestion. He waited until the pony and trap had gone out of sight before commencing his journey. The driveway, which was unsurfaced, had its share of potholes. He took pains to avoid them. Under his feet the clay was baked hard – it had been an unusually dry May – and on his right the river continued to mirror high clouds and the blazing yellow of gorse. He walked slowly, stooping a little beneath his seventy-two years, until he reached a stand of trees grouped together on a spit of land reaching into the river. Here he paused and looked carefully about him. When he was satisfied there was no one to observe him he picked his way across exposed roots until he found what he was seeking. It was a gnarled beech with a deep hollow bole. The trees surrounding it, he knew, would screen him from anyone who might chance along the path. He inserted a hand into the bole and groped about until he found and removed first a piece of canvas sacking, and then the metal box it had been covering. He opened the box and, among the several letters it already contained, he placed the second note he had written in the hotel. It bore no address but had the name Norris Curtis inscribed on the envelope. He closed the box, restored it to its hiding place of many years and replaced the piece of sacking. He took up the shopping bag he had been carrying and picked his way from the dimness back to the path and the light, where grove and river basked in a sunlit emptiness.

Frank inserted his key in the door and let himself in. There was no one at home. He knew it immediately but called down the hallway for her just the same. As he did so the telephone rang. He went to it.

'Hello?'

'Frank. Has anyone been in touch?'

It was Evelyn.

'No,' he said. 'And Margaret isn't home. She telephoned me at the office but I was out at Mass. Then after lunch I had calls to make that took up the whole afternoon. Where the hell is she? And where is Paul?'

'Little Paul is here,' Evelyn said. 'She left him with me while she went to Mass, but she didn't return. Then the nursing home phoned. You have a new baby daughter. I think she was born in the taxi. But everything is fine and they're both well. You should go in to her.'

'What about Paul?'

'I'll keep him for the night.'

'Will he stay?'

'At a year and eight months or so he's hardly going to stomp out, is he?'

'I mean, will he be trouble? I'm sure—'

'I don't mind. Poor Margaret. Two in less then two years. Tell her Paul is safe. And give her my love.'

Margaret said Evelyn always exaggerated. It hadn't actually happened in the taxi. It just started in it. Or a little before. But, anyway, everything was fine. They brought the child in for him to see. He took it shyly and uncertainly. Margaret smiled at his unease.

'Your new daughter.'

'She's lovely, Peggy. A sister for Paul.'

'She wasn't supposed to happen though, was she?'

'No. But she has. And we'll manage.'

'I hope so. But she makes bits of the credibility of natural birth control,' Margaret said. 'So much for bloody Halliday Sutherland.'

Simon Morrissey knew the world about him and had learned how to limp his way through it with fortitude and determination. His experience as a boy (he often hinted) had been confined almost exclusively to his father's horsebreeding business at their stud somewhere among the rich, pastoral expanses of County Tipperary, and had been of no help at all when he set about finding a place for himself in the City. The hip injury, which had occurred in childhood when the horse he was riding either threw him or rolled over on him, had led to long spells in hospital that left him short on the customary educational qualifications for landing a job.

Nevertheless, he would admit, hospitalisation had provided the opportunity to read through a range of subjects which gave nourishment to a naturally lively and inquisitive mind. A course in journalism and another in advertising resulted, after a couple of lean years, in a flow of articles and ideas which began to find acceptance. These dealt predominantly with the leisure pursuits of the gentry and their recurring sporting seasons: fishing, grouse shooting, partridge shooting, hunting, cricket. Some of the stories he had tried his hand at around the same time found favour with the literary magazines and attracted mild interest also, so that he began to be noticed in what were regarded as intellectual circles. Even his physical handicap turned into an advantage of a kind. It helped to distinguish him from the generality and led to his first worthwhile opening in advertising, which resulted eventually in his partnership in Kenny's long-established agency. Here his circle widened to include not only literary editors but trade union officials, business interests and political representatives – whose distinguishing characteristics, he soon decided, were hypocrisy, piousness and, in the matter of religion, an automatic and abject conformity with the expectations of society.

He saw no alternative, for the present at any rate, but to go along with them. Conformity was crucial to his livelihood. But though he was careful to express the right sentiments and always nodded his head at the correct moments, he hid behind an apparently comfortable acceptance of the prevailing order a cold, and at times barely containable, contempt.

Francis McDonagh

Avonmore House
May 18th, 1950
(Ascension Thursday)

My dear Frank,
You will be surprised to have this letter after so long a time, and from someone by now so far outside your world. Let me explain.
Since the death of my dear friend Norris Curtis, in spite of the stretch of years, I have felt time after time this longing to meet again and talk with someone who knew him. The same is true of your own dear father. He and Norris and I – all three of us – were once such stalwart friends.
Do not let them tell you that time is the cure-all. Time brings age; age in turn adds its own problems – lack of mobility is one of them. At least for me it is. Nowadays I must rely on Miley Langan's pony and trap which makes Dublin about as accessible as the moon.
What I am coming to is to ask you to visit me when you can, and as soon as may be convenient. My sister and I are hardly ever away. Stella, poor soul, is feeling the attrition of age even more severely. But then she is three years my senior.
The days are turning benign and I think you would find the cycle

run rewarding. The gorse and hawthorn are in bloom. Everything is fresh and pleasing. A telephone call will be sufficient.

Please give my kindest regards to your mother who was so good to Norris in his last illness and so hospitable to all of us throughout so many years.

I hope to hear soon that you will come.

Yours sincerely,
Lemuel Cox

Margaret was dubious.

'What's he like, this Lemuel Cox?' she asked.

'For years his father tried to point him in the direction of the priesthood. He resisted. But a lot of it took hold.'

'That isn't very promising, is it?'

'He doesn't push it at you.'

'And Norris Curtis?' She stopped suddenly. 'What peculiar names—'

She sounded more uncertain still.

Chapter 2

Lemuel Cox lived quietly with his unmarried sister in their remote house at the end of the driveway which followed the course of the river almost bend by bend. The remoteness of the house seemed to increase as the years accumulated. He found it worthwhile to marshal his activities and spread them over the available hours. In the mornings after breakfast he worked in the study that had once been his father's, usually on notes about local history and lore which he had been acquiring, for no particular reason, over a lifetime. After lunch he would read the morning paper (if it had come) and then, the weather being suitable, he would either work a little in the garden or take a long solitary country walk. In the evenings, when they had eaten, he would listen to music on the gramophone or on the radio, or play it for himself on the piano while his sister knitted and listened. She was now seventy-five, just three years older than he and unable to get about without her stick and the support of the furniture. Once they had been good friends, but isolation and her progressive incapacity combined to drive them apart. They spoke to each other but they seldom conversed. Her incessant knitting while he was playing especially irritated him. How could a mind bent on the rituals of dropping and purling lend adequate attention to Mozart or Beethoven? If he selected Chopin (a favourite of hers) she would sometimes stop. But it was when, stirred by a sentimental recollection of his own, he rooted in the piano stool to produce albums of melodies now crumbling from fifty years or more of damp that the knitting needles were left totally aside. These old tunes touched her so deeply that he would wonder at the sudden, pathetic transformation of her features. That was her nature. She had stored the petals of long-dried-up bouquets lovingly between the pages of the romantic novels of her girlhood. She also kept a collection of old paper fans on her dressing table. They were all that time had left her of yesteryear's house parties and theatre visits.

But it was not this looking backwards for a lost life that irritated him. After all, he harboured his own soft-spoken ghosts of times past. No. It was her resistance to any deviation of habit whatsoever. As when, near the end of the night, his customary pouring of a glass or two of whiskey for himself drew her unfailing disapproval. And why? Simply because their long-dead father, though he would indulge on occasion himself, had disallowed the practice because he feared its addictive potentialities. On that score, however, she no longer allowed her feelings to show. She knew it did no good and only made him more disagreeable than ever. He had seen to that.

Sometime near the end of June, when he had returned from yet another trip to the village with Miley Langan and was playing the piano after their evening meal, the telephone rang and he went to get it. On his return he said, 'You've heard me speak of young Frank McDonagh—?'

Curiosity put a temporary stop to the knitting needles. 'I remember,' she said, 'that your friend Norris Curtis and his parents lived together.'

'Not together. In the same house – but in separate flats.'

'That is what I meant.'

'Some time ago I asked him to come here to visit me. He has just phoned to say he will.'

'Will he find his way?'

'It occurred to me to give him directions.'

'It will be most agreeable,' she said, and to show she understood, 'you can talk to him about his father and poor Norris. You'll like to do that.'

'And I suggested he should bring his wife—'

'His wife? You never mentioned a wife.'

'At some stage or other he acquired one. Many young men do.'

'Of course.'

'It isn't at all remarkable—'

'I suppose not,' she said.

She ventured no more.

But later on, as always, her eyes followed with imperceptible scrutiny when he moved to the drinks cabinet. Even when the bottle and the glass brushed together and released a little clink of surprise she kept an impassive face. Nevertheless her disapproval reached him. He would have liked her company in a glass now and then, but she was not partial so that was that. He rooted in the piano stool for some Bach and began to play it. She was not partial to Bach either.

The room Mrs Holohan showed them into was long and low, its walls white, the wide window looking out on a sheltered garden. Although the sunlight streaming in through the glass was warm, a fire burned in the grate and woodsmoke was a wisp in the air, the merest ghost. The magazines on the sidetable included the literary monthly the *Bell* and its newest rival, *Envoy*. Margaret also recognised two regular Catholic publications: the quarterly of the Jesuits, *Studies*, and the Dominican monthly, *Blackfriars*, which Frank was about to pick up when Lemuel Cox came in. He had been down the garden and the housekeeper had had to search for him, he explained. His sister was taking her afternoon rest but would join them later. He offered them drinks and hoped they had had a pleasant cycle run.

A tallish, thin man, Margaret noted, with a mild and decorous manner.

They both declined.

'Then let me show you around.'

'If you wish to speak with Frank,' Margaret offered, 'I can quite easily look after myself while you do so.'

But he said the afternoon was far too pleasant to spend indoors.

In sunlit silence he led them along the driveway until it entered a wood and narrowed to a track between ripening frocan bushes and fading gorse blossom. He stopped at a point where the river, foaming over a rocky shelf, formed a miniature waterfall and spread out into a pool of golden brown water. They viewed it from among the trees.

'When we were children,' he said, 'my sister Stella and my two brothers Godwin and Jonathan, used to swim here. It was our Pooka's Pool.'

It was hard to imagine Lemuel Cox playing in a world of goblins and pookas. He seemed to be experiencing some difficulty with the thought himself and stared at the silver ribbon of the river as though in disbelief.

At last he beckoned them forward and they continued, clearing the wood and walking in file along the narrow pathway that led to other favourite haunts of his childhood. Ahead of them the valley widened out and sloped down gently to scattered thickets and broad, well-fenced fields, but at that point he felt it was time to get back to his sister.

She was waiting for them with Mrs Holohan in close attendance. To Margaret she spoke mainly about the city shops, not as they were today (she would be utterly lost, she confessed), but as they used to be when she was young and liked to sit in one of the coffee shops, Bewley's perhaps, or Robert's, surrounded by bustle and chatter.

Her talk with Frank was of politics. The present government, she feared, was determined to adopt the welfare state ideology of Great Britain, in spite of the repeated warnings and disapproval of the Catholic hierarchy. Even in Mr Costello's party sinister left-wing elements were at work, of that she was quite convinced. It seemed very strange to her and she had never thought to hear herself confess it, but she now wondered if the defeat of Mr de Valera had been so desirable after all.

'And now, Lemuel,' she suggested, 'you wished to have your little talk with Frank. Margaret and I can keep each other company.'

They retired to the study. It was a place of whitewashed walls and bare, polished floorboards. A plainly carpeted bench occupied one side of the fireplace. A crucifix dominated the mantlepiece. Along one wall, under a small window, stood a narrow bed with an iron headrail and rough blankets. In the opposite corner a harmonium supported photographs of two young men in British Army uniforms of the first world war.

'My brothers,' Lemuel Cox explained. 'This is Godwin. He died at the Somme in 1916. Jonathan here survived a little longer. He was killed in Flanders in 1917. It was on the 27th of July and it was his 27th birthday. The coincidence, for some reason, made the news even more distressing.'

He went down on his knees to coax some life into the smouldering fire. On bookshelves to the left and right of his head, Shakespeare, Swift and Ibsen were the secular authors. The rest were uncompromising representatives of religion and the Ancient Fathers: Cyprian of Carthage, Augustine of Hippo, Ignatius of Antioch, the Sermons of Saint Chrysostom, Saint Basil's Homilies, a study of the liturgy of the Greek Church—

Lemuel Cox, having repaired the fire as best he could, rejoined him.

'My father's books,' he explained. 'To me they were quite overpowering but he seemed to relish their company. He was excessively religious, of course, and a follower of the ideas of Edward Martyn. They campaigned together at the beginning of the century to have the music of Palestrina restored to the Mass in Ireland. They also agitated for the reform of clerical dress which they urged should be in the Roman style and confined rigidly to the cassock and the shovel hat. In the end they obtained their Palestrina, but at the cost of having to endow a permanent Palestrina choir in the Pro-Cathedral. In the matter of clerical dress they got nowhere. To the Irish cleric, cassocks and shovel hats were expressions of the operatic vulgarity of the Italian nation. Won't you sit down?'

Frank went to the fire and did so.

'Everything here is much as he left it,' Lemuel Cox added as he joined him.

'You wanted to speak to me about Mr Curtis,' Frank prompted.

'Ah yes. Norris. I wrote to you for that reason. Now that you're here it seems sufficient just to bring him to memory.'

Nevertheless he went on to talk at length: of his once apparently frequent visits to the Curtis bookshop on the quays, so dusty and disordered and smelling of second-hand volumes in their ancient leather covers; of visits to various recreational events with Norris and Frank's father, especially to rugby internationals at Lansdowne Road, a thing he would never have thought of doing if left to himself. It was clear that he was a very lonely man groping back through the years for a world he had lost somewhere along the way.

'Some time ago a strange thing happened,' he said. 'I was walking by the river and saw Norris. There is this grove of trees and he was standing by it looking at me with a smile on his face. I thought he was about to speak so I stood still and remained silent. He continued to smile and then, on an instant, he had gone. Later I had a Mass offered for him. Then I wrote to you. I hope you didn't mind.'

'Not at all,' Frank said.

'When I had written to you, I decided to write to Norris as well.'

'To Norris?'

'You think that was eccentric?'

Frank hesitated.

'If it helps . . .' he said.

'It helps very much.'

'Then – why not?'

'As you say – why not. As a matter of fact, I've been writing to the dead through most of my life.'

When they rejoined Margaret and his sister he remained conversational and relaxed. He even sat at the piano to play for them. Briefly, though. One must not overdo it.

They began the cycle run home much later than they had intended.

It was a balmy June night, with the hedges sentinel and sweet-smelling and the stars spread high in the sky.

The air in their bedroom hung warm and heavy after their absence and the undisturbed heat of the day. Frank, opening the window to cool the room, heard the hall door being closed as Margaret thanked the babysitter and saw her out.

'I put the bikes away,' he said, when she came in. 'What about Paul?'

'He's fine.'

'And Aoife?'

'Fed and in bed', she said, 'both of them will sleep – I hope.'

He had not turned on the light nor did she. He sat on his own bed by the window, listening across the darkness of the room to her preparations for the night and looking out at the star-crowded sky.

'We haven't slept together since Aoife,' he said. 'Isn't it all right by now?'

'Not tonight,' she said.

He continued to regard the stars.

'I'm tired,' she said. 'The cycle run was harder than I expected. Besides, it isn't the right time.'

She meant it was not, according to the Halliday Sutherland system of birth control, her infertile period. They followed the Sutherland system because it was tolerated by the Church as being in accord with the Natural Law and, therefore, not sinful. The trouble with Vatican Roulette, as it was known, was that it was highly unreliable.

He lay in the darkness weighing her reply. The cycle run, the right time? Doubt formed. But he did not care to express it. Not yet. He knew, however, that she was not yet ready for sleep. It communicated itself across the room. After a while she stirred and said, 'It isn't really because of the bicycle trip.'

'I thought not.'

'And the time is all right according to the system. Which means, as we know, that it could be all wrong.'

That was true.

'You see what I mean?'

He saw what she meant.

'I simply can't believe any longer in bloody Halliday Sutherland and his theories about safe periods.'

She waited.

'Can you?' she asked.

She was waiting for his answer.

'No,' he said.

And where, both wondered, was that going to leave them?

Lemuel Cox banked down the fire to keep it in for the morning and wheeled his sister's chair to her bedroom where she would manage her disrobing in private.

'I find it strange,' he remarked, out of the blue, 'that she should be called Margaret.'

'Why strange?'

'I think of Margaret Penrose—'

'But Miss Penrose was called Margot.'

'It's the same thing. It struck me almost immediately how alike they would look if one could see them together. Don't you think?'

'I can't remember,' his sister said, 'it's such a long time ago.'

But Lemuel Cox could, clearly and painfully. Her presence lingered everywhere: by the river, in the woodlands, on the winding mountain track. Margaret Penrose. He had written to her through the secrecy of his metal box many times. He believed he would find her again. In all her loveliness and her tenderness. Some day.

Chapter 3

After an interval of almost three months Frank was able to bring home some good news. Morrissey's efforts had suddenly borne fruit. He was to receive a retainer from Kenny of four pounds a month for submitting ideas to the agency's own magazine *Laughter Parade* and, in addition, individual payments for humorous copy accepted for publication. He would be paid a further five pounds a month for taking on responsibility for getting the monthly issues of the *Bulletin of the Allied Construction Workers' Union* out on schedule. The *Review* was beginning to look hopeful too. It was on the point of making room for a trial run of a short series of his political cartoons – no offer in the matter of fees as yet, but it would receive attention.

The improvement began when Kenny was pleased enough with his handling of the request for ideas for *Laughter Parade* to arrange to pay the regular monthly retainer. A little later the *Review* responded favourably to the satirical element in his political cartoons, commissioned a series of them and then extended the run.

They were able to change their accommodation to a more comfortable and convenient house in Rathmines where Mrs Cleary, the old lady who owned it, was content to occupy the two basement rooms and rent the rest to them. She was unusual in a landlady in that she enjoyed the children and liked to babysit, a useful convenience when the extra money made it possible to get out together at least a couple of times in the week.

But their improved circumstances, if they helped to ease one part of the problem of Aoife's unscheduled arrival, could do nothing to resolve the moral dilemma it had given rise to: how to regulate the size of their family while still remaining within the teaching of their Church. By varying their Confessors every time they went to the

Sacrament they canvassed the widest range of advice. Some responded curtly and unyieldingly. Others showed sympathy and understanding but remained equally immovable. For the time being they practised abstinence when they could and *coitus interruptus* when they could not.

It was now late into autumn and the narrow pathways around Mount Pleasant Square were thickly carpeted with fallen leaves which scattered and spun in fairy circles when the little winds made ambush. Their multi-coloured patterns, the autumnal skies, the serried spears of the iron railings enclosing the square and the rustle of the leaves underfoot as he walked the last few hundred yards home never failed to stir Frank's memory. Margaret had lived in the Rathmines neighbourhood in the days of their courtship and it was territory he and she had wandered constantly: on their way to the cinema in Rathmines or Ranelagh, or further afield to Terenure; on their evening rambles along the banks of the Dodder River from Dartry to Rathfarnham or, in the longer days of summer, their hikes by way of Templeogue and Brittas into the wilder mountain stretches of Glenasmole and Glencree. It was a world already well sown with reminders of their earliest tenderness and happiness, one into which they felt they could settle with easy faith in their marriage and trust in their love.

There was a world outside, however, which was poised to threaten both. They had walked in the autumn evening by Palmerston Park on their way to the Dropping Well for a drink. The leaves were piled along the pathways of Temple Road and Richmond Avenue and a red sun, low in the sky, made smoky silhouettes of the almost bare trees. Near Milltown railway station a train on its way to Bray dragged its string of lighted carriages past the fence bordering the road they were walking on with a speed that hardly outpaced theirs and with as little noise. It stopped briefly at the wayside station before moving off slowly to cross the long bridge spanning the Dodder River.

'You're very quiet,' Margaret remarked when it had left the evening to them once more.

'I know,' he said, 'I'll tell you when we're sitting down.'

Their drinks were brought in and she looked expectantly at him.

He said, 'On my way home this evening I thought I'd slip in to confession. I hadn't bargained on the reception I was going to receive.'

He had guessed almost from the start that he was in trouble. The priest, elderly, heavy breathing and so stout that the confession box could hardly accommodate his bulk, grunted continuously as Frank went through the customary procedures of asking the priest's blessing, stating the length of time since he had last confessed, and making the ritual self-accusation of sinfulness. Then he got to the matter of *coitus interruptus*. The grunting stopped.

'How many times?'

'Three times, Father.'

There was a silence in which he could feel a swelling tide of anger.

'That is the sin of Onanism. It is told in Genesis that Onan spilled his seed upon the ground, a deliberate and blasphemous act so abhorrent to Almighty God that he punished Onan with death.'

Frank said nothing.

'What led you to commit this most abominable sin?'

'We are trying to space out our family.'

'How many children have you?'

'Two, Father.'

'Two. You have only begun. My own mother, God be good to her, had nine and thought no more about it. How many were there in your own family?'

'Six of us, Father,'

'And did your mother complain?'

'We're barely three years married, Father. Our first child is only two years of age. Our second is four months—'

'What did you think you were marrying for if you were unwilling to raise children?'

Frank again remained silent. He was not expected to answer.

'You must shun that perverted practice and put it out of your life. Abstain from the marriage act until you are ready for more issue. Frequent prayer will sustain you and strengthen you. But if you find you are not prepared to make such a sacrifice, if through weakness and selfishness you are unable to forego your indulgence of the flesh, then there is the natural system of birth control which the Church is prepared to tolerate to a limited degree. You and your wife should take instruction in that.'

'We have tried the rhythm system but it failed, Father. My wife is frightened of it. She refuses to trust it any more.'

'She refuses? And who, may I ask, is the master in your house? Is it your wife? Who wears the trousers? You must have the gumption to insist on what is yours by right of marriage.'

Frank wondered how he was supposed to insist. By force? Rape? He kept his head bowed and detached himself from what was being said, concentrating instead on that state of self-surrender which was required for the full efficacy of the Sacrament.

He was given absolution on this occasion, on the condition that in future he would reject all solutions other than total abstention or the natural method tolerated by the Church. And he must be man enough and master enough to manage his wife. For his penance he was to recite the rosary in honour of the Immaculate Conception and to frequently invoke Our Blessed Mother's help as he went about his daily affairs.

'You poor darling,' Margaret said. 'What a stupid pious old bully.'

'Never mind, I stepped into the wrong confession box. Have another drink.'

'I certainly will.'

Later she said, in a voice pitched low from anxiety, 'What are we to do?'

'I've no idea.'

'I can't go back to relying on that cockeyed rhythm system.'

'I don't expect you to.'

'I'd go out of mind with worry.'

He nodded his head.

'It seems to me we can't go on sleeping with each other unless we use some more reliable procedure. There are plenty to choose from.'

'There are,' he agreed, 'but they're all forbidden.'

His tone was lugubrious, as though he felt they were beyond serious consideration. She let it rest. For the moment she had said enough.

Morrissey stuck his head around the door early in the afternoon and briefly acknowledged the presence of Jackson and Miss Downey before addressing himself to Frank.

'How are you fixed?'

'Ready right away,' Frank said.

They went down to the street together and set off towards the centre of town. As they were passing the broadcasting building in Henry Street, Morrissey smiled and said, 'If I remember correctly, tonight is to be the big night for our national radio station?'

'Precisely at six o'clock,' Frank answered. 'Jackson disapproves wholeheartedly.'

For over a year the radio authorities and the Archbishop of Dublin had been discussing possible arrangements for broadcasting the Angelus once a day. It was the Archbishop's wish that it should be relayed from the bell of the Pro-Cathedral. He also wished that the first bell be struck precisely at six. Such accuracy made it necessary not just to relay the sound from the broadcasting studios, but to start and control the bell strokes from the studios by remote control. An elaborate mechanism and three underground cables were required to accomplish this.

'It's the cost to the taxpayer that Jackson can't stomach,' Frank added.

Morrissey smiled. They were on their way to the office of the *Review*. Morrissey wanted to call and had suggested that Frank, who knew the editor only through correspondence, should come along to meet him personally.

'You'll find Andrews a bit of a mystery man,' Morrissey warned. 'He was a Brigade Commander in the War of Independence and took the anti-treaty side during the Civil War. Nowadays he has Communist contacts which he does little or nothing to hide. He's not afraid to be unpopular. It helps to make him a good editor.'

But when they got to the *Review* office it was in disarray. Andrews had gone missing. It happened occasionally and unpredictably. On a gas ring, perched dangerously among discarded envelopes, contributors' scripts and outdated copies of the *Review*, O'Halloran, telephone answerer and all-purpose office help, was boiling tea. He was elderly and embittered. There had been a time in the active days of the War of Independence when the editor and he had been on friendly enough terms. Now he was only one of the ex-comrades-in-arms who had been left behind in the peacetime jockeying for position, depending on the patronage of Andrews for a job which kept him barely on the edge of penury. When he was introduced to Frank he shook hands until the name had sunk in and said, 'Ah. Our young cartoonist.'

Then he began his litany of complaint about Andrews, 'He was only supposed to be gone for two days and now it's five.'

'And you don't know where he is?'

'Off plotting some mischief with his cronies, I expect. Do you know any of them?'

'I don't think so,' Morrissey said.

'It wouldn't do you much good if you did. They're a clannish bloody clique. How long is it now since the Civil War ended – twenty-six or twenty-seven years? – and they still stick together like glue. They want everything that's in the country for themselves while the likes of us can go to hell. Everything must go to Number One.'

'I know the kind,' Morrissey offered, deliberately fanning the flames, 'posing as patriots while they feather their nests. You did your bit in the War of Independence yourself, I think?'

'Bedad I did. My bit and more than my bit. But I was young. And I had my principles. And I wasn't on the make. You'll have a cup of tea.'

He found two extra cups and some biscuits. Frank listened from his seat at the window while Morrissey made a game of leading O'Halloran on. From the window he could see Nelson on his pillar poised high above the endlessly interweaving patterns of people and traffic.

'However,' O'Halloran disclosed, with a note of triumph, 'I made him leave your money because I guessed you'd be in for it. I have the cheque in the press there.'

Morrissey expressed pleasure and gratitude.

'And I made him give me my own into my hand too. There's so little of it you'd be hard set to find it if he left it down. I told him so.'

'You did right,' Morrissey said, not believing a word.

'I'll go and get it,' O'Halloran said, and went to rummage in the press for the envelope.

'Quite apart from the cheque I was anxious to see him,' Morrissey said. 'He hasn't said anything so far about his ideas for the winter issues and I need to know.'

'He's been going on again about the Book Censorship Act and campaigning for reform and about having another symposium on young writers. He'd give you a pain in your arse jawing out of him about young writers.'

'Neither topic,' Morrissey agreed, 'is likely to set the Liffey in flames.'

O'Halloran handed over the cheque. 'I know what would,' he said.

'And what is that?'

'Tell the public what goes on here and who he hobnobs with. Self-confessed commies and latterday gunmen. There's letters *ad infinitum* coming in here from them. That fellow for instance – what's his name – O'Mahony – that the Archbishop made it a mortal sin to vote for. There's invitations every other month to visit Moscow—'

'And he tells you about all these?'

'No. But he leaves the correspondence lying around and I take a bloody good squint at the ones with the foreign stamps. There's things I could tell . . .'

Footsteps sounded on the stairs and O'Halloran froze.

'Jesus Christ,' he said, 'it's him. I know that step.'

He ducked quickly over to his desk and picked up a letter. The editor entered as he was absorbed in its contents, his back to the door. Over his shoulder, in a mild and absent-minded tone, he said, 'There you are, Boss. Good to see you.'

Andrews grunted and turned to greet Morrissey.

'Let me introduce Frank McDonagh, the young man who's been supplying those cartoons.'

Andrews and Frank exchanged courtesies. Then Morrissey added, 'I'm anxious to find out what you may have in mind for the winter season.'

'I've been trying to get down to that, Simon. For instance, how about an examination of the dilemma of the young writer in Ireland – a symposium—?'

'It's not very long since we did a series on that.'

'Well, yes. But I was thinking of some kind of new approach. A fresh look—'

'Whatever we do,' Morrissey said anxiously, 'I feel we should get together about it as soon as possible.'

Andrews agreed. He said he would telephone within a few days to fix up a meeting. They must get together.

Down in the street they found the bustle was growing as the working day came to an end and offices began to empty. A warm August sun and the thickening drift of fumes from the traffic made the air dry and hot. The noise level grew and became unpleasant.

'Let's have a drink,' Morrissey suggested. 'If we go as far as Ryan's on the quays we may bump into Joe Dunne. He likes to look in there for a while at this time of evening if he's free.'

But Dunne was not to be found. Instead they were buttonholed by one of the members of the Executive Committee, a city councillor and plumber by trade, noted for his singleminded ambition to become one of Labour's representatives in government, an end he used every available means to secure. Political and trade union colleagues noted him for frequent and uncanny misuse of the Queen's English. He was sitting at the bar listening idly to a radio which was playing in the background, but looked around at their entry and immediately hailed them. He began to make preparations to join them.

'Christ,' Morrissey breathed when he saw what was afoot.

'Who is he?' Frank asked.

'You'll get to know soon enough. He's Peter Brady, generally known as Ballcock. He writes these bloody political diatribes about housing conditions and such like to attract publicity for himself. When he finds out who you are he'll pester you to get them published in the *Bulletin*.'

Ballcock approached their table.

'You'll have a drink?'

'We only slipped in for a quick one,' Morrissey explained.

But Ballcock would countenance no refusal. He sat down beside them.

'I don't think I've had the pleasure—'

'This is Frank McDonagh.'

'Ah. The new man on the *Bulletin*. I've seen you calling in to Joe Dunne on occasions. Pleased to meet you. As a matter of fact I dropped in here myself because I thought Joe might be here. He's working on the agenda for the Delegate Congress and I wanted to beg him for God's sake not to be going out of his way to draw the wrath of the clergy and the Catholic press on himself and the Union. Every time I share a platform with that man I lose a fistful of votes.'

'Joe Dunne,' Morrissey said, 'is a man of forthright habits.'

'He made a right fah pooh a couple of weeks ago,' Ballcock confided. 'While I was unfortunate enough to be acting as chairman for him.'

'A fah what?'

'A fah pooh.' It's French for making a balls of it. He sang the praises of the British welfare state and said it took the ancient enemy to give us a lesson in practical Christianity. I think he's right, of course, but there were four or five priests in the audience and I was on tenderhooks.'

Impeccably polite, Morrissey inquired, 'On what?'

'On tenderhooks,' Ballcock repeated, 'the oul' nerves jangling. I knew I was going to be made a scrapegoat of.'

'A scrapegoat?' Morrissey repeated.

'Yes. A bloody scrapegoat.' Ballcock insisted.

'But why should you be blamed for what Joe Dunne chose to say?'

'Because I was on the platform with him. And because as a public representative I shouldn't appear to be too closely associated with that sort of oul' guff. The papers all reported him nearly verbintim.'

'But you seem to believe in much of what Joe Dunne was saying.'

'What I believe in and what, as a politician, I can afford to support in public are two separate things,' Ballcock insisted.

Frank observed him closely. He was a small man in his middle forties, wearing a bowler hat and a dark suit with the two strands of a silver watch-chain spanning his waistcoat. He had a greying moustache which he wiped with his handkerchief when he had finished his drink and left down his glass. Morrissey, who did not want it reported to the world at large that he had failed to reciprocate Ballcock's generosity, ordered more drinks from the bar.

'I sometimes think that being a politician is a bloody cod,' Ballcock told Frank, 'and if I had went into some other field of activation I could have given my natural bent a better chance.'

'Some would envy you the influence of a politician on society's affairs,' Frank said.

'Influence? What influence? The real influences in this city – and the same goes for the country – are the masons and the clergy. And of the two, I think the clergy is probably the greater rogues.'

Morrissey returned with replenished glasses. As he did so the indistinct babble from the radio died out and, after a moment's pause, the air about them began to reverberate to the sturdy strokes of a church bell. The other customers fell silent. Frank glanced at his watch. It was six o'clock. He looked at Ballcock who was taking off his bowler hat. It was the Angelus, coming directly from the Pro-Cathedral for the first time. They had both temporarily forgotten about it. But Ballcock had not. Ballcock left his bowler hat carefully on his lap. He closed his eyes reverently and composed his features to convey to the world the unplumbable depths of his devotion and faith. That done, he solemnly crossed himself.

Lemuel and Stella Cox, sitting expectantly by their radio, heard it too. Stella was especially excited.

'If father were only alive,' she said, her affection leaping back over all the years. 'He'd be so thrilled.'

'Mother, too,' Lemuel corrected.

'Of course. Both of them.'

Lemuel, she recollected, although he was affectionate and respectful to his father, had always favoured their mother. The first serious trouble he had got into as a child had been because of his deep attachment to her.

Chapter 4

His father had always called him Lemuel; his mother preferred Lem. He had liked that. She was gentle and indulgent, and when she died she was only beginning her thirty-first year. He was barely nine. The memories of her that persisted wore a nimbus. They were simplicity itself: of walking with her in the woods or along the river if they were occupying Avonmore House, or, when they were in the city in their town house near Lansdowne Road, of visits to St Stephen's Green with paper bags from which to feed the ducks, or to Phoenix Park to see the zoo or to watch the cavalry officers playing polo. She loved railways and trains. One of her favourite trips, which she took both winter and summer, was from Lansdowne Road to Bray. It was his too. Sometimes his father came.

In summer, from the carriage window, he could look out on the great width of the sea and the smoke rising from countless fires along the beaches where fathers boiled kettles for the tea and mothers and daughters prepared rough sandwiches and huge slices of cake. The sea was full of bobbing heads and flashed blindingly when the carriages swayed as the rails curved.

In winter it was very different. In winter, with a sound like thunder, the waves burst against the wall which bordered the permanent way and flung great fans of spray high up into the air, sometimes ambushing the carriage window and causing you to duck back in delighted terror. His mother loved the storm and told him poems:

> It was the schooner Hesperus
> That sailed the wintry sea:
> And the skipper had taken his little daughter
> To bear him company.

> Blue were her eyes as the fairy flax
> Her cheeks like the dawn of day
> And her bosom white as the hawthorn-buds
> That ope in the month of May.

But there had been one old sailor aboard who did not like the look of things at all and said to the skipper:

> Then up and spake an old sailór
> Had sailed the Spanish Main
> 'I pray thee, put into yonder port
> For I fear a hurricane.

> Last night the moon had a golden ring
> And tonight no moon we see!'
> The skipper he blew a whiff from his pipe
> And a scornful laugh laughed he.

But the skipper was very wrong not to pay attention to what the old sailor had to say because soon the storm arose and smote the vessel and all of them, including his pretty little daughter, were drowned.

At any time, winter or summer, the heavy sea mists could roll in and curl about the railway line and blot out the world. Then foghorns would begin to sound far out to sea to save, if they could, the poor ships that had lost their way and might run on to the rocks, and his father, with the tiniest of smiles, would nod his approval as his mother said:

> The maiden clasped her hands and prayed
> That savéd she might be
> And she thought of Christ who stilled the wave
> On the lake of Galilee.

His father was very holy and said they must grow up to be good Catholics who were well informed in their religion and its practices. So after lunch on Sundays they were required to assemble in his study for instruction. They sat from left to right in accordance with their ages: Stella first, then himself, then Godwin and later on, when he was old enough, young Jonathan. They were instructed in the seasons of the liturgical year, in the use of their missals, in the vessels, vestments and furniture of the Church and in the Cultus of the Saints. Early Irish Monasticism was dear to his father's heart and dear to his own, too, because it interrupted indoor instruction from time to time and led to fieldwork and visits to various oratories

28

and monastic settlements. He found his father's religious earnestness less stuffy in the fresh air.

His mother was never stuffy. She was pretty and full of jokes and fun and she played popular tunes on the violin as well as classical. Nevertheless she joined with his father in instilling within him the love of God and a special love of the teaching of the Catholic Church. She told him of a young French boy, noted for his great piety, who constantly put pebbles in his shoes when he was taken out walking, so that he could offer up the pain they caused him as a sacrifice to God, to balance against the wickedness of evil men. This was discovered by his nurse who began to wonder why he was limping.

The lives of the early Irish saints were of special interest to her and she told him stories about them, some of them interesting and some even entertaining.

She also spoke of old religious observances and peasant beliefs. Once, when they were walking together along the river bank under a night sky that was cold and clear and crowded with stars, something drew their attention at the same moment and they looked upwards. A star was tumbling down through the galaxy in a graceful parabola. He asked his mother if it had become unstuck, but she told him no. It seemed it was not a star at all but a poor soul just released from Purgatory and making its joyful way to Heaven. He wondered to himself how this could be. It was going in the wrong direction. Had his mother forgotten that you go *up* to Heaven. Not *down* to it. Unless, perhaps, the poor soul, so very overjoyed at its release, was totally confused.

Twice, perhaps even three times, during the next few years, his mother had been taken away to a nursing home for days at a time. His sister Stella, who was three years his senior and who knew everything, told him on two such occasions that their mother had a miscarriage. She went on to explain that this meant she had lost two babies. He suspected that Stella knew more about the matter than she was prepared to reveal. Babies were a phenomenon that constantly puzzled him. Even at his youngest he was not so soft in the head as to believe, as some elders seemed to expect, that God hid them under cabbage leaves for eventual discovery. But the explanation that the doctor brought them in his black bag seemed more reasonable. Doctors were always carrying black bags around with them. However, the question arose: where did the doctors get them? And a miscarriage – what did that mean? A carriage was a conveyance. Had his mother mislaid the babies by putting them in the wrong prams?

Twice his mother went away and returned to them looking thin and pale. But she recovered each time, more or less, and they resumed their walks in the forest and their explorations of the maze of deep paths and goat-tracks that the feet of generations had imprinted on the mountains. One evening she was watching them, Stella and Lemuel and little Godwin, from the river bank while they were swimming in the place they called the Pooka's Pool when Stella dived in and was so long under the surface that she became quite agitated and called out to the other two to see if anything had happened. When Stella surfaced at last she had made an exciting discovery. There was a ledge of rock protruding from the bank some four or five feet beneath the surface on which she had been able to remain seated by pressing her feet into the fissures below it and gripping firmly with them to maintain her position. When her mother declared it dangerous Stella denied it and dived in again to demonstrate. They peered anxiously into the water and located her shimmering figure which they saw to be seated on the ledge as she had reported. Not only that but she was able to wave both her hands at them to show that she could hold on adequately with her feet alone.

Lemuel tried it too and mastered the knack after three or four attempts, but Godwin was much too small to reach the fissures with his feet and had not yet the skill to control his breath for the underwater stay. They gabbled excitedly to her all the way back through the woods to the house. It was late evening and the August sun had dipped low in the sky. Its rays slanted between the trees in golden bars in which pollen floated and insects wove constantly changing patterns. As they picked their way fallen sticks cracked underfoot with an echoing sound from time to time. An unseen pigeon behind camouflaging foliage cooed a sad lament for the passing away of a day that would never, ever, come again.

Some months later, when his mother began to swell and swell in a most peculiar fashion, Stella let him in on a secret to which every little girl in her class in the convent school was privy: babies, as he had guessed anyway, were not found under cabbage leaves nor were they brought in black bags by doctors on request. They grew over a period of months inside your mother where God had planted them. The privilege, it seemed, belonged to married ladies only. It was the first explanation he had heard which had a ring of truth and he accepted it unreservedly. Stella made him promise he would not tell his mother.

'I'll have your life if you breathe a word to her,' Stella said.

'But surely she must know already,' he remarked.

'Adults don't like us to meddle in such things,' Stella told him, 'and they get very cross.'

So, although his mother was unable to go about with them as she used to, he remained much in her company as she sat in the garden or, later on, lay in the afternoons on the sofa. He made no reference to 'it', but otherwise talked freely to her as he had always done.

When his birthday was coming near, she asked him what he would like. He said he would like a bicycle.

'Don't be ridiculous Lem, a boy of your age could never control one of those monsters. The front wheel would be bigger than yourself. What if you fell off?'

'They have other kinds of bicycles now,' he told her. 'Both wheels are the same size and they are moved by a chain, not by levers. I read about them in the *Boy's Crafts and Hobbies Magazine*.'

When he came to visit Mother, Uncle Crispin, her older brother, confirmed what Lemuel had read. He was an enthusiastic wheelman himself, a council member of the Irish Cycling Association, 14 D'Olier Street, Dublin, and an honorary associate of The Cyclists' Touring Club which had over 50,000 members and its headquarters at 47, Victoria Street, London SW. On one visit to Mother, a couple of years before, he had come decked out in the full sartorial style favoured by wholly dedicated wheelmen: knickerbockers to allow maximum freedom to the legs, a military-style tunic ribbed laterally across the front, a pillbox hat and an impeccably groomed moustache. Except for the moustache, Mother remarked afterwards, the outfit made Uncle Crispin look like an overgrown version of the young boys employed as bellhops in the bigger hotels – the Shelbourne, for instance, or the Gresham.

In his support for the idea of a bicycle for Lemuel's birthday, Uncle Crispin became a mine of information. He explained the mechanism of the Bowden brake, the intricacies of the pneumatic tyre only recently invented by J.B. Dunlop, a surgeon, and the utility of the spring clip evolved, he was proud to say, by an Irishman, the Rev. Mr Hanlon. The most scientific saddle yet produced had been designed by a Mr Gerrard, a shoemaker of Chelsea and was called—

'Can you guess what it is called?' he challenged them.

Mother gave up immediately but Lemuel had two guesses.

31

'The Lancer?' he ventured.

'No,' Uncle Crispin said. 'But that's very good – the Cavalry connection.'

'The Cossack?'

'No. That's not quite so good,' Uncle Crispin decided. 'I don't think Cossacks actually use saddles.'

He decided to enlighten them. 'Mr Gerrard called his saddle – and I am proud to report it – the Crispin saddle.'

He undertook to look after the ordering of the bicycle himself and to check at every stage. The first and chief consideration must be the height of the frame, the sovereign rule being that the saddle should be fixed at such a height as would allow the foot to follow the pedal throughout a complete revolution of the crank with the heel placed on the pedal spindle. He then gave his entire attention to painstaking measurements of Lemuel's various moving parts, a task that took almost half an hour. That completed, he renewed his promise to supervise personally the whole intricate business, and after some general conversation with his sister he took his leave.

Uncle Crispin was as good as his word. His personal gift was a timepiece which he described as a dress watch.

'I bought it on my last visit to New York,' he told them. 'They were very much the rage over there. It adds distinction when worn on a slender silver chain when you're togged out in evening dress for formal occasions. As you can see, it's quite strikingly slim and elegant and doesn't make that ugly bulge in your waistcoat pocket. You'll appreciate that when you are old enough to wear it.'

The bicycle which arrived in his personal care punctually on the birthday was so perfect that Lemuel found it hard to leave its saddle, even for meals. He practised by riding up and down the river driveway, then he ventured on to the public road, and then he went all the way to Edmundscourt and back, a visit which brought the villagers to windows and doors, and normal activity to a standstill. When at home he gave frequent demonstrations of his growing skills to his mother, until her time came and she was confined to her bedroom. Visits were not supposed to be allowed, but when he poked his head around the door on his way to bed she always beckoned him in and asked him where he had been on the bicycle that day.

'I allow Stella to have a turn at it every day,' he confided on one occasion.

'I don't wish that child to grow up into a tomboy,' she warned. 'But it's good not to be selfish and to share with your sister.'

Shortly after that there was much coming and going of doctor and nurses and when it ended his father called the three of them – Stella, Lemuel and Godwin – into the study to tell them they had a new baby brother who would be baptised Jonathan in due course.

'The child is healthy and strong,' he told them, 'and gives no cause for anxiety. But your mother is weak and requires careful nursing. That will be provided at once, and the most qualified that can be got. Our part will be to kneel down together each day in prayer for her recovery. If we do so as earnestly as our love for her dictates, God is sure to bend His ear to our pleading. We'll begin at once.'

They knelt down together and he led them with a voice that had lost its characteristic firmness. It was soft and, at moments, tremulous.

She died three days later. Just before it happened Stella and Lemuel and Godwin were allowed briefly into the room. A carbolic smell and odours of medicines hung in the air. Her forehead and hair glistened damply. She was not aware of their presence.

During the next three days relatives and sympathisers called continuously and the house was busy with extra servants engaged to attend to their needs. There were important visitors, friends of his father, who included Douglas Hyde, Edward Martyn and Arthur Griffith. Lady Gregory sent a telegram of sympathy from Gort and there was more than a sprinkling of priests. When full honour had been paid to the established rituals of sympathy they ventured briefly into more general topics, the most frequent being the pending suit for divorce from his wife which had been filed by Captain O'Shea and which cited Charles Stewart Parnell as co-respondent. It would come to trial in November.

'What's to happen to the party?' Lemuel heard his father ask. 'The bishops won't tolerate his continuance as leader.'

But a grave and important-looking Monsignor expressed some reservation.

'That is not by any means certain,' he informed them. 'Arch-bishop Walsh is counselling the utmost caution.'

He was referring, Lemuel knew, to Doctor W.J. Walsh who was Archbishop of Dublin.

Uncle Crispin was one of the first to arrive. He came on his bicycle, wearing the appropriate wheelman outfit. He was quite unaware of the consternation he was causing.

'Poor Jonathan,' he said, shaking hands with obvious sympathy. 'We'll all miss dear Celia and her loving and generous spirit, but you he most deeply and sorely of all.'

'Crispin,' his father managed after a struggle, 'the bicycle, this sartorial impropriety – it cannot be. It's entirely and outrageously inappropriate.'

'My dear Jonathan, you can't possibly believe I intend to go about like this. I have the conventional mourning paraphernalia here in the travelling basket.'

He indicated a suitcase in a carrying contraption which was balanced above the back wheel. 'I intend to change.'

'I should be infinitely indebted if you would do so right away.'

'Certainly,' Uncle Crispin agreed. 'Just allow me to dispose of the bicycle.'

When he next appeared he was dressed in impeccable accord with the sadness and solemnity of the occasion: black suit, black tie, white shirt and black socks and shoes. They led him to the room where his sister was lying in a brown habit with her rosary beads entwined about her joined hands. He crossed himself and prayed silently. Lemuel could see that his father was mollified, and when they left the room and sat for a moment to talk he was kindly and courteous.

'Why don't you stay here and be near her until after the funeral,' he offered. 'We have plenty of room.'

'That's a kind thought. I could help with the ordering of some of the details and leave you more time for your guests and for rest.'

'There is much to be done,' his father agreed. 'Cabs to be booked and a host of other arrangements.'

'We can discuss them whenever you feel ready. One of the obvious things I could do is look after the children on their way to and from the cemetery.'

Lemuel's heart jolted with alarm at what his father said next:

'No. That won't arise. It is not the custom for teenage girls to attend on such occasions. And the boys are too young.'

'But I want to go,' Lemuel protested. 'Please, father.'

'You are too young, Lemuel.'

'I'm nine.'

'Your mother would not wish it. It is harrowing even for those of us who are grown up.'

Lemuel looked pleadingly at Uncle Crispin. But Uncle Crispin knew it was not the moment to intervene. And later, when he judged the time to be more propitious, he was unsuccessful.

Lemuel stormed heaven for help. For two nights he cried himself to sleep. His mother's now tenuous presence in the house was dwindling minute by minute. Soon they would come to take her away and that would mean absence forever. She would never again tell him poems about disasters at sea, or explore the forest and mountain tracks with him, or walk with him on nights of sparkle and frost under star-crowded heavens.

When the moment came, he watched from a window in the company of Stella and Godwin. The hearse stood waiting and the horses were plumed and their shining silver harnesses jingled when they tossed their heads. Behind them the cabs with their mourners manoeuvred one by one into orderly procession. In the driveway, Uncle Crispin watched and supervised. When all was ready he had some words with the driver of the hearse and went to join their father in the chief mourning coach. The hearse man whipped his whip. The cortège set off. It was too much for Stella who began to sob. Her grief upset Godwin who joined her. When the crunching of wheels on gravel began to fade in the distance their sobbing eased. Lemuel said, in a low voice, 'I'm going to the funeral.'

Stella caught his arm in a terrified grip.

'You mustn't, Lem. Daddy has enough to bear and you'll only distress him further.'

'He won't know. I'll watch it from the top of Donnellan's lane.'

'Besides, they've started off and you could never catch them up.'

'They have the Mass to attend before they go on to the cemetery. I'll use my bicycle to catch up.'

'Lem – you mustn't. Please don't upset Daddy. Not at a time like this.'

'I told you – he won't know,' Lemuel insisted.

He pulled his arm free and left them standing at the window. A little later he passed by. He was riding the bicycle and did not look around.

The little church and its surrounding churchyard were peaceful under the warm morning sunshine. The mourners had already gone inside; the cabs and their drivers waited on the gravelled forecourt. At well-spaced intervals the light-toned bell tolled a single note to let the countryside know that a funeral Mass was in progress. Between strokes, while the cabman smoked surreptitious cigarettes, the birds in the hedgerows entertained them with chatter and song.

Although from halfway up Donnellan's lane Lemuel could view anything that went on about the church, he knew a better vantage point higher up. He left his bicycle to tackle the steeper gradient ahead on foot. It took him to a wooden gate and field with a rough track which wound across it and disappeared down its slope. He used the track until he came to a rowan tree which bent over it with clusters of bright red berries. The churchyard was now directly underneath and the tree hid him from sight. For him, as for the cabmen below, the occasional solitary bell stroke and the unheeding chatter and birdsong lent an air of loneliness and isolation to the sunlit fields. He wept and watched.

He had almost forgotten about the mourners when they began to emerge from the main porchway, following a bier on which his mother's coffin had been laid. They walked in silence the short distance from the porchway to the newly opened grave. They grouped about the priest who was officiating, hiding him from his view. But the priest's voice drifted up to him, as did the murmurs of their responses. Then there came to him the scrape of a shovel against something hard, and after that the first sharp thud of clay on wood. The sound of the shovels continued for several minutes. Then it ceased. The priest said a final prayer after which the mourners began to make general conversation and to drift away in small groups. The priest walked with his father and Uncle Crispin. On the fresh grave behind them the mass of floral tributes made a riot of colour in the morning sunlight.

He had done as his heart had bidden him. Now he wished to get back to the house before they missed him. He would have preferred to start off ahead of them but was afraid he would not be able to outpace the horses on his bicycle, and that they would catch up and discover him. It would be better to follow behind, making sure to keep out of sight. He returned to the lane and made his way down again to recover his bicycle which he had left leaning against one of the many wooden gateways that opened on to it. He quickened his pace to get there sooner. When he reached it, it took several seconds to realize that the bicycle had gone.

He searched carefully at first, walking twice up and down the whole length of the lane. It was fruitless. Despair sent him aimlessly around fields he knew with complete certainty he had not been in. He peered into ditches in the wild hope that some practical joker had been at work. But by late afternoon he surrendered to hunger and reality and began the long trek home on foot.

Stella, who had been watching out for him without respite for some hours, waylaid him halfway along the river driveway. His appearance shocked her. His boots and stockings were grey with dust from the road. His face was tear-stained and lined with exhaustion.

'Lem – everyone has been asking where you were. What happened?'

'I had to walk home—'

'But your bicycle—'

'I left it leaning against a gate in Donnellan's lane. When I got back it had gone. Somebody stole it.'

'Nonsense!' Stella said. 'The people around here don't do such things. Did you search for it?'

'For hours and hours. That's what kept me so late.'

'Father said you were to see him the moment you got back. What on earth will you find to say to him?'

'I don't know. I don't much care.'

'Did you go to the funeral?'

'I watched it from a field above the church. That's how my bicycle was stolen. Did you tell Father where I had gone?'

'No, Lem. I wouldn't do that.'

Of course. Stella would never do such a thing. She turned to walk towards the house with him.

'Have something to eat first and then see him,' she advised. 'And wash and tidy yourself. You look awful.'

'I'd rather get it over with.'

'Well, all the guests have gone, so he's probably in his study.'

He was. He opened the door to his knock and waved him in to the room in silence. Lemuel could feel the grief and anger and personal hurt that were all bundled together in the eyes his father turned on him.

'I am wondering what explanation you will have to offer. On the day on which your dear mother was buried and the house was full of guests you go missing for several hours. Did you think your absence would go unnoticed? Did you not realise that people would believe you had scant regard for your poor mother's death, and no respect at all for the feelings of your father? Where did you go?'

'I went out on my bicycle.'

'And stayed away most of the day.'

'It wasn't my fault. My bicycle was stolen. I searched for it for ages. Then I had to walk back.'

'Where was it stolen from?'

'From Donnellan's lane.'

'And what business had you there?'

It would be best, however painful, to face up to the matter. Deception would only make things worse.

'I went there because you refused to let me go to the funeral. From the top of Donnellan's lane I could see the church and the churchyard.'

'So you defied my wishes.'

'I wanted to be present. I wanted to be with her as long a
possible.'

Having to say that overwhelmed him and caused the tears to flo
uncontrollably. His father waited in silence for the attack to pass
When it had almost subsided he said, 'Dry your eyes, child. I am no
going to chide you. You've suffered for your disobedience.'

'I'm deeply sorry, Father.'

'You're forgiven,' his father said. Then in a gentler mood he sai
the loss of the bicycle must be reported and steps taken to retrieve it

'Your Uncle Crispin is staying on for a few days longer. In th
morning I'll speak to him. He'll know what should be done.'

Uncle Crispin said the first thing was to give the fulles
information to the police. He could supply the frame number an
all technical particulars to them – he had all these details noted. H
wondered, however, if the machine had really been stolen. For suc
a thing to happen in this small country community was quit
unprecedented. Besides, what use would the bicycle be to the thief
He could never ride about on it openly himself and if he tried to sel
it it would arouse suspicion immediately. His conclusion was that i
had been taken by some wandering tinker or tramp, who woul
soon begin to wonder how on earth he could manage to get rid of i
again and avoid detection.

Lemuel listened without hope and almost without interest. H
went to his bedroom as soon as it was permissible and sat quietly b
the window. His mother's image filled his mind persistently an
made his need to communicate with her in some manner or othe
imperative. At first he talked to her in whispers, but gave it up whe
he became convinced that she was unable to hear him. He decide
to write a letter to her. If he hid it somewhere, she might come alon
when no one was about and read it. He began:

Dearest Mother,

*I am writing this to you so that you will know how much I mis
you and also all the things that happened to me today, the day yo
went away altogether from me and from all of us . . .*

He set down the day's events and told her of the bicycle and wha
Uncle Crispin had said, and that his father, although angry at first
had forgiven him and spoken kindly to him. He wrote two pages an
then began to wonder where best to hide it. When his bedroom
seemed to offer nowhere suitable he thought of an old box whic
had been lying forgotten in a corner of an ancient woodshed. Th

shed had been unused for years. He left the letter there for the night but next morning became uneasy and racked his memory for a more secret and safe lodging place. The hollow bole of the beech tree in the copse by the river came to mind. He had played alone among the trees many times and knew everything that was there. He got the metal box out of the woodshed and into the hollow of the tree undetected. The accumulated leaves that carpeted the ground about the trunk provided an effective covering to hide it from any intruder. It was to be the first letter of many another, but for the moment it lay all alone in its metal box in the heart of a beech on the tree-crowded bend of the river.

Some mornings later Stella stood beneath his bedroom window calling out to him in wild excitement.

'Lem,' she shouted again and again.' 'Come and look. Oh hurry up, you old slow coach. Hurry, hurry. I have your bicycle.'

He pushed the curtains aside and poked out his head. His heart jumped. Stella was holding the bicycle, one hand on the handlebars, the other on the saddle. As he dashed down to join her he shouted outside Uncle Crispin's door, 'Uncle Crispin. Stella has my bicycle. She's found my bicycle.'

She had been up early and decided to walk as far as the entrance gates to breathe the morning air before having breakfast. She could hardly believe her eyes when she found it lying against one of the gate pillars.

'I thought as much,' Uncle Crispin commented, when he had arrived in his dressing gown and was told the story. 'Some tinker or tramp found it too hot to handle, and left it back during the night.'

But Lemuel knew better. It was his mother had left it back. She had read his note and was sorry for him and had found it and restored it to him. Dead people, if they wanted to, could do such things.

Chapter 5

Margaret, in company with Maeve and Teresa, sat at the long circular table in the convent parlour and listened with feigned interest to the elderly priest who was addressing them. The parlour, as always, bore the cleanly and Christian odour of beeswax. From its walls sacred subjects in dull colours kept an eye on what went on.

The priest had addressed them on so many occasions that by now they had adopted a name for him among themselves: Father Profundus. For Reverend Mother who, as usual, was presiding, they used one they had given her way back in their schooldays at the convent – Mother Splendiferous – although by now her once proud and regal carriage had been bent and crippled by arthritis. On either side of her sat an attendant sister: she on the right being Sister Loquacious: she on the left Sister Inconspicuous. Giving them such names helped to lighten the tedium.

Like Margaret, Maeve and Teresa had been recruited into the Legion of Mary by the good nuns when they were about to leave their classrooms for the last time to confront the temptations and pitfalls of the great world beyond. Like Margaret also, they had remained in membership, though largely through inertia. At first the objectives of the Legion had been simple: Sanctification of Self and the regular practice of charity to others. But more recently they had come to be expected to help in humble but positive ways in the propagation of official Church thinking in such areas as moral philosophy, social ethics and social science. Grave threats to faith and morals were always being uncovered, usually in the columns of the *Irish Catholic* or the *Standard* or the *Universe* and these, of course, had to be combatted. Father Profundus would be summoned to arm them with instruction and they, in turn, in the course of their regular charitable visitations, were expected to explain in broad and general terms the nature of the Church's teaching and the duty of according it undeviating support and loyalty.

Why they had been selected as intermediaries between the lawmakers and the humble faithful was a mystery to all three. Teresa was gentle and pious and dutiful and well aware that even the simplest of philosophical formulations gummed up her mind within seconds. Maeve was happy to go through the accepted round of religious practice but was bored to death by analysis and argument. Margaret found the official viewpoint on a succession of subjects becoming more and more simplistic and overbearing, and had begun to feel guilty and hypocritical about her own prudent silence.

Last time around Father Profundus had for his subject the spiritual welfare of emigrants who were leaving the country at a rate which was increasing alarmingly year by year. These, it was feared, would have to live and work in non-Catholic environments and thousands of souls would be at stake unless they were directed to hostels and organisations that would provide spiritual support.

This time it was contraception, abortion, the duties of married couples and the rights of the unborn child. He instructed them in how to reply to the Malthusians, whom they were bound to encounter, and how to defend the raising of large families by quoting them the special edict of the Lord Himself. Had he not commanded them to increase and multiply? Could anything be more explicit than that?

He impressed on them the unacceptability of divorce under any circumstances whatever, and the grave sinfulness of birth prevention.

'It is totally forbidden,' Father Profundus warned, in a voice which laboured for emphasis, 'by the direct pronouncement of the Holy Father himself, to use the matrimonial act in any way that deliberately thwarts its natural purpose of generating life. Those who do so offend against God's law and the law of nature and are branded with the guilt of grave sin.'

He proceeded to quote the Holy Father's assurance to them on the efficacy in all dilemmas of the grace of God, 'No difficulty can arise that justifies the putting aside of the law of God which forbids all acts that are intrinsically evil. There are no possible circumstances in which husband and wife cannot, strengthened by the grace of God, fulfil faithfully their duties and preserve in wedlock their chastity unspotted.'

Abortion, he said, was so heinous, so unutterably depraved and evil that he would not talk of it at all in the presence of three simple, good-living young wives and mothers such as the three of them were. Instead he led them in a short prayer and, because of another pressing appointment, declined to join them for tea and sandwiches. Reverend Mother felt unequal to a more prolonged evening also and hobbled out after him.

But Sister Loquacious and Sister Inconspicuous remained briefly while a couple of old serving Sisters brought in tea and sandwiches, together with a fruit cake which was specially recommended by Sister Loquacious.

'It was made by Sister Paula,' she told them, 'and Sister Paula makes perfectly gorgeous fruit cakes'.

'I thought Reverend Mother looked very tired and ill,' Teresa said to Maeve. 'Did you?'

'She is far from well,' Sister Loquacious put in. 'Some days ago one of my pupils, a flighty little rogue, came into class wearing earrings. At eleven years of age, if you please! I asked Reverend Mother if I should send the little wretch to her for correction but Reverend Mother took no interest whatever. Send a note to her parents, was all she said.' Sister Loquacious shook her head gravely, 'I thought it so unlike Reverend Mother that it must surely be a bad sign.'

'Shall I pour for you?' invited Teresa.

'No, thank you,' Sister Loquacious answered. 'Today all of us in the community have arranged to take part in a general fast. It is for a special intention that the community would wish to come to pass. In fact we both have to leave you to attend a session of evening prayers that all are agreed to. But I'm satisfied you won't be inconvenienced. After all these years you know your way around the convent better than I do myself. Come, Sister.'

She turned to address Sister Inconspicuous. But Sister Inconspicuous had already gone.

Margaret sat in silence. The parlour had hardly changed since her girlhood: the heavy crucifix on the wall; the large picture of Christ in brown cloak and red under-mantle with his arms crossed on his breast and his hands so faded and pale beneath the varnish that they were barely visible. There were the two familiar statues: the Madonna, and the Good Shepherd. There were the heavily framed paintings with their sacred depictions. And the never-absent odour of beeswax. Unease and guilt troubled her. Teresa noticed. 'You're being very quiet,' she said. 'Is anything wrong?'

'The Reverend Profundus,' Margaret said. 'He has me troubled.'

'Why on earth should he have you troubled?' Maeve asked.

'Because I'm practising what he's spent the evening preaching against – birth control.'

'It's all right if you use the rhythm method – isn't it?' asked Teresa.

'Is that what you do?'

'Well, John and I don't agree with it. We know it's permitted, of course, but we both prefer to leave it in God's good hands.'

'You've four children already. Where do you think you'll end up?'

'We don't mind, really, so long as we're able to manage. Are you and Frank using the rhythm method?'

'We were, but it's far too unreliable. Now we abstain, or we turn to *coitus interruptus*.'

'I don't know what that is,' Teresa said.

'I do,' said Maeve. 'It's highly unsatisfactory.'

'So what do you do?'

'Peter uses condoms – except that he calls them French letters.'

'Yes, I've heard of those,' Teresa said brightly, pleased at this evidence of her own sophistication.

'Is it satisfactory?' Margaret asked.

'Not altogether. It's like having it off with a fellow with a sock on it. But it's better than yours.'

'One thing seems clear,' Margaret said. 'I'll have to leave the Legion, which wouldn't upset me one little bit. What bothers me are the questions and the cross-examinations it'll draw from people like Reverend Mother and Father Profundus.'

'Just stay put and keep your mouth shut,' Maeve advised.

'I can't go around preaching maxims to poor bitches that I'm not honouring myself. I couldn't do that.'

'I can,' Maeve said. 'I know it's dishonest but it's convenient. I'll just have to put up with being a whited sepulchre.'

Frank, who had been sitting on the other side of the fireplace most of the evening writing on a pad which rested on his knees, left his pen aside and said to her with relief, 'I have that stuff for *Laughter Parade* finished – the limericks Kenny asked for. Care to look at them?'

'Just read them out to me,' she said.

43

'It's no use reading them out,' he explained, passing one of them over to her. 'The joke is really in the spelling gimmick. That's what caught Kenny's fancy.'

She took it without enthusiasm and read:

Foyled

> Said a harrassed professor named Coyle
> I'm heartsick of trouble and toyle
> The contempt in this college
> For learning and nollege
> Would make a poor teacher's blood boyle

She passed it back.

'I've got four of them done. At half a guinea each that's two guineas for an hour or so's work.'

He passed her another.

'Well, what do you think, Peggy?'

'I think,' she said, 'it must be pleasant to have so little on your mind.'

He retrieved the page and put it in his briefcase with the pad and the others. He said quietly, 'I think I'll take a walk for a while. I won't be long.'

She nodded. But as he opened the door she said, 'Frank – I'm sorry.'

'That's all right.'

'Would you mind taking me with you. Perhaps we could have a drink?'

He hesitated. Then he said, 'Of course.'

She crossed the room and kissed him. He took her in his arms. After a while she disengaged herself and said, 'I'll get my coat and tell Mrs Cleary.'

They walked in silence for a while, and then took a bus to Neary's of Chatham Street for a drink. As they passed St Stephen's Green they looked down from the upper deck on the railings around it. Moonlight glinted on the leaves of the evergreen bushes. The bare trees were dark silhouettes which cast skeleton-like images across pathways and grass plots. A light frost rimed the statues.

As they drank they were at pains to show their tenderness to each other: she to make amends for her show of bitterness; he to let her know he understood her unease and depression.

'I know it's going to be hard to run the gamut of all the probing and whispering that will go on when you tell them you're going to leave the Legion,' he said, 'but you'll be doing what's best.'

'Maeve said I should just bluff it out. That's what she intends to do.'

'That may do for Maeve. It wouldn't suit you.'

'I should have left long ago.' She was quiet for a while. 'We won't spoil our drinks by going on about it,' she decided. 'Let's think of something else.'

'Right. I've had something at the back of my mind. How would you like us to get a car?'

'We couldn't possibly afford it.'

'If things continue as they're going, we just might – a cheap, second-hand yoke which could totter from place to place. I think a car would be a help at the moment. That's why I'm turning out as much as I can for Kenny.'

She put her hand on his sleeve.

'I'm sorry for being snotty about your limericks.'

'Never mind.'

'Can you remember the other two? Let me hear them.'

'But I told you. Hearing isn't the point. The gimmick is in the spelling.'

'Then write them down.'

For conciliation's sake he agreed to scribble one of them on an empty cigarette carton which he tore open for the purpose.

She read:

Looking Blough

Said the captain, this forward we've signed
Is driving me out of my migned
He's so slow going through
The best we can dough
Is to push the damn fool from behigned

She smiled. 'It's quite clever.'

'Kenny likes them. If he stays that way and I can keep on perpetrating enough nonsense of the kind, plus the stuff for the *Review* and the editing I do for him each month, a car of sorts might be a possibility.'

They enlarged on the advantages: summer evening spins with the children; weekend drives; camping holidays which would cost them half nothing; a new interest to tide them over the difficulties that could threaten their relationship. They went home talking about it as though a car was theirs already.

As they prepared for bed the moon still rode high and clear in the

45

sky. They undressed and watched it together from their bedroom window.

'It's so beautiful,' she said to him.

He took her hand.

'You know, Madge,' he answered, 'we marvel at the sun and think of the planets and stars as the uncountable lamps of heaven. But the moon is magic. I think adding in the moon was an inspired touch – even for God.'

'That's probably blasphemous,' she decided, 'nevertheless I agree.'

When they were in bed and he had turned to her she said, 'Don't withdraw tonight.'

'Are you sure?'

'Yes,' she said, almost in a whisper. 'I don't think I could bear it. Tonight I think God would let it go.'

In the days that followed she was anxious and unusually silent. But on the due date all was well. God, or Fate, or Chance, or whatever, let the offence pass.

Chapter 6

The car was ready for collection on the last day of April. It was an Austin Seven with a sunshine roof, 1948 vintage and so already three years old. Jackson came with him to drive it away; Morrissey came out of curiosity. The weather was unwaveringly hostile. The wind blew coldly, fusillades of hail battered the trees along suburban roads, tore their delicate blossoms to shreds and stained the pathways with squandered petals. When they drove to Phoenix Park so Frank could take a turn at the wheel, rain pelted the windows and exploded in spurts on the roadway in front of him. He craned forward in his effort to see what lay ahead.

'Tomorrow, the calendar tells us,' Jackson remarked, 'is the first day of summer.'

'You could have fooled me,' Frank commented, still peering.

They were to have collected Margaret and Morrissey's companion Penny to take a run by Pine Forest and Glencullen when Frank had had his hour or so of practice, but the weather ruled out country rambling. Instead, Morrissey suggested they should have dinner in a hotel he knew in the Bray area.

'I'll stand treat,' he offered.

'Are you mad?' Jackson asked.

'Special occasion,' Morrissey said. 'To mark the acquisition of the automobile. We'll charge it to office expenses.'

Jackson took over again and they collected Margaret, who was standing by the window watching out for them.

'I thought you'd never come,' she complained.

'We're giving Glencullen a miss because of the rain,' Frank told her. 'Instead Simon here has offered to stand us dinner in a little place somewhere near Bray. We've only to collect Penny first.'

When they went in for Penny, Morrissey, to cap his genial mood, offered them drinks. The thought that Penny and he were actually living in sin shocked Margaret a little. She had known about it from Frank, of course, but in a remote way. Now she was standing in the middle of the den of iniquity itself: a tastefully arranged room with better furnishings than she or Frank could boast and drinks from a Waterford glass decanter with its matching set which must have cost a fortune. Penny, who worked as a feature writer with one of the fashionable women's magazines, looked quite expensive herself. But she was outgoing and welcoming, with a trim figure and pleasant face. Margaret found herself liking her. Penny admired the car.

'It's gorgeous,' she whispered to Margaret. 'I'm going to pester Simon.'

At dinner they spoke, in common with everybody else in the city, about the recent collapse of the government following the clash between the Minister for Health and the hierarchy over his proposed maternal and child welfare proposals.

'The general election is likely to be around the end of May,' Morrissey said to Frank. 'You can expect Joe Dunne to come up with a great outpouring from the Left.'

Then they talked of other things and the meal went well. Jackson offered to give driving lessons to Frank in the park on three or four evenings a week. He had already had a little experience from time to time and would pick up the knack of it quickly. When they were parting Penny suggested to Margaret they should meet for coffee occasionally.

'You could come to me, of course,' Penny said, 'but dropping down town to Bewley's or Robert's is probably more interesting. Would you phone?'

'Of course,' Margaret said. 'I'd love to.'

The great pre-election outpouring came about as predicted. The trade union activists and the intellectuals of the radical Left, though they disagreed among themselves violently enough at times to come to blows, had certain distinguishing marks in common. Some of these Frank particularly observed. Almost all of them walked around with protruding newspapers and magazines dragging down their overloaded pockets and, though the hues varied a bit from one to the other, the ties they wore were predominantly red. They addressed one another as 'comrade' or 'brother' usually for emphasis, but sometimes when they had lost their temper with each other and were about to come to blows. Their favourite haunts were Ryan's public house on the quays or a little cake and coffee shop in a laneway near the river. Here, in normal circumstances, they discussed unemployment, emigration, inflation, their determination, despite the disapproval of Catholic social theory, to lay the foundation, of a welfare state similar to that across the water.

But in May the general election, the Mother and Child Scheme and (as they saw it) the arrogance of the bishops, united all their thinking.

In the opposite camp, as election day drew near, opinion became equally heated. The Maternal and Child Welfare Scheme was denounced as a cloak to cover a softening towards birth control and abortion. It was condemned as being opposed to Catholic social teaching. It was the thin edge of a wedge to set up a welfare state by individuals obsessed by socialist philosophy which would be evil and pagan and designed to strip man of his dignity and his autonomy. It was further reported that the Minister for Health had allowed himself to be photographed shaking hands with the Protestant Archbishop of Dublin. When the Scheme was dropped and the Minister forced to resign, one of the politicians, speaking for himself and on behalf of his colleagues had said, 'We are quite proud of what has happened.'

The country, Frank decided, had lost its marbles. Ballcock, who had failed yet again to gain a nomination, thought so too.

Dear Frank,

What an exciting possession – a car of your own. As soon as I'd left down the telephone I told Stella and she found it hard to believe. When she and I were growing up, young couples such as yourselves could never afford the luxury. Indeed, only a tiny minority of people could do so. How times change.

I'm sure Margaret is getting greatly excited, and now that you possess such a wonderful asset I would hope you both will call on us much more often. We'd love to see you. And, of course, we cannot wait to set eyes on the motorcar. So call as soon as you can.

Sincerely,

Lemuel Cox

They responded by calling near the end of June, on a Sunday when the sun made solemn promises in the early morning and kept to them steadfastly throughout the long day. Cycling clubs came out in their hordes: the boys and girls, men and women, their heads bent forward over low handlebars and their buttocks cocked high in the face of heaven. The bicycles were brightly painted and the costumes variegated: light shorts or corduroy pants, baggy pull-overs or tight blouses, hairbands or jockey-style hats. They wobbled about at times and caused Frank, who was still far from confident, to swear roundly as he swerved in panic himself. They stopped by the way to have a picnic and let the children breathe the country air. At Avonmore the sun seemed even warmer so they both took the opportunity to swim in the Pooka's pool. Lemuel Cox came to look on.

And at supper he was interested in what books were being read in the city. Frank remembered that the paperback issues of Evelyn Waugh's works had led to a rash of devotees on the beaches, on park benches, in restaurants and on buses and trains, all with their noses dug into his pages.

'You've read Waugh, of course?' he asked.

'The truth is, I have not,' Lemuel confessed. 'That is one of the disadvantages of being both old and isolated. I am no longer able to make my way in to the city on my own account, and it's difficult to arrange it otherwise. I've become hopelessly out of touch.'

Frank looked at Margaret.

'Now we've the car you could come in with me some time,' he offered. 'I'd call out for you and you could stay the night.'

'Mrs Cleary only uses two of the rooms,' Margaret said, 'there are plenty to spare.'

Lemuel thought that would be a wonderful treat.

'And you, Miss Cox?'

'Don't worry about me,' Stella said, 'I'm not really able for going around. And I'll have Mrs Holohan to look after me.'

It was agreed they should telephone.

They drove home by the small country roads which were well nigh deserted. The open window of the car let in the light breath of flowers and hedges, the air was balmy, the children slept.

'I'm glad you asked him,' Margaret said. 'He looked so pleased and excited. In fact I think one day is hardly worth while – you should invite him to stay a little longer.'

'I could phone him tomorrow,' Frank said.

'I think you ought to.'

She covered the children with the car rug and a coat. They were tranquil and secure and breathing quietly. She leaned forward to touch his knee. He smiled. Then she lay back and watched the beam from the headlamps racing along walls and fences and hedges.

He came in August and stayed four or five days. Frank had booked a

couple of theatre nights in advance: Marlow's *Dr Faustus* at the
Gate, and the Belfast Arts Theatre's visit to the Peacock with Jean-
Paul Sartre's *In Camera* (*Huis Clos*). The Dr Faustus he was
familiar with from beginning to end, but the Sartre was unknown
territory.

'I know he's a leading Existentialist,' he said, 'and I know the play
provoked a lot of controversy some years back, but that's about all.
I'll be very curious to see it.'

'The setting is Hell,' Frank explained, 'which is depicted as a
room with three characters locked up in it, a man and two women.
One of the women – she's called Inez – is obviously lesbian. It will
be interesting to see how that goes down with our pillars of society.'

'Indeed,' Lemuel Cox said.

He felt he was on holiday and ready for anything.

The mornings and afternoons he spent revisiting places that were
part of the life he had lived when they stayed in their Lansdowne
Road house. His father had bought it in 1883 to be convenient to
schools when Stella was eight and Lemuel five. Godwin was still
only three. It remained their town house until it was sold on his
father's death forty years later.

Lemuel went to see it on the first morning after his arrival. It
stood well back from the road, a substantial semi-detached
building, two upper storeys of red brick above a ground floor front
of cut granite. Its heavy steps mounted high above the entrance path
between their wrought-iron handrails. They had been painted black
and white. In childhood the halldoor at the top seemed set at a dizzy
height. It took fourteen steps to reach. He had often counted them
as he climbed.

The little railway station with its white wooden gates guarding
the level crossing was almost beside it. Sometimes at night, when
they were returning from a children's party and listening to the clip
clop of the horses' hooves through a veil of sleepiness, his mother
would say, 'See that you have all your things, Stella. And you Lem –
we're almost there.' And they would straighten up to wonder once
again at the pretty little station with the lanterns on the gates
spilling their light in little pools about them, and dark shapes of the
rising trees behind the coloured lamps on the arms of the signal
posts. Sometimes the gates would be closed and they would have to
wait until the sound of the train rose from a mere quiver in the air to
a great roar as the lighted carriages rocked and swayed and
thundered past them, each after each after each, until a red lamp on
the rear of the last of all flicked past and the sound began to die

away and the gates shuddered for a moment before opening to let them across.

Further down, past the rugby ground, was the River Dodder with the laneway leading down from the road to the water's edge which carters used when they had occasion to water their horses. It was there that Uncle Crispin had seen the ghost.

'I saw a ghost last night,' he told them at breakfast.

'Where?' Stella and Lemuel demanded together.

'What nonsense, Crispin,' their mother protested. 'Do you want to frighten the children?'

'It was after midnight and I turned to cross the bridge. As the entrance to the lane down to the river came in sight I saw a horse and cart turning off the road to go down it. I saw the carter shake the reins. When I had passed the passageway it struck me that it was a peculiar hour of the night for a carter to think of watering his horse. So I went back to look. There was nothing there – no cart, no horse, no carter, nothing. As you know, the river forms one side of the track and the wall of the rugby ground runs along the other, so the only way out is back up to the road. I went down to have a closer look. Not a thing. So where had they gone? Then as I turned to go back to the road, I realised there had been something odd about it. There had been no sound at all, no creaking of the cart, no horses' hooves – complete silence. I had seen a ghost.'

'Pay no attention,' their mother advised. 'Uncle Crispin saw nothing of the kind.'

'A ghostly manifestation,' Uncle Crispin insisted. He was quite serious.

After that Stella and he kept vigil from time to time; never in the dark though – they were not brave enough for that – but sometimes in the gathering dusk of an autumn evening. They stayed close together on the bridge with their elbows on the parapet and their eyes fixed on the slope of the lane from its beginning at the road level to its ending at the bank of the river. A smell of decaying vegetation hung in the air about them, and in the gloom the brown current was edged with white foam where it ribbed against the stanchion of the bridge. Once, when they leaned over the parapet to look, a carter who had been there already was turning his horse and cart away from the edge of the water to come back up to the road. They heard the crunch of wheels on the gravel and the creaking of shafts. They waited transfixed as the cart reached the bridge and began to approach them. But as he passed, the carter gave the reins a little tug and the bell hanging from the horse's harness made a tinkling sound. He was in a jovial mood and waved over to them out of the dusk.

'Hardy oul' evening,' he shouted across to them.

After that they kept away from the bridge.

How close to one another he and Stella had been in those far-off days. And well into adulthood too. How had he come to be so intolerant of her, and so antagonized? How had she changed? He wondered about it on his way back crossing the canal bridge at Leeson Street and passing the entrance to the Catholic University School which he had attended until his eighteenth year. He and Stella had walked or cycled together by the same route numberless times: on their way to Stephen's Green or to the cousins they visited frequently in Harcourt Street. Or to have afternoon tea with the O'Gradys at a later time when Stella and John O'Grady were beginning to get sweet on one another. She confided in him about it but he had already guessed and he had been very pleased for her sake and because he liked Johnny.

The visit to the Gate Theatre to see Dr Faustus, in which Godfrey Quigley was the Doctor and Aiden Grenell played Mephistophiles, was the highlight of his short stay.

Sartre's play ran into trouble. There had been rumbles of disapproval before it opened. Then it was reported that there had been a misunderstanding. The players believed they had booked the theatre through the Abbey. The Abbey said no. They could not let them use it at present because it had to be closed instantly. It had been discovered to be a fire trap. They succeeded in hiring the theatre of the Royal Irish Academy of Music as an alternative, but once again the hidden censors got to work and the Board of Governors of the Academy told them they would allow them to present the play, but only on condition that the name of the play and author would be removed from the posters. The players felt they had to comply. When Margaret and Lemuel and Frank attended on the second night, the theatre was nearly empty. At supper afterwards they wondered if it was because the play took liberties with the accepted notions of hell, or because it portrayed a lesbian character, or because the author was an Existentialist with views incompatible with those more generally held and orthodox. Then a thought flitted suddenly across Lemuel's mind.

'It's odd,' he remarked. 'Both the plays I've attended were about hell.'

'Has that some significance?' Frank asked.

'No. But I hadn't noticed it until this moment.'

When he was presenting some flowers to Margaret at his departure he said to her, 'I know it is not regarded as suitable to tell one young lady how closely she resembles another young lady, but it struck me at your very first visit to Avonmore, and it has fascinated me all the time I've been here.'

'Do I know her?' Margaret asked.

'No. She died very many years ago, long before you were born. She was only eighteen. Her name was Margot Penrose and she was very lovely.'

'And you loved her?' Margaret suggested, smiling.

'Very deeply,' he said.

He told Stella about it when he returned to Avonmore. She was not greatly interested. But when he spoke of going to see their old house on Lansdowne Road and asked her if she remembered their vigils on the Dodder bridge in quest of Uncle Crispin's ghostly visitation, she smiled sadly and said she did.

'I have many memories of Lansdowne Road,' she confessed. 'They come into my head at odd moments for no reason at all. Especially when I'm alone and sitting here at the fire.'

One of those memories, he felt sure, would be of the farewell party for Uncle Crispin and young John O'Grady. He felt a moment of compassion for her, a tenderness which had not troubled him for many and many a year. Later, when he sat at the piano he played a little Chopin for her, and then to please her more some of the songs she had sung and the popular tunes she had danced to when a girl and which she still adored.

Dear Margot,

I have returned from a visit to my young friend Frank McDonagh and his wife Margaret and I feel compelled to leave this for you to let you know that she is not only a charming and most lovely young woman, but bears a resemblance to you that I find quite uncanny. Of course she's older than you were, but this hardly makes any difference. I ask myself if there is such a thing as reincarnation after all. Could she be you? Is she you? One way or the other it brings me back to a time of great hopes and exquisite happiness, and evokes the sweetness of our all-too-brief relationship. I see you so clearly once again and that is worth the pain which must accompany such vivid remembering. I am a doddering 73, with the heart of a lovelorn lad of 17.

God pity all who are born.

I love you still.

Lem

Chapter 7

Margaret attended her usual Wednesday morning health and beauty class in the Rathmines Town Hall, but left a little early to have time to walk to her coffee appointment in Bewley's with Penny. The door closing behind her cut off suddenly the jangling of the piano and the rhythmic patter of the director which echoed in the large room. She stepped out by the side door into narrow lanes which brought her to Mount Pleasant Avenue. The October sun lit up the dome of the Church of Mary Immaculate, Refuge of Sinners, which rose in green and massive dominance above Lower Rathmines Road. It lent unseasonable warmth to the streets and dazzled her with its reflection on the water as she crossed the Grand Canal at Charlemont Bridge. In Harcourt Street it played on the weathered facades of the old Georgian houses, painting them with hues of red and orange and slaty blue. After lunch she would take the children for an airing in Palmerston Park. The leaves would be deep along the pathways, all yellows and reds and browns, arousing in her a joy and delight that had remained with her from childhood.

Penny was seated with a woman of around her own age. The air was heavy with odours of coffee and sticky buns.

'This is Denise,' Penny said, 'a friend of mine.'

'We bumped into each other. I hope I'm not butting in,' Denise apologised.

'Of course not,' Margaret said. She sat down.

'Margaret has been at her health and beauty class,' Penny explained. 'Wouldn't you know it. Look at the glow on those cheeks.'

'I walked down,' Margaret explained.

'From where?' Denise asked.

'From Rathmines. It's an absolute pet of a morning. And besides,

I'm full of the joys – I've discovered I've an elderly admirer, a charming old man who thinks I'm the spit and image of a boyhood sweetheart of his. She was very beautiful, he tells me.'

'Has he money?' Penny asked.

'Oodles of it,' Margaret declared.

They laughed together. But then Margaret thought of the ingenuousness of Lemuel Cox and felt a twinge of shame. It was wrong to poke fun at it.

'If it becomes a problem,' Penny added, still smiling, 'Denise here is your woman. She looks after the agony column for the magazine, among other things.'

'I'm Auntie Jane,' Denise supplied. 'Take a good look.' She raised her eyes briefly towards the ceiling.

'I would have thought that should be full of interest,' Margaret said.

'It would be if you were allowed to deal with the real problems.'

'And are you not?'

'Most of the real problems are taboo. I can talk about cures for dry skin or dandruff. Or even how to cope with a sagging bust line, thought that is regarded as sailing close to the wind. I can deal in a discreet way with a kid who thinks she's in love with two boyfriends at the same time, or who wonders if she should tolerate the overtures of a married man who swears he loves her to distraction and whose wife, he says, doesn't understand him. But the real problems can't be properly answered. Take the teenagers. A young girl asks if she can become pregnant through allowing French kissing; or a frightened boy wants to know if masturbation leads to blindness. The words French kissing and masturbation are barred. The editor won't print them. I'm allowed to reply privately, and I quite like writing letters, but very few youngsters supply addresses.'

'Are they usually sexual problems?'

'With young people, yes. But I can't discuss birth control in the column. It's taboo also. But I write to those I can contact, especially the ones who are denying the marriage act to their unfortunate husbands and running the risk of wrecking their marriage.'

Margaret controlled her face and the tone of her voice as best she could.

'What do you tell them?' she asked.

'Among other things, I tell them that husbands who don't get it at home usually go elsewhere for it.'

'I would think so too,' Margaret said.

She pitched her voice to make it sound detached and judicial. But the sunlight on the large window and the savour of her coffee were both noticeably diminished.

The day remained unusually calm and sunny. Palmerston Park was deserted. She wheeled the pram there in the afternoon with the children seated one at either end of it and the pathways so peaceful that the faint squeaking of one of its wheels was clearly audible. The rustling of leaves as she walked, and the coloured carpet they spread about her feet pleased her as always. But what Denise had said occupied much of her mind.

'Your friend Maeve telephoned,' Mrs Cleary told her when she got back. She returned the call.

'It's about the Legion,' Maeve said. 'You've probably guessed.'

'Is it Father Profundus?'

'Well, no – not yet. It's Mother Superior.'

'Has she been told I'm not attending?'

'It seems so. She was questioning me about it. I told her I thought you'd been ill. Perhaps you should drop her a note – any old thing to put her off.'

'I meant to do so earlier. I'll write telling her the truth,' Margaret decided.

'Don't be foolish. You'll only have herself or the Reverend Profundus making life a misery for you.'

'Let them. It may as well be faced up to first as last. I'm not going to be bullied.'

She wanted to talk to Frank about it but he was in bad humour when they sat down to their evening meal together and she decided it would be inopportune. He was in trouble over a cartoon of his which had appeared in *Laughter Parade* the previous month. *Laughter Parade* had been carrying an advertisement for several months in which the government regularly promoted its backing for the revival of the Irish language. All further insertions of the advertisement had been cancelled. The cartoon, they complained, had derided their campaign and they were not prepared to continue to do business.

'Kenny is bloody furious,' Frank said.

'With you?'

'With me, the government and with himself. He admits it was his responsibility as editor to decide whether to publish it or not. But he feels, no doubt, that I should have had more savvy.'

'Will it do you damage, do you think?'

'At present, no. But Morrissey let me know today that Kenny had decided anyway to advertise for an additional artist-cum-copywriter. When they get him that will make three of us on tap – myself, Jackson and the new recruit, whoever he'll happen to be. It'll hardly arise before the New Year. But when it does things are likely to become a bit crowded in Kenny, Morrissey & Co.'

'Life's no picnic, is it?'

'You're feeling a bit down, too?'

'Yes. A bit.'

'Look,' he suggested, 'let's go into town. The Abbey has been playing at the Queen's since that fire at their own theatre and I'd like to see how they're doing. We'll take a chance on getting seats.'

They made their way down to the old variety theatre where Boucicault and the patriotic melodramas of his lesser rivals had once thrilled their parents and grandparents. Tonight's offerings were Shaw's curtain raiser *Village Wooing* and Sean O'Casey's *The Shadow of a Gunman*. The house was reasonably full; the bar did a crowded and noisy trade; the orchestra (all five members) larrupped through a Rossini overture and a selection from Guonod's Faust, neither of them very relevant to the content of the plays and a suite of Irish airs, which were.

'While the Abbey is still here,' Frank remarked as they were leaving, 'I must suggest to Lemuel Cox that we should take him along sometime. I've heard him talking about his father patronising the old Queen's in its heyday.'

It was midweek in early November. The streets were not very busy. Fog was creeping down and spreading lightly about the lamp standards and empty shops and offices. They drove home saying very little. But their silence was companionable. They were both a little happier.

Dear Frank and Margaret,

When I said yes to your kind offer to take me to the Queen's theatre over the Christmas season to see the Abbey Theatre Company in action, I thought they would be presenting one of their regular plays. However, the paper now in front of me tells me that they are staging their seventh annual Gaelic Pantomime, this one being Reamonn Agus Niamh Og, the story of the daughter of Niamh Cinn Oir who returns after centuries from the Land of Youth and decides to marry a present-day Irishman. It assures me that, though the script is in Irish, the programme will carry a synopsis of the story in English and this, together with the acting and the use of mime, should enable non-Irish speakers to follow the action with very little difficulty. The presentation through the medium (I am further assured)'will be no bar to enjoyment'.

Despite such benign urgings I find my love of native tongue and homeland – powerful as both are – unequal to the undertaking of a long journey in the deeps of winter to sit through the performance of some whimsicality in a language I do not (shameful confession though it be) speak.

But the same notice informs me that plans for 1952 include the revival (probably in the spring) of such plays as The King of Friday's Men, Friends and Relations *and* The Righteous are Bold. *(The last, as I remember, is about an exorcism). I should much prefer to wait for the spring and one or other of those.*

Meanwhile, however, I would dearly love to see you both over the Christmas – it can be a more than usually lonely time out here at Avonmore. If you wish to bring a couple of friends along, that would be lovely. I'll invite one or two old neighbours and we'll have a party. Please say yes. Stella would love it, too.

Wishing you both every blessing for Christmas and the New Year.

> *Sincerely,*
> *Lemuel Cox*

They made the journey to Avonmore on New Year's Eve in the company of Morrissey, Penny and Jackson. Frank was glad to have Jackson along. He had volunteered to do the driving and, being a non-drinker, his offer would reduce the possible hazards of a long drive home after a night of celebration.

Lemuel Cox proved determined to make it so. The windows were ablaze with light as they approached up the driveway. High-stacked fires were burning brightly inside. Bottles were ranged on tables and glasses sparkled under lamps. He had engaged extra staff to cook and serve their needs. And he had invited some people of his own.

'This is Canon Deegen,' he said in introduction, 'our parish priest. And Mr and Mrs O'Byrne, two good neighbours who own and manage our excellent hotel and licensed premises. We may have Doctor Slattery along later – it depends on sick calls. Please sit down.'

When they were all supplied with drinks he raised his own glass to them and said, 'May I wish you, one and all, a happy and successful New Year.'

'And to you,' they said.

Mr O'Byrne left his glass down and said generally:

'Do you know what I'm going to tell you. That's a wish I've heard year after year for more years than I care to admit to. And I never hear it now but I wonder to myself how many more New Year's Eves are left of what the good Lord has set aside for me. It's a sobering thought.'

'So long as we're prepared, Larry,' the Canon answered sternly, 'we've nothing to be apprehensive about.'

'You're right, Canon,' Mrs O'Byrne put in. 'We do well to keep a heedful mind on what may come hereafter.'

'You remind me of a story a priest, a friend of mine from the west, once told me,' Jackson contributed. 'He went to great trouble to persuade his oldest parishioner to go inside the church for Mass on Sundays and not to just stand at the door. But it had no effect at all. Sunday after Sunday the old man took up his usual position outside the church door and remained rooted until the Mass ended. At last my friend decided it was time to admonish him. So one Sunday morning he went over, stood beside him and said, "John, how many times do I have to tell you that it's wrong to remain outside during the Mass. Do you never give a thought for the next world?"'

But the old man was unimpressed.

'"Yerra, Father," he said at last, "wan world at a time."'

Jackson had tobacco-stained teeth which he sucked when he was excited. He did so now. He had the habit, too, of putting his hands deep in his trouser pockets and scratching vigorously. He did that as well. The rest laughed at his story but the canon would have no truck with anyone who treated the Hereafter as a joking matter, and fixed him with a disapproving stare.

Dinner turned into a prolonged ceremony with glasses being frequently topped up. Then they retired to the sitting-room where Lemuel performed on the piano and accompanied Stella, whose voice was still reasonably good, when she sang: 'There is a flower that bloometh'. At the Canon's suggestion they honoured the nature of the season by trying some carols all together, after which Mrs O'Byrne was persuaded to oblige and selected:

> Open the door, Alannah
> Somebody wants you, dear.

'You were asking me recently about the Queen's Theatre,' Lemuel said to Frank when the song had finished. 'And that song brings it very clearly to mind. Dion Boucicault incorporated it in his play *Arrah na Pogue*.'

'I travelled many a time myself to Dublin just to attend the Queen's,' Mr O'Byrne put in.

'Boucicault was a fine dramatist,' Lemuel said.

'There were other fine plays,' Mr O'Byrne insisted, 'and other fine dramatists too. Where do you leave P.J. Bourke and his *For Ireland's Sake*. I remember seeing it in 1914; J.F. Mackey's Company of Irish Players performed at the Queen's in *The Croppy Boy* in those years. Ira Allen's company gave us *Father Murphy* or *The Hero of Tullow*. Then there was *Erin Machree* – I forget who wrote that – and another one about that notorious regicide and Bible-thumper Oliver Cromwell. Yes – *For Ireland's Liberty* – that's what it was called.'

'They were all highly patriotic,' Lemuel remarked. 'It became a bit overpowering at times.'

Lemuel, who felt that Mr O'Byrne was monopolising things, turned to the Canon.

'Would you agree with that, Canon?' he asked.

'You forget we have the Maynooth Statute which forbids the attendance of the clergy at theatrical performances,' the Canon answered, 'a view I shared long before the Statute was enacted. I've never attended presentations of the kind and so I cannot assess their effect.' The Canon tightened his lips. 'However, my information has always been that they were frequently salacious.'

Mr O'Byrne looked shocked.

'Goodness gracious, Canon dear, but you wouldn't find that kind of thing at the Queen's. The Queen's would have no truck at all with that class of carry on. Am I right, Lemuel?'

'I myself certainly never came across it,' Lemuel supported. 'There would be plenty of treachery and trickery portrayed, plenty of villainous rogues with crooked and unworthy designs. But never loose talk or offensive innuendo. Villainy was always circumvented. Virtue always triumphed.'

'That is not as I was told,' the Canon persisted. 'Nevertheless, I must accept your assurance.'

The tone of his voice conveyed that he was going to do no such thing. Stella did not want the pleasant atmosphere spoiled by the Canon's sourness. It was New Year's Eve, a time for goodwill and fellow feeling. They were all companions drifting forward to unpredictable and individual fates on a silent flowing river. It was the eve of yet another year which would take up its position at the head of others which stretched back one behind the other in unalterable order. Far down the file she was a child again, all on her own, the first born of the four. Then she was teaching Lemuel how to unclasp the hasp on the nursery toychest which always gave trouble. Later she was a schoolgirl and wearing a green bow in her hair on St Patrick's Day and singing in the convent choir. Later still she walked with John O'Grady in St Stephen's Green and he asked if her family would be at the Norton's New Year's Eve Ball again this year and she said they would and yes, she would be with them.

She looked across at Lemuel and said, 'Dr Slattery seems to have been delayed, after all.'

'He was anxious about old Mrs Hegarty.'

'So you said. Whatever is to happen, I hope it won't happen tonight.'

But when Dr Slattery eventually arrived, it had.

'She went very quietly,' he told Lemuel, 'there was nothing I could do.'

'People shouldn't die on New Year's Eve,' Stella said, 'it doesn't seem right.'

'You'll want something after your hard work,' Lemuel offered. 'I suggest a stiff whiskey.'

'I wouldn't say no,' Dr Slattery agreed.

When Lemuel had gone to fix it he turned to Morrissey.

'I hope you'll pardon me for asking,' he said, 'but when Lemuel introduced us I wondered if you might be related to the Morrissey family from Glendowan, which is about twenty miles from here. There was a Simon Morrissey there when I was a very young doctor—'

'That was my father,' Morrissey said.

For a moment the doctor seemed uneasy.

'I thought there was a resemblance. We've met before, long, long ago. I attended you briefly when you were five or six years of age.' And he smiled.

When Lemuel returned with his drink he said to him, 'I've discovered that Mr Morrissey here's a son of old Simon Morrissey of Glendowan.'

'Then I must have seen you around when you were a child,' Lemuel said to Morrissey. 'You had a sister – Alice, was it?'

'That was her name.'

'There. My memory is not yet totally destroyed,' Lemuel said, pleased with his own performance.

They turned on the radio a little before midnight and waited through its offering of nostalgic melody until the preliminary clamour of bells and hooters warned that the New Year was on the threshold. When the first stroke of midnight sounded, Lemuel struck up Auld Lang Syne on the piano and they shook hands as they wished one another a Happy New Year.

Dr Slattery stayed on a while for a nightcap and conversation after the rest had left. Stella kept them company. She was concerned about old Mrs Hegarty.

'Poor woman,' she reflected. 'She led a lonely life and was as poor as a church mouse. I don't think she had another of her own in the world.'

'An elderly cousin,' Dr Slattery told them. 'As old as herself and twice as poor. I think the parish will have to see to the funeral.'

'Dear goodness,' Stella said, very moved, 'what an end for her. The family was once comfortable and highly respected.'

'I'll have a word with the Canon about it,' Lemuel decided.

'That old sourpuss,' Stella complained. 'I wish you luck.'

'A formality. He'll simply pass it on to the parish committee. They'll see it's looked into.'

'An entirely self-centred old man,' Stella persisted. 'If the other guests weren't so forbearing, he would have spoiled the whole evening.'

Lemuel turned to Slattery.

'You were quick enough to recognize young Simon Morrissey after all the years.'

'The name struck a chord and the hip trouble set me on the trail. He was only a child when I attended the family but it had already affected him by then.'

'Poor child. A fall from a horse was the cause, I understand.'

'Not at all,' Dr Slattery said. 'It had developed long before he was old enough to handle a horse.'

'I'm sure Frank McDonagh told me it was the result of being thrown by a horse.'

'Nothing whatever to do with horses. It was a tubercular hip.'

'You tell me so?' Lemuel said, greatly puzzled.

'The father was a well set-up man when I first knew them. He was steward to the Bowden estate with a comfortable house to go with the job and highly regarded for the way he discharged his duties. But he fell into unbecoming habits.'

'The drink?' Lemuel supposed.

'The drink, yes,' Dr Slattery confirmed, 'but then to make sure the job was done properly, he began gambling heavily as well.'

'I didn't know that,' Lemuel said, 'but then my own acquaintance with them was long ago and very brief.'

'The upshot was he lost his stewardship and the steward's house.

But he was well enough treated. They gave him a cottage on the estate and the chance to earn a little doing odds and ends. It wasn't much of a cottage but it was a roof over their heads.'

'Well, hip or no hip,' Lemuel decided, 'young Simon seems to have done well for himself in the end of it all. I must find out more from Frank.'

Frank was adamant about it. Morrissey had referred many times, though never very specifically, to a riding accident. But when he cast his mind back he recalled other vague but positive references to a former background of privileged forms of recreation of the hunting, shooting, fishing variety. Now he began to wonder about their validity. Were they to be believed? Or were they meant simply to impress the audience?

Chapter 8

At teatime in their Lansdowne Road house his mother began to refill their cups, doing so – as always – in strict order of seniority: their father first, then Stella, the eldest at twelve years of age, then Lemuel who was nine, and, lastly, Godwin, who was only seven, and saying as she did so, 'Jonathan dear – more tea? Stella? Lemuel . . ? You, Godwin. . ? I declare to goodness there are times when I wonder did I marry Jonathan Cox or Jonathan Swift.'

That, Lemuel knew, was because his father was so devoted to the life and writings of Dean Swift and so proud of having been called Jonathan himself that he had given them all names connected in some way or other with his hero: Stella because that was the pet name Swift had given to Esther Johnson, his lifelong companion and (as he had declared) his 'truest, most virtuous and valued friend'. Lemuel was Lemuel Gulliver, surgeon and captain of several ships and explorer who had voyaged to Lilliput and other distant kingdoms. Godwin, an uncle of Swift's, had been greatly disliked by his nephew and died insane. Even the little dog they had was called Dingley after the brainless little woman who was Stella's help and companion.

He spoke frequently to them about Swift and tutored them in the details of his life. He now looked across at Godwin.

'Godwin, you are very young and I know the subject may be too advanced,' he said, 'but tell me something you now know about Jonathan Swift.'

Godwin puzzled over it for a while.

'I can't think, Father,' he said eventually.

'Of course you can think,' his mother urged. 'You've listened to your father reading *Gulliver's Travels*. Who wrote that?'

'Jonathan Swift,' Godwin remembered.

'There, you see. You must learn to think more carefully when asked a question.'

'Who can remember where Swift was born,' their father asked next. 'You, Lemuel?'

'In Dublin, in 1667,' Lemuel answered promptly. He and Stella liked being asked questions about Swift. Frequently the correct answer brought such pleasure to their father that it would earn them a prize of sixpence or even a shilling.

'Excellent. And where did he die. Do you know, Stella?'

'Yes, Father. In Dublin in the Deanery of St Patrick's Cathedral in 1745.'

He beamed with pride and pleasure and said to their mother, 'We are blest, my dear Celia, with clever and well informed children.'

The result was he felt they were now grown-up enough to be brought on trips to places associated with the dean. He engaged a carriage to take them to Laracor where Swift had been incumbent, and to see the remains of the nearby house where Stella had lived. This involved the adventure of a picnic by the wayside which they loved. He also hired a carriage to visit Marley Abbey where Esther Vanhomrigh, the ill-fated Vanessa, had lived. This time they picnicked on the pleasant banks of the River Liffey. Another time they went by horse and tram to the Phoenix Park to see the Magazine Fort about which Swift, who had gone to inspect it when it was first built, wrote a much quoted quatrain:

> A monument to Irish sense
> Here Irish wit is seen
> When nothing's left that's worth defence
> They build a Magazine.

Reciting this to them reminded him of another verse which also referred to the park. Swift had performed a marriage ceremony under one of the trees there on an afternoon of torrential rain and storm. Later on, it seemed, someone expressed a doubt that a marriage ceremony carried out in such eccentric circumstances could possibly be valid. Their father quoted for them the answer Swift had given:

> Under the oak in stormy weather
> John George and Jane were wed together
> And only He who made the thunder
> Can part John George and Jane assunder.

From the park he walked them along the quays of the Liffey to the cathedral where Swift had been dean for over thirty years. They left behind the broad green acres and the trees freshly in leaf with the river winding its thread of silver below them and the mountains raising their blue and graceful shapes away in the distance. The quayside streets were a bustle of hooves and wheels. They passed a row of red-and-blue-painted barges marshalled along the river wall for loading with barrels of Extra Stout from the sprawling yards of the Guinness brewery. Intermingled odours of brewery and river and steaming horse dung ascended with them as they climbed the steep hill to High Street. Here the distillery in Bow Street added its sour smell of leftover wash. At Francis Street they stepped into a world they had never suspected could exist. It led through a foul web of streets where tenement houses stretched line on tottering line with rags and sheets of cardboard stuffed into broken window panes to keep out the weather, and hallways which had long lost their front doors exhaled the malodorous breath of poverty, rotting woodwork, overflowing cesspits. Lemuel looked across at Stella and they both held their noses in disgust.

'I agree with you,' their mother remarked. 'How can poor human creatures be so reduced.'

Children in rags emerged from laneways that were spattered with mud and excrement, to surround Jonathan and beg from him.

'They are the unfortunate outcasts of a rapacious society,' he said in answer to their mother, when he had distributed what coins he was carrying in his pockets. 'You'll find no fouler breeding beds of disease in the whole world.'

The cathedral squatted in the centre of an improvised market place, where stalls under ramshackle canopies offered assortments of second-hand goods. Vendors and their baskets obstructed the footpath. Their tethered horses with rickety carts attached were spread out along the kennels. Beggers hawked broadsheets of the latest street ballads. A boy of ten or twelve performed with passable competence on a tin whistle, but Jonathan had already given away all his small change and Celia never carried any herself when she was with him, so the performance had to go unrewarded.

Inside the cathedral the polluted air of the streets became a wraith-like presence which stirred above them as the entrance doors closed with a dragging sound. It hung motionless when they sat to rest a little and to take in the surroundings.

Accumulated monuments and statues of past centuries crammed its dim and pillared length. Lemuel found them depressing and dreary. But the helmets and banners and swords of the Knights of St

Patrick which displayed their bright heraldic colours above the choir stalls thrilled him, and the flags of famous Irish regiments hanging in rows high up on the walls of the nave filled his imagination with gunfire and battlecries, bugle calls and the thunder of charging cavalry. These had flown above a hundred battlefields and were much more engaging than the tomb of Swift near the entrance porch, or that of Stella almost beside it. His father read out the Latin epitaph which Swift had written for himself and then translated it for them:

> Here lies the body of Jonathan Swift,
> Dean of this Cathedral, were fierce
> indignation can no longer lacerate his
> breast. Go, traveller and imitate, if you
> can, his utmost endeavours in the defence of
> liberty.

Lemuel marvelled, not for the first time, at his father's fluency in the Latin language.

The little tin-whistler was still playing his music dressed in an assortment of rags which bore no recognisable resemblance to any original garment. But at least the evening sun was adding a pleasant warmth and the air in the street was calm. Stella, thinking of the boy and his tin whistle while they were inside in the cathedral, had suddenly remembered the sixpenny piece that was stored away in her inside pocket. She found it and held it out to her father.

'I'd like you to give him this,' she said.

'It's your sixpence,' her father told her. 'You must give it to him yourself.'

She went over shyly and dropped the silver coin into the box at the boy's feet. He stopped playing, smiled and touched his forelock to her.

Kenny, seated at his desk in his shirt sleeves, had the others ranged about him in his office and was conducting one of his policy review conferences. Morrissey, as the junior partner, sat beside him. Frank and Ernie Jackson faced him. Miss Downey was to one side busily taking notes which P.J. had never been known to read afterwards. What he wanted, he said, was a drive for more business.

'We're doing fine,' he conceded, 'but we can do even better. One thing we must not do is lose our regular customers.' He directed his full attention in Frank's direction.

'Don't misunderstand me, Frank. I'm not harping on that little business of the Irish language cartoon. I was editor. I accept responsibility. Let that close the subject. But situations of a like kind can arise elsewhere. We do business with both ends of the construction industry, for instance, with the employers through their individual firms, and with the construction workers through their union bulletin. We should avoid, wherever possible, publishing what may please one side but give offence to the other. We've got to be cute about this and remain always conscious of the need for cuteness. I won't labour the point.

'Next we must go out for new business – prestigious business – the very highest. What about Hospitals Trust, Simon – I spoke to you about that?'

'I looked into it,' Morrissey said. 'Their copywriting isn't breathtaking for a start.'

'Maybe not, but the radio show is damn good. What's that signature tune:

> Makes no difference where you are
> You can wish upon a star—

When I hear it I want to dash out and buy a ticket myself.'

'I have a sample here of their selling approach,' Morrissey persisted. 'They listed in this particular ad the benefits we can all gain through buying a Hospitals Sweep Ticket. Just listen—

> *Family Happiness*
> *Luxury Travel*
> *Enjoyable Leisure*
> *A Dream House*
> *Ideal Old Age*
> *Alms For Charities*
> *Hopes Fulfilled*

'These are the highest aspirations of the bloke-next-door,' Jackson commented, 'all except the Alms For Charities bit, which is there to salve the conscience by suggesting a Christ-like element. It's clever enough.'

'I don't agree,' Morrissey said, 'it's too transparently cynical. The bloke-next-door cops on right away.'

'Matter a damn,' P.J. interjected, 'I wouldn't say no to having their account.' He looked at his watch. 'Anything else before I round off?'

'There's one area I feel could be explored,' Morrissey suggested, 'the sporting one – the hunting, shooting, fishing set. There was a time when their needs were supplied mainly from the workshops of small craftsmen living locally. It was so, I remember, when I used to go as a boy to my uncle's place in Roscommon. Duck, snipe, plover and the like were there aplenty. A few miles away on Lough Ree we'd first-class fishing. My father went down regularly to stay and took me with him.'

'I'd forgotten about your huntin', shootin', fishin' side,' P.J. bantered.

Morrissey smiled wistfully.

'I couldn't get around as well as the rest,' he confessed, 'but I did well enough. What I have in mind is that in those days the local workshops had no necessity to advertise, and no means of doing so, if it comes to that. But today the individual craftsmen have been absorbed into more centralized groupings which still don't use advertising to any significant extent. It might be worth trying to plant the idea of doing so among them.'

'Do you think you could?'

'I could try. After all, I grew up in the middle of it.'

P.J. thought the idea was worth a closer look. Morrissey agreed to develop it.

'Finally,' P.J. said, 'in addition to serving our clients' technical needs, I think we should involve ourselves more personally. At various functions, for instance, where our presence would be acceptable – the idea being to display our continuing interest. That sort of thing should create enormous goodwill.'

'Frank here has been doing something of the kind,' Morrissey commented, 'He's attended a number of construction workers' meetings to cover them for the *Bulletin*. Joe Dunne suggested it.'

'That's the sort of thing,' P.J. approved, 'provided we're careful to avoid giving our more conservative clients the idea that we are harbouring socialist tendencies.'

'Of course,' Morrissey concurred.

'Which brings me to my final item,' P.J. resumed. 'What I have been suggesting calls for more staffing. You'll know that over the past couple of months Simon and I have been considering applications for the position of an additional draughtsman-cum-copywriter, the final decision being mine. I've now made my selection. We'll have that extra help as from Monday next.'

He began to gather up his papers. Miss Downey stopped taking notes. Frank picked up his scribbling pad and said to P.J., 'May I ask who he is?'

'Of course,' P.J. said, 'but my choice may sound a bit unorthodox. It isn't a He. It's a She. A Miss Patricia Lennon. She's young and she'll need some initial guidance, but I know she's going to turn out extremely well.'

He beamed at all around him.

Margaret listened with only half an ear. No one in the office took P.J.'s review meetings very seriously. But when Frank mentioned that the new appointment had been made at last, her interest flickered.

'Do you know him?' she asked.

'It's not a Him. It's a Her.'

'A Her. You mean a woman?'

'A woman. A Miss Patricia Lennon.'

'I didn't realize women had access to that kind of work.'

'The odd one or two get in. She's probably one of these arty and crafty young ladies from some private tutor or other. P.J. tells us she'll need some initial guidance—'

'Who looks after that?'

'Certainly not Morrissey. Probably Jackson or myself. However, don't worry. If she's only a trainee, she's unlikely to pose any threat, which was what has been bothering me this while back.'

'And when does she start?'

'On Monday next.'

'So soon,' Margaret said.

She was suddenly thoughtful.

Their Lansdowne Road house had been fine. From it you could walk to Sandymount and its great strand in ten minutes, and then follow it along the coastline for as far as you pleased. Or you could head out along the suburban roads and in no time you were rambling the winding country lanes which led into the silence and solitude of the mountains.

But the sweetest days ever had always belonged to Avonmore. Those long summer days and the simple entertainments of country living; the garden parties, the visiting circus, the dog trials, the handicraft exhibitions, even the poultry shows. Young friends came to stay for a while and Stella and Godwin and he would take them roaming the mountains and swimming in the Pooka's Pool, revealing to them the special haunts they had discovered: a camouflaged den in the depths of the wood, an ancient path lost in the wild spread of fern and heather. One secret only he held back from all of them, even Stella. It was the hollow hideyhole in the beech tree, a personal possession of magical properties, until little Jonathan's birth and his mother's consequent death changed the magic into holiness and the hollowed bole into a shrine. Margot Penrose alone shared its secret.

The ground floor of the Union premises was deserted and Joe Dunne's office in darkness, but from the first or second floor above them the sound of a brass band drifted thinly. It grew massively in volume as they climbed, and became a sudden ear-splitting din when they opened the door to the rehearsal room. Bandmaster Fogarty was conducting, a duty that had been his for over forty years. He was too engrossed to notice their entry until the piece had finished and he stopped to leave down his baton and mop his brow. When he saw them he came across to greet Frank with obvious pleasure.

'Let me introduce Miss Lennon,' Frank said. 'She joined us very recently in Kenny Morrissey's and I'm showing her around. Patricia, meet Bandmaster Fogarty.'

Bandmaster Fogarty extended his hand. He was the remains of a once tall, well-built man, soldierly in bearing, who had become an institution, referred to always and only as the Bandmaster.

He said, stiffly and gallantly, 'A pleasure to meet a pleasant and beautiful young lady. Can I be of help?'

'If you would,' Frank said. 'We had an appointment with the general secretary for eight o'clock but he's not in his office.'

'No,' Bandmaster Fogarty confirmed. He's above addressing a meeting of Mullett's men. There was a sudden stoppage there today and he's trying to sort things out.'

'Is there any point in our waiting?'

'Let me see to the lads here first and we'll try to find out.'

Bandmaster Fogarty announced a break of fifteen minutes to the players and led the way to the floor above, where cigarette smoke billowed out of the overcrowded assembly room when he pushed open the door. Through the blue haze they could make out the platform at the far end from which Joe Dunne was addressing the members. Bandmaster Fogarty picked his way through the thickly pressed pack of bodies and waited his opportunity to intervene. He had a whispered exchange and returned.

'He sends his apologies,' he explained, 'but hopes, if you can hang on for fifteen or twenty minutes, to get away to talk to you.'

They went back to the bandroom to wait. Music stands were spread about in disorder and pools of water surrounded most of the chairs. Bandmaster Fogarty steered them clear of this disagreeable array.

'Saving your presence, Miss Lennon,' he apologised, 'but blowing a brass instrument for any length of time is a watery class of an occupation. There's no alternative but to shake the stuff out of it from time to time.'

Miss Lennon smiled and said pleasantly, 'I wonder the poor men don't dehydrate altogether.'

'You'll find they've already taken themselves over to Ryan's public house with that problem in mind.'

He turned to Frank, 'I think you told me you play yourself?'

'The flute,' Frank confirmed.

Miss Lennon was agreeably impressed and looked at him in admiration, 'My goodness,' she exclaimed, 'what a lot of talents you possess.'

'I'm not very good at it,' Frank said modestly.

'I'm sure that's not so,' Miss Lennon contradicted with resolute charm. 'I'm sure you are being simply too modest to own up'.

'Are you a music lover yourself, Miss Lennon?' Bandmaster Fogarty enquired.

'My father was a great enthusiast and we had lots of music at home throughout my growing-up. He used hired professionals for our musical house parties – chamber music especially. Mozart, I think, wrote three very agreeable flute quartets: one in C major, one in D major and one in A major. Do I remember correctly, Frank?'

'You do indeed,' he confirmed, much impressed.

They sat down.

'The flute is one of the more genteel members of the wind family,' Bandmaster Fogarty observed.

'No puddles on the floor,' Frank agreed. 'You're a lifetime in music yourself, I'm told.'

'It began when I was a young lad in the British Army,' Bandmaster Fogarty admitted. 'That was before the First World War. When I was in civvy street again, in 1910, I landed this job as tutor and conductor with the Union band. They were hard times for taking on that kind of thing – strikes and lock-outs everywhere and bloody confrontations. The police couldn't stand us. Then, after the big lock-out of 1913 the Union was broken and the band dismantled, so I took to soldiering again and ended up at Suvla Bay and later in France. As did many another, I might add.'

Bandmaster Fogarty began to wander at random over his own past and that of the band. The stories of far-off encounters and personalities who were now part of history became fascinating. When the flow ceased for a moment, Frank was tempted to ask if anyone had ever featured the band in the *Bulletin*.

'I mean, the band and the highlights of the past and your own long years of service?'

'No,' Bandmaster Fogarty answered, 'and I've often thought they should. It's sad to see all that part of the past gone out with the tide.'

'Would you mind if I suggested to Joe Dunne that it should be written up?'

'Not in the least.' Bandmaster Fogarty was well pleased.

Members were returning. The sound of tuning and a cacophony of different passages filled the room. Frank and Miss Lennon stayed on. Ballcock Brady came in to convey a further message from the general secretary and to express his apologies. He was obliged to postpone their appointment after all. Ballcock sat with them and remained listening until the rehearsal ended.

'I come to listen to them rehearsing whenever I happen to be here and they're at it,' he told them. 'Do you like the sound of a brass band?'

'Very much,' Frank confessed.

'Yes indeed,' Miss Lennon agreed.

'I love it myself,' Ballcock told them. 'But far and above even that, I love the sound of strings. The violin is a gorgeous instrument. I often say to the missus: I'd give my right arm to be able to play the violin.'

Miss Lennon looked at Frank. Frank smiled.

'Bandmaster and I will be going for a drink and a chat together later on. Would you and the young lady care to join us?'

Miss Lennon felt a drink would be just the thing. Frank agreed. He would also welcome the opportunity to talk a bit more with Fogarty about the band's chequered career. It was the kind of thing, he knew, that would win the whole-hearted approval of P.J.

In Ryan's, Bandmaster Fogarty took over and talked until closing time brought the matter to an end. The hour was late. Frank was the only one with a car. In the circumstances he felt he should offer to drive them home, but by the time he had done so and inserted his key in his own halldoor it was after midnight. The house was very quiet. Margaret had gone to bed.

Next morning, at breakfast, she said, 'I didn't hear you coming in. You were late?'

'I stayed on to discuss a feature for the *Bulletin* with a character called Bandmaster Fogarty. We went for a drink and Ballcock

Brady, who was hiding in the woodwork as usual, joined us. It was quite late so I felt I should drop them home. It's one of the disadvantages of having a car, I'm beginning to discover.' He omitted to say he had also left Patricia Lennon home. Later in the day he began to wonder why? The omission irritated him.

Margaret denied to herself that the arrival on the scene of Miss Lennon was causing her a moment's uneasiness. Nevertheless she began to note the occasions when Frank was delayed or late. Much to her surprise, she found herself talking to Penny about it.

'Have you met the new girl yet – the one they've taken on at the office?'

'Miss Lennon – not yet,' Penny answered. 'Have you?'

'No. Frank seems to see quite a lot of her. He and Ernie Jackson are taking turns to introduce her to the clients and teach her the various routines.'

'Are you unhappy about it?'

'For goodness sake. Why should I be unhappy—'

'I thought you sounded a bit.'

She had betrayed her anxiety. It would be best now to continue.

'Well – a bit perhaps. I remember what Denise said that morning in Bewley's and wondered could she be right. About husbands who don't get it at home going elsewhere for it.'

'That's the agony column portion of Denise's mind. It conjures up problems all over the place.'

'You think so?'

'I do. Nevertheless,' Penny decided, 'I think perhaps it's time to have a closer look at young Miss Lennon.'

Her solution was to hold a small dinner party with Frank, Simon and Ernie Jackson in attendance to formally introduce Miss Lennon as the new member of the office family. Morrissey had revealed that Miss Lennon was not a pupil of the College of Art, nor a trainee of one of the commercial offices. She had been a private student with a one-time pupil of Orpen – a veteran survivor who had found a profitable balance between the creative and commercial opportunities on offer. Miss Lennon saw good sense in the compromise and hoped to repeat its success. Her background was well-to-do. She intended that her own adult style should be the same.

She was not as either Penny or Margaret had visualized. They had expected some eccentricity as to hairstyle or jangling bracelets or cascading necklaces, perhaps even drapes. They found instead a two-piece suit, a pretty hairstyle and a fetching elegance. In artistic matters Miss Lennon was superbly well informed. Over dinner she discussed the work of Hilary Heron, whom she regarded as Ireland's only modern sculptor; she deplored at some length the absence of any connection whatever between people in real life and the characterless presentation of them in what passed currently for modern religious art; she reported a conversation she had had with Patrick Swift at a recent R.H.A. Exhibition, during which he told her there was nothing of any worth there with the exception of a couple of pictures by Yeats and the odd canvas by Le Brocquy. Then she turned to Frank and said:

'I was looking at those things on your desk, Frank. You have a lovely sense of caricature. Really you have. I feel you conceive the comedy pictorially and then leave the caption to come later. That's how Cornelius Veth believes it should be. Have you read him?'

'He defined caricature as the human creature's amusement with itself and its environment,' Frank replied.

'Veth,' Ernie Jackson pronounced, 'is a consequential bore.'

'I don't agree, Ernest,' Miss Lennon said severely. 'Would you, Simon?'

'My dear Patricia,' Simon said, 'when you are a little older and a lot more cynical you will have to come to realise that pronouncements and definitions are relative and largely useless, and always a bore.'

They had Veth for another twenty minutes. Penny and Margaret hung about on the sideline; Margaret noting with some anxiety the first-name nature of Miss Lennon's exchanges, Penny drinking a little more than was usual in her effort to be bright and interested in their high-minded shop talk.'

When the others had gone and it was time for a nightcap together at the fire, Penny said to Simon, 'What dreary tabletalk. Who in Christ's name was, or is, Cornelius Veth?' She was the slightest bit tipsy.

'I told you – a pursuer of definitions, who believed among other things that caricature is rooted in amusement. My own view is that if it is rooted in any one thing it's rooted in uneasiness, the kind you feel when you look too closely at human pretension.'

'Simon, please. Don't start that again—'

'What puzzles me is why you wanted a goddamn dinner party in the first place.'

'Be a dear,' she asked, 'and give me just one more drink and then I'll tell all.'

He did so.

'Poor Margaret and Frank,' she explained. 'Margaret is worried. Poor dear nice Margaret is worried. She's afraid she's going to lose poor dear nice Frank.'

'Why should she lose poor dear nice Frank?'

'Because they are both very good little Catholics. They are trying to space their family, but are doing their best to work birth control through abstinence.'

'Dear God—'

'But big mouth Denise told poor nice Margaret that men who don't get it at home usually ferret it out elsewhere. So she doesn't like the fact that Frank has to be spending so much time training pretty Miss Lennon because she fears Miss Lennon might decide to be loving and giving as well.'

'Penny, you're getting tiddley—'

'I know. It's all that Cornelius Veth fellow's fault—'

'And you can tell Margaret there isn't the slightest chance of Miss Lennon throwing herself at Frank.'

'Oh. You think not?'

'Patricia Lennon will play her cards with exquisite care until someone who is rich and highly influential in the world of art or high-class advertising or something comes along. Then she'll concentrate her charms and attractions and sail into matrimony with all flags flying. Miss Lennon hasn't the slightest intention of wasting time on a young married man who has a wife already and two children and a very modest share of the world's wealth. She'll flatter Frank and coax him while he has some useful information to pass on to her. But the fact that he is also a man won't occur to her even remotely. You can tell Margaret I said so.'

'I couldn't do that, Dunderhead,' Penny said, 'she'd know I'd been talking about her.'

Margaret found Miss Lennon becoming an almost hourly pre-occupation. If Frank were late home, which began to happen more and more frequently, she found it impossible, however much she tried, to resist questioning him about it. If she found he had been in her company it made her miserable; if he said he had not it made her even more miserable because she wondered if she could believe him. When he arrived home at a normal hour she began to find everyday conversation difficult and took instead to spending long periods talking to Mrs Cleary in her small living room downstairs. If he was not at home before ten o'clock she went to bed on her own. When he spoke to her she answered in as few words as possible. After a while he gave it up and began to match her silences. One evening, when they had been sitting together for almost an hour without any exchange and she rose quietly to go down to Mrs Cleary, he lowered his paper and called to her. She stopped at the door and turned to face him.

'Margaret,' he said, 'what have I done to offend you?'

'Nothing. Nothing at all.'

'That couldn't be true,' he said, 'you wouldn't go on as you are if it were. Won't you tell me?'

She hesitated. Then, feeling foolish and ashamed, she forced herself to tell him.

'If you must know, I don't like you to be so much in the company of Patricia Lennon.'

'But why?'

'I simply don't.'

'P.J. has me tutoring her in the cunning ways of Kenny Morrissey and Company – you know that.'

'Why you? Why doesn't Ernie Jackson do his share?'

'But he does.'

'It seems to take up such a lot of time.'

'It does. A damnable amount. But it won't for much longer. P.J. is sending her off to London for a fortnight as from tomorrow. His contacts there will give her a finishing look around and that should see the end of it.'

He left his paper down altogether and pushed it aside. 'Look, why don't we go out for a walk and a drink.'

She hesitated again. Then she said, 'I'll get my coat.'

They took their old route to the Dropping Well by suburban roads where dusk and quiet mingled in silent companionship. It was October again. Along the way a carpet of leaves muffled the tread of their feet. They paused briefly on the bridge as they always had done to gaze down at the brown and glimmering glow of the Dodder. All was familiar and reassuring.

Her renewed confidence continued for a weekend, then melted away. She accepted what he had told her: that Miss Lennon was in London, but that need not prevent him phoning her from the office. One evening, when he became quite engrossed in something he was writing, the thought that it was a letter to Miss Lennon became a conviction. But they had returned to their habit of mutual silence and she had no way of probing at it without betraying her thoughts. She watched until he rose at last to go out for his evening walk. He folded the letter as though to put it in his pocket, then changed his mind and left it on the side table. It hypnotised her. She heard the door closing behind her. She had never in her life read anything belonging to him unless specifically invited to do so. Now, temptation choking and overmastering her, she went over and picked it up. She opened it. It was not a letter after all but several disjointed attempts at cogent expression which had ended finally in complete success. She read:

You Beath

I wish that some millionaire's daughter
Would throw herself into the waughter
To save her from death
I'd get myself weath
And her Pa would reward me, or augther.

After that she felt she had to tell someone. She selected Penny, who went into hysterics.

Painfully embarrassed, Margaret said, 'I know. It's ridiculous. But don't laugh. It's not funny. What am I to do?'

'Do what I did, my dear. Go to Belfast and have a diaphragm fitted. You'll find peace of mind. I'll give you an address.'

She told Maeve over coffee and showed her the address. Maeve was firm.

'Penny is right. Go up without delay and get the bloody thing.'

'You think so?'

'Not only do I think so, I'll go up with you and have the same job done on myself. Peter is fed up with condoms. He says they're only for students or soldiers on foreign service.'

'I'm wondering about Frank. When it comes to religion his inclination is usually to stick to the rules.'

'Then why tell him?'

The prospect of Maeve's company and support decided her. They made their appointments, told husbands and friends it was a shopping trip and took the train together. The examination, the intimate probing, the subsequent lesson in practical application and the consciousness of heinous doctrinal disobedience filled Margaret with guilt. Some integral part of her upbringing was being assailed.

Maeve took it in her stride and laughed about it on their way home, 'I'm wondering what Reverend Mother would think.'

The same thought had come to Margaret. It triggered no gaiety.

For some weeks she said nothing to Frank and there was no way of making use of her acquisition without him finding out. The preliminary drill, she believed, would betray her if nothing else did. She sought out acceptable ways of breaking the news to him. She read the agony columns, seeking some mention of her dilemma, believing it must surely be widespread. Nothing turned up. She paid short visits to churches on her route when out shopping, and prayed for guidance. Through long habit she solicited the assistance of St Anne and the Mother of Good Counsel by lighting candles at their respective shrines, seeing nothing inconsistent in turning to them for help. They stared stonily back at her. Meanwhile Frank and she resorted again to old-fashioned interruption of the marriage act from time to time. After one such session she thought she would tackle the matter obliquely.

'I've been thinking, Frank,' she said, 'making love in this way is all sin and no satisfaction.'

'I know. But what can we do?'

'I could go to Belfast and have something or other fitted. Penny did.'

'Penny isn't a Catholic.'

'Penny isn't even married. What difference does it make? If we're bound to sin one way or another we may as well get some good out of it.'

'They are not one and the same thing,' he said. 'There's a difference between a sin that has some spontaneous element to excuse it and one which is premeditated and deliberately prepared for.'

'I don't follow that at all,' she said, becoming angry. 'I'm going to Belfast. Lots of people have done it.'

'Margaret,' he said. 'You know you can't.'

She lost control.

'I bloody can,' she shouted.

'You bloody won't,' he shouted back.

She looked at him with sudden hate.

'You can't bloody stop me,' she screamed, 'because I already bloody have.'

He was stunned momentarily into silence. Then, incredulous, he asked, 'You have what?'

But by now she was bawling her heart out and couldn't hear him.

The diaphragm – small, soft, rubber-domed – lay undisturbed in its container well into the New Year. They had patched things up between them in their own way and adjusted to getting on with their personal relationship despite their disagreement. She insisted on showing him the diaphragm as part of their undeclared truce. He said nothing at the time, but referred to it ever afterwards as her engine of delight. She didn't really mind. Then one evening he returned with news of Miss Lennon which proved Simon Morrissey's powers as a prophet. She had never returned to Kenny Morrissey and Co. from London and now word had come that she was engaged to be married to a highly fashionable and influential agent she had met there.

'So I was right, was I not?' Simon Morrissey boasted to Penny.

'Were you ever wrong?' she approved wholeheartedly.

Margaret threw out the diaphragm and instructions manual and told Frank what she had done. They never spoke of it again.

Part Two

Chapter 9

Avonmore
May 14th 1953
(Ascension Thursday)

Dear Frank and Margaret,

Today being the one it is has set my mind back to your visit. What a nice Eastertide we spent all together, you and Margaret and the two children and Stella and myself. And what lovely children. Aoife is still too young, of course, to project any very revealing hints of where her later interests are likely to lie. But Paul (I know he has just past his fifth birthday – many happy returns to him) is giving clearer indications. He watched every move you made when driving us around in the car. In the house the piano was the focal point and drew him irresistibly. Please forgive Stella's odd bout of irritation. She found his sudden and somewhat cacophonous impromptus startling. To me they were merely the first faltering steps on the road to keyboard mastery.

How they enjoyed the bonfire on Easter Saturday. When Stella and I and Godwin and young Jonathan were children and my mother still alive, my father used to light one for us to commemorate the Paschal fire St Patrick lit on the hill of Slane before beginning his Mission to the Irish in that miraculous year of 432.

There was another important fire I helped to light in times gone by which returns persistently to haunt my memory. It was a bonfire for St John's Eve long, long ago (to be precise, June 23rd 1895 – I was seventeen at the time). When you bring the family for the Whit weekend in ten or so days time, I may tell you about it.

With warmest wishes to you both and looking forward to that visit.

Sincerely yours,
Lemuel Cox

The June day on which the house guests were to arrive began a little uncertainly: at breakfast it was too bright for such an early hour (his father thought) and later showed signs of cloud build-up on the nearer mountains. But by noon the good weather got the upper hand. The sun was drawing delicate drifts of vapour from the brown surface of the river and flooding the spare bedrooms, which were being made ready by the house staff. Mrs Stephens sang at her work in the kitchen – a good sign.

Stella had stayed with their cousins the Nortons on Stephen's Green, and had her young friend Margot Penrose to stay with her. They were to travel on the Westland Row line to Bray with the two brothers of the O'Grady family, John and Eddie.

'How are they to manage from there?' Godwin asked.

'They'll take a couple of outside cars from Bray to Edmundscourt and two of McGinty's pony traps to here.'

Godwin was fifteen. He liked to sound worldly wise and disillusioned. 'If they can find him,' he remarked. 'McGinty, I've been told, is seldom sober on Mondays.'

But McGinty deputed two of his workmen to drive them so they arrived in good order and in time for afternoon tea, which they sat down to when bedrooms had been allotted and rough unpacking completed. Jonathan remained in his study and would do so until Uncle Crispin arrived, but Lemuel and Godwin sat with them and allowed little Jonathan to join them. The O'Grady brothers were familiar and popular company, especially Johnny, who at twenty-three was the older of the two and enjoyed the added glamour of being a young lieutenant stationed at the Curragh. The complete newcomer was Margot Penrose. Lemuel had seen her before in Edmundscourt, but only at a distance and usually in the pale blue shirt and grey tunic of the pupils of the Protestant Boarding School. Now she wore a white blouse and long navy skirt and a straw hat with a pink band and a yellow rose. He knew she was around sixteen, but the clothes added a couple of years. They also revealed something he had not been in a position to note before: that she had very lovely features and eyes that were lively and humorous. The fact that she was Protestant caused Stella to hesitate before venturing to ask her as a guest, but their father had been surprisingly offhand about it. Watching her now while tea was being poured and scones passed about, Lemuel felt in quite a detached way that it was going to be interesting to see how things would turn out.

Uncle Crispin was the one to be late. The two workmen had not yet returned when he reached Edmundscourt so McGinty, who, as Godwin had predicted, was almost footless, insisted on stepping into the breach by escorting him personally. The only remaining vehicle was an outside car. With some misgiving Uncle Crispin strapped his luggage and bicycle on one side of it and mounted the other himself. McGinty took the reins and for three miles or so swayed dangerously in the driving seat but managed to stay aboard. Then the car lurched violently over an unexpectedly large pothole and McGinty, with a loud yell, shot out of his seat and into the ditch, taking horse and car, passenger and contents with him. He also broke a wheel and a shaft in the process.

After a fruitless hour waiting for help of some kind to pass by, Uncle Crispin decided to abandon his belongings temporarily and complete the journey on his bicycle. Before doing so he threatened to have McGinty arrested if his belongings were not sent on at the earliest possible moment.

But by dinner time his good humour had returned and he entertained the table with the details.

'The answer, of course,' he decided as he concluded, 'is to get oneself a motor car.'

'You mean one of these horseless carriages?' Jonathan remarked. 'I'm surprised you haven't done so already.'

'I couldn't see the point of sitting at the wheel of an ingenious piece of engineering, capable of a speed of twenty or more miles an hour, being forced to creep along at three miles behind some thickhead chewing a straw and carrying a red flag,' Uncle Crispin replied. 'However, I now have information from a source very close to Sir David Salomons that a proposed Locomotives On Highways Act will do away with this red flag nonsense and allow motor vehicles to use the public roads without them quite shortly.'

'It'll frighten the horses,' Jonathan foretold, 'and slaughter the unfortunate pedestrians.'

Uncle Crispin ignored him.

'That, and the replacement of electric power by petrol or paraffin and the enormous technical advance of the pneumatic tube, is going to revolutionize road transport. Have you met John Boyd Dunlop?'

Jonathan had not.

'A most interesting person. He's living at present on the Ailesbury Road in Donnybrook. Number 46. He told me he thought of using steel at first but came to rule it out because it would never stand up to the constant bouncing and bending on the road. That's how he hit on the idea of a triple tube – rubber, canvas and rubber again,

87

filled with compressed air. He cycles quite regularly about the city himself.'

'Is he an engineer by profession?'

'No – a veterinary surgeon. If I'd been he I'd have kept the discovery strictly to myself.'

'Why so?' Jonathan wondered.

'Because eventually it will replace horses altogether.'

'What if it does?'

'John Boyd Dunlop will make yet another discovery: that he has deprived himself of a large part of his veterinary practice.'

Uncle Crispin made it sound so droll that everyone at the dinner table laughed. Miss Penrose in particular, Lemuel noticed. He found her merriment infectious and pleasing.

Jonathan and Uncle Crispin stayed on to talk after dinner but the young people went walking. They strolled by the river and for a short distance along the public road. The air hung warmly and the evening light seemed destined to tarry forever in the infinite stretches of the June sky. It would be Midsummer's Day in a few days time, Stella remarked, the longest day of the year.

'I don't bear to think about it,' her friend Margot told her. 'I'd prefer the longest of lovely summer days to stay ahead of us for ever and ever and ever.'

But John O'Grady thought differently.

'Most of us would wish pleasant things to remain forever, but endings are necessary.'

'Why so?' Lemuel questioned.

'I don't properly understand,' John O'Grady admitted, 'but Byron remarked on it and the reasons he sets out are persuasive:

> So, we'll go no more aroving
> So late into the night
> Though the heart be still as loving
> And the moon be still as bright
>
> For the sword outwears its sheath
> And the soul wears out the breast
> And the heart must pause to breathe
> And love itself have rest.

'I like that,' Lemuel said. 'Is there more?'

'Just one more verse.'

'Well—?'

John O'Grady continued:

Though the night was made for loving
And the day returns too soon
Yet we'll go no more aroving
By the light of the moon

'That's lovely,' Miss Penrose said, 'but it's very sad.'

John's brother Eddie spoke for the first time. 'Pity we don't have a moon.'

They all smiled politely. All, that is, except Stella, whose adoring gaze was fixed on Johnny O'Grady, her young lieutenant with Byron's poems at his fingertips.

As they turned off the road through the entrance gate once more, a pony and trap swept past them in the dusk at a hectic pace and clattered down the driveway.

'What was that?' Stella asked.

The rest were equally startled. Eddie O'Grady watched the trap's progress and its erratic swinging from side to side.

'Could it be McGinty?' he suggested.

It was. When they arrived back at the house, Uncle Crispin's luggage was lying in the hallway and he was doing his best to sort it out. McGinty (he told them) had allowed himself further refreshment to soothe the shocked state of his nerves when help had come at last. He had now been put on a mattress in the stable behind the house to sleep it off in the company of the replacement pony which was feeding contentedly on the hay that lay plentifully about. It was not an unprecedented situation, Jonathan explained. It had happened from time to time in the past. McGinty would wake up in due course and be sober enough to find his way home.

Uncle Crispin heard him doing so somewhere around five o'clock in the morning. The wheels crunching as the trap swung about on the gravel and the sound of hooves working up to a trot awakened him. Framed in the bedroom window, the pale upreaching fingers of dawn were spreading out to show McGinty his way.

Margot Penrose heard him too. She had slept hardly at all and knew she could not possibly spend another night in the same room. The embarrassment of having to say so to Stella would be dreadful, but it could be endured, whereas another session of listening to scratching and scampering in almost total darkness could not. She was afraid of mice. Irrationally so, she conceded. Nevertheless mortally and incurably so. Mice terrified her. And there was one — at least one — in her bedroom.

Stella was very understanding about it. She was even apologetic.

The guest rooms were simply not used frequently enough, she explained. They should be inspected regularly but of course they were not. Servants forgot or didn't bother, and country mice, who were as clever as you please, got to know this quickly enough and took every advantage. The solution was to make a change of rooms. She would arrange it without delay.

In the course of the morning she spoke to Lemuel. She could not offer her own room because little Jonathan slept in the nursery which opened directly off it, and it would be unthinkable to have a five-year-old wandering in and out of a guest's bedroom whenever the fancy took him. Since there was no other room to spare would Lemuel swap around and surrender his own for the duration of the visit? Lemuel was perfectly agreeable. It was only a matter of transferring a few odds and ends from one room to the other.

In the course of the morning the transfer was effected. In the afternoon Stella suggested they should bathe in the river and have a picnic on its banks. Jonathan had work to attend to in his study and Uncle Crispin wished to go exploring on his bicycle. The young people set off in pairs: Godwin with Eddie, Stella with John; Lemuel with Margot Penrose.

'You were very kind to swap your room,' she told him as they filed along the narrow woodland path which wound between fern and frocan bushes.

'My pleasure, Miss Penrose,' he assured her.

'I'm aware that to have to give up one's room because some silly female. . .'

'My dear Miss Penrose—' he protested.

'I apologize most sincerely.'

'There's no necessity.'

'And it makes me feel more guilty still when you keep calling me Miss Penrose.'

'What then, should I call you?'

'I think Margot is perfectly suitable.'

'Very well then – Margot.'

'Good,' she approved, 'that looks after formality. May I call you Lemuel?'

'As you wish. I prefer Lem.'

'Lem it is. What I want you to let me say is this: I feel a great fool about my behaviour. I feel I must appear to be acting the part of the defenceless, dependent female, who needs to be reassured and defended. I am not. This ridiculous terror of a little creature quite incapable of doing me harm is inexplicable. But I have suffered it as

90

long as I can remember and there is nothing I can do about it.'

'I'll set a trap for your visitor tonight.'

'I think there are more than one.'

'Then for them. You'll have their heads on a platter.'

'Stop,' she appealed, 'I don't want such a thing.'

'Very well. I'll dispose of them secretly.'

'Now you are making fun of me.'

He smiled broadly, saying nothing.

'The funny thing is,' she admitted, 'I keep a scrapbook and I've a couple of poems about mice in it. One of them starts:

> All dressed in grey, a little mouse
> Has made his home within my house;
> And every night and every morn,
> I say, "I wish that mouse were gone".'

She stopped and shrugged her shoulders.

'There's more but I can't remember it. I must look it up when I get back to the house.'

'Do you always carry your scrapbook with you?'

'On holidays. On visits. Back with me to school. Everywhere. I'm like a magpie, I have to gather things together. Do you?'

He was about to say no but thought of the growing trove of notes and comments hidden in the bole of his tree.

'In a sort of way,' he admitted.

'I'm told I should really call my scrapbook a chapbook, but I'm not quite sure what it is.'

'I think it used to be a collection of ballads and jokes and stories and prayers and such odds and ends hawked around by chapmen in days gone by.'

'That's exactly what my scrapbook is,' she admitted, 'so I must be a sort of chapwoman.'

They reached the clearing where the others were already sitting about on the grass awaiting their arrival before undressing for their swim.

'The Pooka's Pool,' he told her, indicating the miniature waterfall and the spreading river. Stella took her to a more private area where they could change into swimming apparel with maidenly circumspection.

The men had changed and were already in the water. They were familiar with the pool from earlier visits and were showing off its entertaining features. Eddie O'Grady clambered on to the rock in the centre which rose some feet above the surface. He dived back in again with practised skill and surfaced several feet away. Godwin swung back and forth from a supple branch overhanging the water and allowed Lemuel to push him repeatedly outwards until its limit was reached. When this happened he relinquished his grip, went flying through the air and plummeted into the water with an earshattering splash. Since Stella had been the one who first discovered the underwater ledge and mastered the feat of being able to sit on it without a stir for several seconds, she was allowed to demonstrate it to Margot before the rest showed their mastery in turn. They urged Margot to have a try herself, but she refused all their offers of help.

'Leave it be,' Lemuel told them, 'it's her first time in the pool. She'll have a try later on, I'm sure.'

'Not on your life,' Margot insisted, 'Never. I'm an unflinching coward.'

They had their picnic later on the bank and went exploring in a group when they had finished. The day remained calm and the trees in the woodlands, silent and motionless, reached up into the blue-and-white-filled deeps of the sky. As they ascended, the sunlit countryside spread a tranquil pattern of green fields and golden maturing crops below them.

'What a beautiful place to live,' Margot said to him, when they stopped briefly to look and rest. Then they returned downhill to retrieve the picnic baskets from the river bank and make ready for dinner. Lemuel found himself with his hand on her bedroom door before remembering that for the present it was no longer his. He went on to the room vacated that morning by Margot Penrose. There was a weekly magazine of hers left forgotten on a chair and a hint of her perfume still faintly discernible in the air. He found a tie to wear for dinner and went to the mirror to put it on. He examined his own image curiously as he adjusted the knot. He could feel her lingering presence in the silence and warmth of the room.

'There was this curious well,' Uncle Crispin told them while reporting at dinner on his afternoon's explorations. 'A holy well, obviously; probably a place of pilgrimage at one time or another. It was high up on the mountainside and a faint track led up to it – that's how I found it. There were rags of all shapes and colours tied to the bushes, most of them worn threadbare by the elements. There were medals and coins lying at the bottom of it – the water was so clear I could make them out without difficulty. And around it an extraordinary mixum-gatherum of objects had accumulated:

rosary beads, more medals, crutches, bandages, a pair of spectacles even.'

'Tell me how you got there,' Jonathan asked.

Uncle Crispin was explaining in great detail when Jonathan cut him short.

'Say no more,' he put in. 'I know the well you came across. It's the well of St Brigid – or one of them. Wells of St Brigid are too numerous to be counted.'

'This one seems to have been highly successful.'

'I remember it from the old days,' Jonathan told them. 'Hundreds of pilgrims went up and down to it. I'm told they even came from America to take bottles of the healing waters back with them. But the biggest event was the annual procession up to it to keep the vigil and light a bonfire on St John's Eve. They carried lighted turves which they'd soaked in pitch, and they prayed and sang hymns as they went. It was quite a spectacle for a young child to see their massed torches winding up into the darkness.'

'And why was it discontinued?' Uncle Crispin wondered.

'Need you ask? Whenever our countrymen gather in numbers for any purpose, sacred or profane, it's never long until drink and faction fights and worse become part of the routine. Add to this the belief in these parts that sin is suspended for the duration of St John's Eve and you don't need help from me to imagine what the go-boys would be up to. Eventually the vigil was banned by the local clergy. St John's Eve is, of course, the eve of Midsummer's Day, an old pagan feast in its time.'

'Which St John are we talking about?' Uncle Crispin inquired.

'St John the Baptist,' Jonathan answered. 'A man uniquely honoured by the Church.'

St John, he told the assembled, is the only creature, besides Our Blessed Lady, whose birthday is a feast of the Church. In fact he had two feast days: his birthday, which was Midsummer's Day, June 24th, and the feast of his martyrdom on 29th August. The lighting of bonfires on the eve of his birth was a custom of the Middle Ages which still persists in many places even today.

'I have a superb idea,' Uncle Crispin announced.

They looked at him expectantly.

'St John's Eve is only four or five days away. I have not had the thrill of lighting a bonfire for far too long. Let's go all together on St John's Eve with torches and climb to the well and light a bonfire there in his honour.'

'It's six or seven miles away,' Lemuel warned.

'A couple of traps or outside cars will take the lot of us.'

Jonathan was uneasy.

'It might appear to be a lark,' he objected. 'We mustn't scandalise our neighbours.'

'If we let them know that what we have in mind is simply a pious commemoration of an honoured custom of our grandparents and forebears, they won't object. In fact, we can invite them to join in.'

'Uncle Crispin,' Stella put in quietly, 'you are forgetting the position of one of our company—'

'Miss Penrose,' he recollected. 'I meant no offence.'

'There is no offence and no reason in the world why I shouldn't go,' Margot said. 'In fact it's most exciting. No one will stop me.'

'But your parents—' Jonathan reminded her.

'My parents, I regret to say, Mr Cox, take little interest.'

She was polite but firm. The subject was folded away.

After dinner they sat around and chose their own forms of amusement. Uncle Crispin and Eddie O'Grady played chess. Stella sang a little while Lemuel played the accompaniments. Then she slipped out to go walking with John. Margot joined Lemuel in some piano arrangements for four hands: a couple of them made specially for students which were agreeably easy, and a Rossini overture and a Schubert symphony which gave them trouble. Jonathan sat and listened. Then it was time for bed. Margot took her leave of the company.

'Lemuel stood and said, 'Sleep a little better tonight.'

She smiled and whispered, 'Don't forget the mousetraps.'

'They're set and ready,' he assured her.

He spent some time tidying the music before fetching a candle to light himself up the stairs. The mousetraps were still tenantless. There was a note on the floor which someone had pushed under the door. Puzzled, he left the candle on the bedside locker, opened the envelope and unfolded the sheet of paper it contained. As he read he began to smile:

The Mouse

All dressed in grey, a little mouse
Has made his home within my house
And every night and every morn
I say: 'I wish that mouse were gone'.
But why? a quiet soul is he
As anyone may wish to see

94

My house is large, my hearth is wide
There's room for him and me beside
Ah! yes: but when the lights are out
He likes to slyly creep about
And help himself to what he sees
Without once saying, 'If you please'.

In the morning, when they were alone for a short while she asked if
he liked the little mouse poem.

'Thank you – yes.'

'I copied it out from my scrapbook.'

'Are the other items you've gathered together all like that?'

'Some. Not all though. There are quite serious things.
Philosophical things. Or what I think are wise sayings.'

'May I see it?'

'Well – I don't usually let others read it. But I'll make an
exception. You said you gather things too. Have you made a book?'

'Not a book.' He hesitated, then decided, 'I'll show you before
you leave.'

The house party divided for the morning. Eddie O'Grady
borrowed Lemuel's bicycle and he and Godwin went off exploring
with Uncle Crispin. John and Lemuel escorted Stella and Margot to
the pool. This time the behaviour was more sedate: they swam
without the previous day's skylarking. When they had dried off and
dressed, Stella and John decided to go walking together for a while.

'I thought they'd do that,' Margot remarked when they had gone.

'That's a coincidence,' Lemuel said. 'So did I.'

She had brought her scrapbook in her carrying bag.

'This is of no interest to anyone except me,' she told him, 'but I
promised and I'll just give you two or three examples.'

She opened the book and read out whatever happened to be
written on the random pages:

Note: When I was a little tot in school I learned a song about
finding one's way:

This way's east and this way's west
Soon I'll learn to know the rest
Soon I learned that if I stood in the morning time
with the sun on my right-hand side, my face would
be to the north and my back to the south. Later
on I was able to determine where the north was at
night by finding the plough, and drawing an imaginary

line upwards from its two back stars to find the very
bright star known as the polar star. And that became
the limit of my equipment as a navigator.'

'A very useful piece of information,' he approved.

She turned the pages and stopped.

'As you might expect,' she went on, 'there are a number of
Shakespeare's sonnets and lots of things like this:

> Love me not for comely grace
> Nor for my pleasing eye or face
> Nor for any outward part
> No, nor for my constant heart
> For these may fail or come to ill . . .

and so on. These are sentiments which afflict most young girls of
thirteen or fourteen, and two or three years ago I was no exception.'

She turned the pages again and said, 'There's something of
Thoreau here:

> It is not that we love to be alone but that we love to soar. And
> when we do soar the company grows thinner and thinner till at
> last there is none at all.'

She turned again.

'Here's a little nursery song I was taught a long time ago. This will
be the last:

> Come, little leaves said the wind one day
> Come to the meadows with me and play
> Put on your dresses of red and gold
> For summer has gone and the days grow cold'

She closed the book and put it away.

'There,' she pronounced, 'I made a promise and I have kept it.
Will you do the same?'

'I will. The drawback is there isn't really anything like that. It's
just a place that is secret.'

'Now you have told me that I can't wait.'

They began to walk back.

'Then we'll change the subject,' he suggested.

'I think we should.' She pondered a while. 'You haven't told me if
you caught the mouse?'

'I did more than catch the mouse. I caught his brother as well.'

'So. I was right. There were two.'

Then, with unfeigned and inconsistent pity, she added, 'The poor little creatures.'

Next evening, when they were all together again at dinner, Jonathan let it be known that he had discussed the bonfire suggestion with the parish priest.

'Father Nulty is an old friend and I thought it as well to mention it,' he said. 'At first he was dubious. However, when I explained the intention was not to resuscitate the custom on an annual basis, but simply to commemorate and recall it in a personal way, he decided it could be regarded as a private act of devotion. In which case, of course, it would be prudent for himself and Father Finlay, his young curate, not to be involved.'

'Good,' Uncle Crispin said. 'And you'll attend yourself?'

'I will. But I'll wait at the bottom for your return. My days for climbing mountains have faded and gone.'

On the day before St John's Eve Uncle Crispin organized men to gather wood and leave it up at the well in readiness for the making of the bonfire. On the eve itself he had a closed cab as shelter for Jonathan while he waited at the bottom of the mountain. He himself accompanied him in the cab. Two open traps accommodated the rest: Stella, John and Eddie travelling in one, Lemuel, Godwin and Margot in the other. They travelled in procession and were joined shortly by three others, becoming a contingent of six. Dusk deepened on road and fields as they journeyed; trotting hooves beat out their cheerful rhythm, harnesses clinked in unison. Lemuel was at the reins, Margot sat close beside him. She leaned forward and said:

'This is so exciting. How much further?'

He could see her face in the meagre light reflected from the paraffin lantern on her side of the car. Her eyes sparkled. Her face was eager.

'Not too long. About half an hour.'

'I wish it were longer,' she said. 'I could sit here listening to the clip-clopping and the sound of those wheels all night.'

Three more cabs drew out from the side of the road and called out to salute them before falling in behind. Not long after, more joined them.

'Someone seems to have been spreading the word,' Lemuel remarked, surprised.

'Lovely,' Margot said. 'Let there be dozens and dozens.'

'I expect it was Uncle Crispin,' Godwin said. 'Uncle C. blabs a bit.'

By the time they reached the open space at the bottom of the

97

pilgrim path, there were over a dozen vehicles to be accommodated. Uncle Crispin automatically took charge. He gave a short explanation of what they were about to undertake. They would form a torchlight procession as they made the ascent. Had they the necessary materials? They had. Then, he said, we'll prepare at once.

'Is it bare-footed?' someone asked.

'I beg your pardon?'

'Do we do the ascent in our bare feet?'

'I wouldn't advise it,' Uncle Crispin answered. 'There won't really be enough light. And the pathway is unfamiliar.'

He called Lemuel to him. 'I'll lead the ascent,' he said, 'and I want you to take the rear. Let us know if you notice anyone in difficulties.'

'How? You'll be way ahead of me at the rear.'

Uncle Crispin took what looked like a police whistle from his pocket and handed it over.

'With this,' he instructed. 'Three short blasts will bring us to a halt. I'll pass the word down the ranks before we start moving. I'll have a whistle of my own up front.'

Lemuel returned and told Margot. He showed her the whistle.

'Uncle Crispin thinks of everything,' she said.

The torches ahead of them were beginning to blaze and grow in number. He lit Margot's, then his own.

'Keep close to me,' she begged. 'I won't know what I should be doing.'

Uncle Crispin blew one long blast on his whistle and the procession began to move forward. Darkness was now complete. A cool night wind played about their cheeks as they gained height. The chain of torches spread upwards and the flames wavered and flattened out as the mild breeze caught them. There was a smell of mingled kerosene and turf smoke in the air. Those at the head of the procession began to sing:

> Hail Glorious Saint Patrick dear Saint of our Isle
> On us thy poor children bestow a sweet smile . . .

Margot looked puzzled and said, 'I thought it was St John we were supposed to be remembering?'

'There are no hymns to St John in the local repertoire. I suppose the national apostle is a reasonable alternative.'

> And now thou art high in the Mansions above
> On Erin's green valley look down in thy love.

At the top they lit the bonfire and as the sparks swept upwards with the freshening gusts of wind, one of them led off the recital of the rosary. They knelt in the bracken and fern and made responses in chorus. At the end some remained kneeling in prayer; others went to drink the waters of the well and to fill the containers they had brought. As they returned down the slope they prayed once more in unison, and here and there torches began to fail and to go out, Lemuel's among them.

They stopped and Margot said, 'Let's sit down for a moment.'

They did so.

'Are you tired?' he asked.

'Only a little.'

'Sorry you came?'

'I wouldn't have missed it. All those torches winding up the mountain. Like an enormous glow-worm.'

'Or the souls of the dead?'

She drew her breath in sharply.

'What a strange thought,' she said.

But after a moment she put her hand on his arm and admitted her agreement.

'Yes, they could have been. I know what you mean.'

He turned her to him. 'You heard my father saying the other day that it was once generally believed that considerable latitude is allowed to all of us on St John's Eve?'

'I do. It sounds attractive.'

'I wish to ask you something?'

'Of course.'

'May I kiss you?'

She looked at him for some seconds, then smiled and said, 'Please do.'

On the way down he took over her torch to light the way for both of them. She linked his arm as they went. They said very little.

Father Nulty, in a trap that was at once ancient and sturdy, rattled up the long driveway with unsacerdotal haste and tethered the pony to the paling post nearest the halldoor. He walked in past the servant who opened to his knocking.

'Your master,' he demanded, removing his tall silk hat and depositing it on the hall table.

'In his study, Father—'

'Stay where you are. I'll find him myself.'

Jonathan was alarmed by his obvious distress.

'Paul – what's the matter. What has happened?'

'May I sit down?'

'Please do. Let me get you something. Some whiskey, sherry?'

'A little sherry would fill the bill.'

The drink was brought. Father Nulty, no stranger to either the study or the excellent sherry, sipped a couple of times before setting down the glass.

'Jonathan,' he said, 'you have me in the height of trouble.'

'How so, Paul?'

'This pilgrimage to the well. I understood it was to have been a private affair, just your family and a few guests. I'm told there were sixty or more people there.'

'I don't know how many. But a surprisingly large number, I must admit.'

'How did they come to hear about it in the first place?'

'I've no idea.' He had, but he intended to keep quiet.

'Half my parish there, it would seem. Saying rosaries, singing hymns, carrying torches and lighting bonfires, making a circus out of our religion. The next thing is they'll be seeing visions. The Blessed Virgin will appear. To a few young ones, very likely, whose imaginations are deranged by the nuns who teach them.'

'I was not at the well-side myself,' Jonathan said, 'but I remained down below all the time and saw all who passed on their way up. There were no young girls.'

'There will be next time – wait and see. Holy God, Jonathan, do you not understand prudence? I'll be in desperate trouble with the bishop.'

'Surely the bishop is not to know?'

'The bishop is extremely likely to know,' Father Nulty answered, 'because my informant was Fintan Drury, editor of the *Weekly Sentinel*. He wanted details from me of this new devotional exercise. He wanted to feature it in next Saturday's edition.'

'But you told him you knew nothing about it?'

'Of course I did. He said that would make it extremely interesting.'

Jonathan replenished his parish priest's glass without bothering to ask. He also poured a glass for himself.

'I know Drury,' he said grimly.

'The whole countryside knows Drury.'

'It would not be seemly for you to approach him,' Jonathan continued. 'I'll do it on your behalf. I'll tell him you want no reference whatever to the well or the events of St John's Eve. I'll tell him it was an unfortunate misunderstanding and further notice of it would cause you extreme displeasure. You'll find there'll be no more about it.'

'You think not? He's a stubborn man. And very lukewarm in his attitude to religion.'

'I'll impress on him the uprecedented depth of your displeasure, and my conviction as to the wide-ranging repercussions it is most certain to give rise to. I'll cool his anti-clerical ardour for him, I'll promise you. He has been critical of the influence of the Church in the past and got away with it. Let him now be given an opportunity to prove his mettle.'

Father Nulty frowned, but then nodded his head thoughtfully. He had begun to see a ray of hope.

'Stay for lunch,' Jonathan invited. 'We haven't had the opportunity for a little conversation for ages.'

Father Nulty consented, and they talked for the whole afternoon. The next day Jonathan made it his business to dine with Fintan Drury. He spoke as a friend. He had heard in person Father Nulty's declared determination to use all the weight of priestly office to wreak a terrible vengeance on anyone attempting to ridicule either himself or the Church he so ardently served. Jonathan, in his quietest manner, urged Fintan Drury for his own sake, and for that of his newspaper, to exercise the utmost caution. Fintan Drury said he deeply appreciated Jonathan's advice. He would carefully consider it. But there remained his editorial duty to serve his readers without fear or favour.

His decision in the end seemed to favour Jonathan's views. The *Weekly Sentinel* made no mention whatsoever of holy wells, or bonfires, or devotional novelties.

On the evening before her departure, Lemuel and Margot walked together to the trees and the spit of land that reached some distance into the river. They took great care not to be observed. A low sun spread its hues on the surface of the water, foam edged the little beaches and rose and ebbed with barely discernible motion among the fragments of purple sandstone. In the gloom among the trees, insects laboured incessantly. She followed behind and watched, fascinated, when he stopped to dip his hand deep down into the hollow in the bole of the tree and take out first the covering of sacking and then the metal box. He opened it.

'This is what I meant,' he said. 'My special scrapbook.'

She gazed down at the contents: sheets of paper of assorted

colours and sizes, and among them a scattering of envelopes. They sat down together, the box between them. He searched for and found the letter that had been the first of them all, the one he had written to his mother five years before. He had been nine then, but now it seemed even longer than five years. He passed it to her and began to tell her the events that compelled him to write it. She listened with obvious compassion.

When he had finished she said, 'I'm glad you got the bicycle back. It would have been just the last straw if you hadn't.'

'My mother saw to that,' he asserted.

She regarded him tenderly.

'And you still believe it?'

'But of course.'

'You're a very strange person,' she told him.

The thought that her visit must end on the next day returned to distress her. How they were to make contact with each other in the months that were to come had occupied them for some days. She would be back once more in her boarding school in Edmundscourt, while he would have returned to the Lansdowne Road house to resume his schooling in the city. Too regular a correspondence would be indiscreet because it would be quietly but closely supervized in her school. It was a dilemma that returned to trouble him as well. He put the box back in its hiding place and covered it once more with the piece of sacking. An idea occurred to him as he did so. He took her arm and led her back to the driveway.

'Margot, when the summer holidays end and it becomes difficult to see each other, there's something I'd like you to do.'

'Tell me.'

'When you have anything special you'd like to say to me, write it down and then, when opportunity offers, leave it in the box here. I'll cycle out from time to time to have a look and to leave my notes to you. Do your best not to be seen but don't worry if you are. The servants know you now and they'll regard it as perfectly normal for you to come to wander around this way when you're out for a trip on your bicycle. Will you do that?'

'Of course.'

'And I've thought of something else,' he continued. 'We must sit down later this evening, or before lunch tomorrow, and work out a code between us. Then, if ever you know in advance there may be a few hours in which you could slip away on your own, you can write to let me know without anyone else being any the wiser. I'll cycle out if there's the remotest chance of meeting you.'

'It's a long, long way from there to here and back again. I'd hate to think of you cycling all those miles for nothing.'

'To be practical,' he acknowledged, 'it would have to be a Saturday or a Sunday to allow me enough time. But, don't doubt me, it'll happen.'

The possibility cheered them both. They walked in easy companionship back to the house, but found no desire to return indoors and continued on past it. The Pooka's Pool was a glimmering expanse of silver under the deepening dusk. The splash of water falling over the curve of its weir was muted. In the air, the faint odours of humus lay cool and pleasant. Their mood was several degrees brighter.

'We still have July and August to make the most of,' he reminded her. 'There won't be any trouble getting to see one another then. Stella will help us. I've only to ask her.'

'What of your father?'

'Father, for all his piety, is not very conventional. His contact with the world is, at best, tenuous. We find it easy to go our own way. Are your parents very strict?'

'My parents don't see anything beyond themselves. They barely know I exist.'

He recalled that she had said something of the same kind when they were proposing the pilgrimage to the well, and his father had asked her if her parents might be offended. He decided to leave the subject alone, at least for the moment.

'Anyway, I'll cycle down if you're able to be free. A few trips of that kind would keep us going until the Christmas holidays. Then we'll have visits to friends and parties. The O'Gradys are great for parties. Stella will persuade Father to let her arrange one in return — or perhaps even two — in Lansdowne Road. I think Christmas parties are great. Don't you?'

She made no response. He sensed her change of mood and hesitated.

'Don't you think?' he asked again.

'We don't have Christmas parties in our house,' she told him. 'We never have had. My father and mother both say they don't believe in them. The truth is they're too mean. So we don't go to parties either. If you go to parties you have to give parties in return. Nor do we give presents. There's never been a Christmas tree in our house, nor Christmas cards on the mantelpiece, nor the smell of turkey or goose or plum pudding. Never. Anyhow, they're mostly away.'

103

'And what happens to you?'

'When I was smaller I was left with a nurse. For the last few years I've been to my aunt. I prefer that. My aunt is no Merry Andrew but she hasn't forgotten how to laugh. My parents have.'

She paused and then said, 'Well, now you know.'

'Poor Margot.'

But she dismissed the matter. 'I'm used to it,' she told him. 'I no longer care.'

Back in the house Jonathan was reading, and glanced up only briefly to acknowledge their arrival. Eddie O'Grady and Uncle Crispin were once again engrossed in chess. Stella and John were absent. So, too, was Godwin. Lemuel, to be polite, announced that he was going to put on a pot of tea and asked if anyone would like some. When nobody did he led Margot through to the kitchen.

As he put on the kettle he said to her over his shoulder, 'When this is ready we'll think about making up our code.'

They agreed there would be three reasonably unobtrusive meeting places: the wood where the box was hidden being the best, its only disadvantage being its distance from Edmundscourt. An alternative was the little tearooms about a mile outside Edmundscourt, which was mainly for summer tourists but which was kept open in the off-season by the passing custom of farmers and their wives on shopping errands to the town. Another was the ruined mill on the town's outskirts, with its almost forgotten walk along the river bank and its maze of now unfrequented lanes. An assignation for the first would be referred to by working the word 'red' into the letter. The word 'white' would stand for the second, and for the third the word 'blue' would do duty. When one of these was being used as a code it would be written and crossed out as though an error had been made, and then immediately written down correctly a second time.

They decided this was quite clever and believed it would work for indicating the day of the week also: if Tuesday was the day, that word would be worked into the text, crossed off and re-written a second time. Quotations from poems would convey the time of the meeting: two lines for two o'clock, three lines for three o'clock and so on. For an hour or more it provided an enjoyable exercise in inventiveness and imagination until they had elaborated to the limit and there was nothing more to be added.

'I defy the wiliest headmistress alive to crack this Penrose-Cox Code,' Lemuel said. 'So let's make a copy each to keep by us for the future.'

'The question is,' Margot wondered, 'will we really find an opportunity to use it?' Her tone was wistful.

After lunch next day their transport arrived and their farewells were made. She travelled in company with the two O'Grady boys. They waved handkerchiefs to each other and called out goodbyes until the loop of the drive hid them from each other. He went back into the house. The silence was oppressive.

Chapter 10

Morrissey had Miss Downey bring in coffee for Frank and himself, but when she did so she discovered she had forgotten the biscuits and became embarrassed and exclaimed, 'Oh dear goodness!' and went off again to fetch them.

'A head like a sieve,' Morrissey remarked, 'Miss Dawny they should have called her.'

But when she returned he treated her with his unfailing courtesy for a subordinate and she retired unrebuked.

'I asked you to drop in because I've booked a cruise on the Shannon for the Whit weekend. It sleeps four and I was wondering if you and Margaret would care to join Penny and myself.'

'Unfortunately,' Frank apologized, 'we're already committed. We've agreed to spend the weekend with Lemuel Cox and his sister.'

'That's a pity,' Morrissey said, 'you'd have enjoyed it. I know the Shannon pretty well. When I was a kid my father had his own boat there. The annual regatta was the big event. Quite international. But we spent a good deal of our time exploring and having picnics on the islands of Lough Ree and Lough Derg. No chance of ditching the Coxes I suppose?'

'I couldn't,' Frank said, 'he was a close friend of my father's, and apart from that he's a kind-hearted, lonely type of person. He seems to have taken quite a shine to Margaret.'

'I'd watch that,' Morrissey said, smiling.

'It isn't that kind of shine,' Frank smiled back. 'It seems he once loved a young girl who died in her teens. She was called Margot and he is convinced that Margaret is some kind of reincarnation.'

'He's a bit barmy, isn't he?'

'Well – eccentric.'

'Oh well. Pity you can't come cruising. Penny will be disappointed. She enjoys Margaret's company.'

'I'd have enjoyed a couple of days on the water myself. Later on, I hope.'

'There are a few other things I wanted to talk to you about but they can wait until I get back from London. One of them is a meeting Con Andrews asked me to arrange to discuss an idea he has for a series of pieces for the *Review*. He'd like you to be there.'

'Any time that suits. When do you go to London?'

'The Monday after Whit. On business, of course, but just in time for the coronation, as it happens. Westminster Abbey, Tuesday June 2nd. Decorations to be worn. They haven't invited me but it's to be televised so I won't be left out. Neither will Penny. She insists on being there.'

He turned his attention to the papers that were strewn on his desk.

'Well, I've some things here that need looking at and then I've to go out. We'll talk again.'

'Enjoy the coronation,' Frank said on his way out.

'If Miss Dawny doesn't forget to book our flight,' Morrissey laughed.

Frank, standing at the window of his office some time later, saw him setting off down the street. He was now well known for his regular perambulations, his limping gait punctuated by an occasional lurching movement as his stick slipped under him with a sharp, dragging sound. He limped his way into the offices of the city, its bars, its better-class restaurants and its places of entertainment, in pursuit of a complex of interests which he knew to be, in essence, irreconcilable. The advertising side of his activity required a well set-up style, a non-confrontational philosophy, even a degree of deference. His intellectual pursuits on the other hand, which ranged from his sympathetic contacts with the trade union movement and his occasional engagements as drama critic for the national broadcasting station, to his work with Con Andrews for the outspoken *Review*, demanded a liberal measure of detachment in his outlook on society, and free play in the matter of criticism. He had to pick his way carefully among the hazards that lay in ambush for the unacceptable opinions he sometimes propagated in a society he despised for its obscurantism and poltroonery. To strive secretly to undermine it was a form of revenge.

They found Con Andrews in crusading form. He had compiled a list of public happenings which he regarded as outrageous or ludicrous or both, and he wanted them challenged in a succession of pieces for the *Review* aimed at the antics of officialdom and public notables over the preceding decade and, as he saw it, their distrust of any manifestation of liberal thought. He was also seeking a fuller report on a booklet which, he had been told, laid down the correct public behaviour to be adopted by Catholic boys and girls. The text, he understood, took the form of a series of conversations in which a fictional Father Oliver delicately enlightens them as to what is acceptable and what is to be avoided in the matter of conduct.

'The terrifying thing, if it's true,' Con continued, 'is that it sold 150,000 copies right away and another 100,000 had to be printed without delay.'

He scanned his list.

'There are several things here that merit attention,' he told them, and went on to read out some examples.

Then he said: 'Well, that's the general idea. What do you think?'

'The items you've read out are all deplorable,' Morrissey conceded, 'but some at least wouldn't stand up to extended treatment.'

'The treatments don't have to be extensive. Anything from half a dozen lines upwards. I was hoping Frank here could supply an illustration for each which would have some humorous or satirical relevance. What do you think, Frank?'

'I can have a try,' Frank agreed.

But Morrissey seemed uneasy.

'It's a bit head-on,' he suggested. 'Not much room for manoeuvre. You'll lose advertising for a start.'

'The *Review* hasn't got much of that to lose. I wouldn't worry.'

'And we'll make enemies.'

'The *Review* has plenty of them already,' Andrews argued. 'What's a few more? However, we'll leave the articles unsigned. There's a fair case for anonymity.'

He rubbed his hands together in anticipation. 'I look forward to this series,' he added, 'it will have the general title: *On The Side Of The Angels*.' Morrissey undertook to give it a trial but when they had reached the street he made his doubts known.

'Con is too rash,' he complained. 'There are other ways. I can see my head being passed around on a platter. Yours too.'

'If they're anonymous—'

'There's no such thing. Not with characters like our friend O'Halloran prowling about the editor's ante-room.'

They crossed the street. Under the portico of the General Post Office a beggar in a ragged coat which was fastened about his neck by a large safety pin, held out a cardboard box to the passers-by. Newsboys among a scatter of evening papers sang out in unimpassioned competition. Riderless bicycles were spread along the kerb of the colonnade and leaned in disarray against its pillars. Morrissey persevered grimly among the press of pedestrians.

They turned into Muldowney's public house and climbed the stairs. Don Maguire of the radio station and some of his colleagues were there in small groups. There were the ageing Catholic intellectuals, most of them Thomists and all of them given to quoting G.K. Chesterton a great deal, and harbouring their early admiration for Belloc and Baring and Ronald Knox and Georges Bernanos and Mauriac, among others. They studied affability and optimism, revelled in paradox and drank copiously. The Catholicism of the Toby jug and the belly laugh, their detractors had labelled it.

The Maguire group leaned towards the less than optimistic T.S. Eliot and the more cynical voices of Auden and MacNeice and their contemporaries. But their favourite entertainment was uninhibited indulgence in public scandal and gossip. Frank and Morrissey found them deploring the growing frequency of political pressures on the radio station, due, they suspected, to an internal leaking of information. The finger seemed to point to one of the lady announcers who, (they believed) might be motivated by a recent romantic entanglement.

Maguire suspended discussion of the matter to greet Morrissey warmly and to invite him and Frank to join them.

'I know what you're here about,' he told Morrissey. 'You want to know when the new season's drama review spots are to be resumed, and I can tell you right away. They start at the beginning of September and I have your first assignment pencilled in for you: it is to review the visit of a Spanish Ballet Company – the first ever performance of Spanish ballet here in Dublin – if I'm not greatly mistaken. Does that please you?'

Morrissey frowned in alarm.

'What pipes, what timbrels, what wild ecstasy,' he responded. 'The only snag is, I know sweet bugger all about ballet, Spanish or otherwise.'

'Nor does anybody else in this town,' Maguire assured him. 'Just make wholesale use of the blurb they're bound to distribute. Phone the Spanish Embassy. Read up about the Bolero and the Fandango and the Zapateado and Flamenco and work it all into the critique. Jaysus man, use your loaf.'

He raised his glass and wished them luck.

'Forgive the bombast,' he added genially. 'I won a long-fought fight and enjoyed the first fruits of it today. I've had a couple of glasses extra to mark the occasion.'

His victory had been over the Office of Public Works. Some years before they had supplied clocks for the new studios with no second hands on them, and minute hands that moved only in half-minute jerks, leaving it to guesswork on the part of announcers and producers to judge how much of the last thirty seconds of any programme still remained before its allotted running time came to an end. A master clock in the General Post Office controlled the studio clocks and the master clock itself functioned in half-minute leaps. After a dogged battle over a number of years, bureaucracy had been at last defeated. Second hands were clicking away on every clock in every studio and Maguire and the others could now tell the exact time while directing the station's programmes. He bought them another drink to express his satisfaction and delight.

'All is radiance, all is light,' he assured them. He was going to treat himself to a bloody good meal in town. Their company would crown his joy and fill his cup to overflowing.

Morrissey said Penny was away and a meal in town would fill the bill nicely. Frank telephoned Margaret who had no urgent need of his presence. They set off contentedly in search of food, passing once again under the portico of the Post Office where the beggarman was still offering his begging box in the name Jesus and his Blessed Mother. This time Morrissey dipped down into his pocket and found half a crown. He pitched it in on top of the sprinkle of coppers where it shone like a silken prince among a ragged peasantry.

'Is that not overdoing it?' Frank commented.

'There, but for the grace of God, go I,' Morrissey answered, declaiming.

'All of us,' Maguire agreed wholeheartedly. 'The whole bloody bagful of us.'

The mood of both was high, Frank noted. Rhetoric was going to be big on the menu.

They continued across the bridge and at Trinity College they turned into Dame Street, their choice wavering between the Dolphin Hotel and the Central.

'The Central, I think,' Maguire finally decided. They went in by the side entrance. The crush of parked cars along the pavement outside the Phoenix Hall told them the radio orchestra was giving a public concert, but the street itself was deserted in the dusty warmth of the July evening. Sounds from main thoroughfare traffic filtering to them over rooftops and sun-warmed slates were muted. Frank paused on the threshold to gaze back at the disorder and clutter of the side street. The sunlight and the comparative silence stirred in him as it always did a ghost-like consciousness of the melancholy inherent in all human activity. He spoke of it to the others while they had a drink and waited for their meal. Morrissey confessed to the same response: a sense of transience, a regret for things gone past, never to return. He believed it had to do with the clutter of objects and the absence of those who had only recently left them there: or the contrast between the silence of the side street and the sounds of the main streets which drifted into the consciousness remotely. Maguire said he would tolerate no pallid introspection and no bloody navelgazing while they were the honoured guests of the hero who put a stop to the gallop of the Office of Public Works.

His mood of lofty disdain persisted as they addressed their meal. Morrissey, unease attacking him once more as he reflected on the idea of being the one to review Spanish ballet, got short shrift when he suggested an alternative critic.

'Is it Martin McVickers?' Maguire repeated. 'What in God's name has Martin McVickers to recommend him?'

'He always seemed to me to have an encyclopaedic knowledge of most things – wherever he got it.'

'From an encyclopaedia, where else,' Maguire replied, banging the table and setting crockery and cutlery dancing about. 'This city – what am I saying – this whole bloody country, is inhabited by a race of brazen humbugs who swot it all up in an encyclopaedia and then pontificate at large. They know nothing beyond the inform-ation they've just cribbed – a crowd of Sir Oracles, a plague of bloody hob lawyers. So let you do the same. Look it all up. Hold forth on Spanish ballet. Take on the McVickers of this world and beat them at their game.'

'If I do that,' Morrissey said, 'I simply become one of the McVickers myself.'

'Never, Simon. You're an honest man for a start; he isn't. And you're not trying to cod us. In my judgement you'll do it better than anyone else I can find. So let that be enough.'

When they came out again the side street had lost the sun and in the sky above it dusk spread its dull silver. The concert had finished, the cars had gone, the silence pressed down on the dusty kennels. Maguire stood still to take it all in.

'Yes,' he conceded. 'I agree with Frank after all: a whisper of something lost; a breath of that melancholy that inheres in all things. We are tempted to look inwards at the desert in our hearts. Another drink is the answer. But where?'

'Come home with me for one at the fire,' Frank offered.

'And your good wife?'

'Margaret will be glad of company.'

Maguire accepted on condition that they had another drink while they got a supply to take with them. But first he insisted on flowers for Margaret and dragged them around the streets until he found a florist that was still open. The mood was high again by the time they were having their drink and ordering a supply for taking away. The bunch of flowers lay on the counter beside Maguire's glass. Frank picked it up to admire.

Maguire, watching him, said, 'Women and flowers go together. That is one of the blessings I lack. A good wife of my own to bedizen with blossoms.'

'Time you put that matter right,' Morrissey admonished. 'You have the wherewithal and there are plenty of tender-hearted young ladies.'

'I have the wherewithal now – as you rightly say. But I didn't always have it. So I made a vow to myself a long time ago that a woman must have money as well as charm. No money – no matrimony. Time and again I have had to admonish the impulsive and affable little god of love: restrain your bow, Cupid, I tell him, until you have a golden arrow.'

They finished their drinks and faced into the streets again; Frank and Morrissey each with a half-dozen bag of Guinness under one arm, Maguire with a bottle of whiskey stuffed into his right-hand pocket and the bunch of flowers in his right hand. Their progress was slow and impeded a little by their burdens.

'We should have called a taxi from the pub,' said Frank. 'Are you all right, Simon?'

'Gameball,' Morrissey answered.

'We'll keep an eye out and flag one down.'

They trailed for several minutes without success until Maguire began to run and shouted back, 'Taxi ahead, up at the traffic lights at the crossing.'

Frank broke into a run to follow him but almost immediately he heard behind him the skidding sound of Morrissey's stick and the crash of breaking glass. Maguire ahead of him heard it too and came back. They found Morrissey lying in the gutter among broken bottles and meandering rivulets of froth-crowned stout.

'One for the road,' Morrissey greeted, raising himself on his elbow.

'One my arse,' Maguire lamented, 'six for the goddamned road.'

Frank, examining the situation more closely, said to Morrissey, 'Your hand is bleeding, Simon, let's have a look.'

There was a nasty gash along the side. They bound it with their pocket handkerchiefs and got him to his feet. He assured them he was otherwise uninjured. They decided to go back to the pub to replace the breakages and telephone for a taxi from there. It duly came. As it passed the scatter of broken glass and its pool of stout in the gutter, Morrissey became embarrassed and said, 'Sorry about the damage, chaps.'

Maguire, surveying the scattered debris in turn, murmured reflectively, 'There, but for the grace of God . . .'

He left it unfinished.

Margaret cleaned the wound and bandaged the hand properly. Morrissey, for all his unconcerned pose, looked shaken. Margaret observed him quietly while they drank and talked.

'I think you should stay the night,' she suggested. 'With Penny away you'll be more comfortable here.'

'I'd like that,' he agreed.

He was tired and a little drunk. As soon as Maguire left she went off to make up the bed. They poured more drinks when she came back to join them.

'The bed is ready whenever you are,' she told him.

'You're very kind,' he acknowledged, and left down his glass. 'I'm sorry you weren't able to come sailing on the Shannon with us.'

'It would have been lovely. But the invitation from the Coxes—'

'Of course,' he interrupted, 'there wasn't much you could do. I got help to come with us and it turned out very well. I was able to show Penny over quite a few of the islands we used to picnic on when I was young. We had our own cruiser then and my father was a first-rate sailing man. In fact, when it came to sport of any kind he was top of the class: riding, fishing, tennis, cricket – an all-rounder. But I'm sure you enjoyed Cox and his sister's company?'

'It was pleasant.'

'Did Doctor want-do-you-call-him turn up?'

'Doctor Slattery? He did.'

'Did he speak of me?'

'He inquired about you, yes.'

Morrissey's eyes narrowed as he considered some thought that had come to him.

'He said last time that he had attended me once or twice as a child, but I have no recollection of it. Did he refer to my accident on this occasion?'

Frank was becoming embarrassed. Margaret stood up to do some unnecessary tidying at the sideboard.

'Only briefly,' Frank answered, 'he spoke of your hip trouble and expressed sympathy. But his recollection has become inaccurate.'

Morrissey leaned forward. 'How so?'

'He seemed to attribute it to tuberculosis.'

'Bloody fool,' Morrissey complained. 'Did you correct him?'

'I saw no reason to,' Frank answered. 'I reckoned he's an ageing man now for whom it's all a long, long time ago.'

'I suppose so,' Morrissey said, appearing to dismiss the matter.

But the high spirits of the early part of the evening had evaporated. He had become suddenly hunched and pale. Margaret offered coffee but he declined, saying he preferred to drink. Later, when Margaret announced that she was going to bed he asked leave to sit on for a while longer.

'Of course,' she said.

'I'll keep you company for a bit,' Frank offered, 'and show you to your room.'

'I'd appreciate that. There's something I've made up my mind to say to you.'

When Margaret had gone Morrissey poured whiskey again, a normal measure for Frank when he declined a larger one, and more generously for himself. Dangerously so, Frank thought. He worried about getting him to negotiate the stairs. Morrissey raised his glass

'Here's to you.'

'And to you.'

They drank. Morrissey left his glass down and pushed it from him very deliberately.

'Doctor Slattery is my subject,' he said. Frank became attentive.

'When I met him at Lemuel Cox's house I didn't remember at first. But since then I've recollected that he *did* come to our house once or twice and that he *did* know my father and mother and family. And he's not remembering inaccurately. My hip was not due to a riding accident. It was a tubercular hip, due to that severe and

114

ntirely unromantic disease – tuberculosis. I was ashamed of it as a
child, and then as a young boy lying on my back in a hospital bed for
hours on end I persuaded myself that a horse I had been riding had had
a fall when taking a ditch and rolled over on me. I began to believe so
fervently in it I could nearly have shown you the place where it had
happened. It did two things for me: it was easier to bear the idea of a
riding accident than that of a base and unbecoming disease. It also
placed me among the priviliged for whom horsemanship is one of the
badges of their superiority. On the Bowden estate, of course, before
this hip involved long absences, I'd been in daily contact with the
landed gentry's style of life. In hospital I began to read what books I
could find about it. It was self-deception, but it helped. It restored the
necessary modicum of dignity and manliness.'

Frank watched and listened and saw an unguessed-at Morrissey
emerging, one whose father had not belonged to the lifestyle of the
gentry as he had so consistently implied, except in his menial
capacity as steward on the Bowden estate, comfortable enough in the
beginning with a dignified house which went with the position and
highly regarded for the competence with which he discharged his
duties. But while his son Simon lay watching the ceilings of a
succession of hospital wards, drink – after long threatening –
combined eventually with gambling to lose both house and job. He
had returned at last to find his parents in a tumbledown cottage
which the Bowdens allowed them to occupy. He caught his first
sight of it through a small back gate on the estate which let him in to
an earthen yard where he found it surrounded by partly collapsed
sheds. A green ooze disfigured the whitewash on its outside walls.
Those inside had patches of damp with strips of carpet tacked on to
them to protect the clothes of any who might rub against them. A
travelling trunk, which had always gone with them on their holiday
stays in Dublin in better times, served now as a seat beneath the
window which looked out on more collapsing outhouses with
wooden doors that time and weather had rotted and partly eaten
away.

They stood looking at him in confusion and embarrassment until
his mother cried out and rushed forward to embrace him. Her grey
hair straggled untidily about her eyes. His father stood with both
hands deep in his pockets. He said nothing. His nose was bulbous in
a purple-veined face.

At tea-time he found out that the Bowdens saw to it that his father
got odd jobs to do which earned a little money. They continued to
llow them a modest share of the produce of the estate: potatoes,

vegetables, a little meat from time to time and firewood for the winter. There were eggs from the estate for tea and homemade jam and cheese from the dairy. His father had put aside a pound of the odd job earnings to offer to him as pocket money for his stay. He tried desperately not to take it but they urged it on him until he realized he seemed to them to be rejecting their love, and he gave in. He could not bring himself to spend the pound except on some essential items that arose. When he was returning to hospital he had enough of it left to offer small presents: some sweets for his mother, a plug of tobacco for his father. He gave them with pity but without love, and wondered at it as he lay back in the bus. They had lost more than job and house and all that followed from that. They had no longer any standing within the estate. They were dependent non-productive menials. And they had lost the love of their only son and their status of parenthood.

Morrissey was now quite drunk. But his mind retained its clarity.

'You'll keep all this to yourself?' he asked.

'I promise you, solemnly.'

'I'm very drunk, Frank.'

Frank had never seen him so drunk before. But he answered with sympathy, 'I'm not entirely sober myself.'

'Right then,' Morrissey said. 'We'll have one more and then we'll hit the sack.'

But he had two before he rose unsteadily.

'Enough,' he said, taking Frank's arm. 'Lay on, MacDuff.' He made the stairs with reasonable control. Frank sat him on the bed and helped him to undress, divesting him of his shoes and white socks and wondering as he did so at the scrupulous cleanliness which, with his handicap, must have been difficult to achieve.

In the morning he chattered so lightly and effortlessly to Margaret that Frank wondered how he had managed to escape the after-effects of his night's drinking. When he rose from the table he waved aside Frank's offer of a lift and elected to walk on his own into town. It was a grand, sunny morning.

'A walk,' he told them, 'is what the doctor ordered.' He would go by Earlsfort Terrace where the University students would be arriving for the first lectures of the day and then through St Stephen's Green, where the flowers would be marshalled in their summer beds and the laburnums in blossom and the fountain embroidering the air with pearly fans.

Frank helped him to the front door and let him negotiate the outside steps on his own. He grasped the upright spokes of the railings and did so step by step. At the bottom he turned to look up and smiled his farewell, pointing his stick at the blue sky above the street and then at the houses on the other side. But then his face drained slowly of colour, leaving the smile fixed and frozen and in some odd way no longer attached to his features.

'Now for the torment,' he announced to Frank and the sky and the rooftops and the world in general, 'of suffering through the length of this God-given day.'

Chapter 11

He had cycled the distance between Lansdowne Road and Avonmore on three Sundays and found notes from her in the bole of the old beech tree on two of them. They told him of small tribulations in the course of the school term and of how she continued to think about him and miss him. A third came direct to the Lansdowne Road address through the legitimate routine operated by the school. Obviously she felt the letter would by now be sufficiently isolated to escape arousing suspicion. It hinted at an opportunity of meeting. She had dated it November 2nd, 1895 and addressed him as Dear Cousin. She made use of their code of cancelled words and verse quotations. He underlined the vital passages:

'While in the village the other day I heard the butcher and the delivery man talking about the British general election and the complete win of Lord Salisbury and the Conservatives and how this might affect relationships between the Empire and the Boer Republic. The butcher thought it would show Europe that we were united under the Queen as never before and would retain the ascendancy that is our due, but the delivery man thought the outlook was quite ~~blew~~ blue and, in his opinion, Germany had now grown quite strong enough to force Britain out of Europe . . .

He underlined the word 'blue'. Further down she had written 'You asked me to remind you about Cousin John's birthday and do so now because it occurs on ~~Teusday~~ 17th (Oh dear, there I go again), on Tuesday 17th which is very soon indeed . . .'

He underlined Tuesday 17th. Further down still she had inserted the lines of verse which he now expected:

With little here to do or see
Of things that in the great world be
Sweet Daisy, oft I talk to thee
For thou art worthy
Thou unassuming commonplace
Of Nature . . . etc.

He counted the lines of verse – five whole ones, one unfinished and the message was complete. She was asking him to be at their agreed spot by the mill at half past five on Tuesday 17th. He would have to dodge school by some means or other. The simple solution was not to return after the lunch break. His absence might not be noticed. If it were he would have some excuse ready anyway.

He took the route through Bray and out along the Wicklow road. It was longer but less exposed to wind and rain for most of the way. The light began to fade while he was still on the trunk road and, as he turned off into the hills, fine rain speckled the light breeze and itched on his eyelids. It took over two hours to reach Edmundscourt and a further ten minutes or so to get to the top of the laneway which led to the old mill. He dismounted and waited in the shelter of the hedge. It was now completely dark. The rain spun softly, sprinkling hedge and roadway. All their imaginings of secret meetings had been on remote roads lit by the evening sun or winding between silvered hedges under moonlight. Almost impenetrable darkness had not occurred to them. Or the possibility of rain.

He kept his carbide lamp trained on the ground at his feet and was wondering anxiously if she would be able to find him, when another bicycle lamp in the darkness fixed his attention. It approached slowly and stopped a little distance from him. He could see no one and waited some anxious seconds before making up his mind.

'Margot?' he called.

She gave a little cry of relief and came forward.

'Lem. It's you.'

She was wearing a green sou'wester hat with elastic drawn under her chin to secure it and a belted mackintosh coat.

'I was scared it mightn't be you,' she said.

Now that they had come together they were unsure what to do next. They stood in awkward silence.

'Well,' she ventured, 'you got here. I'm so glad. It rained very heavily earlier this evening. That's why I'm all geared out. How was it with you?'

'I was well on the road when it started. It was only light. Just as it is now.'

'You'd such a long journey. I'm sorry.'

'We're together. That's worth twice as long.'

The awkwardness melted away. She came to him. He kissed her and said, 'Margot, I love you.'

She smiled.

'I'm sure I smell overpoweringly of mackintosh coat.'

'It becomes you.' They both laughed.

'The thing is what are we to do now?'

'I had thought of a walk along the bank of the tributary that used to feed the mill and then on to the river. I hadn't reckoned on it being so dark.'

'Nor I.'

They hid the bicycles and decided to have a try. But night and the raincloud hovering low overhead quenched every glimmer of light. The lane was enveloped in thick darkness, the water flowing alongside the pathway was black and invisible. They were conscious of the danger of stepping off the path. Worse still, the rain was becoming more determined. The mud of the laneway began to squelch under their shoes.

'I think we should give up,' she suggested.

He agreed. They retraced their steps, finding the return more hazardous than the setting out and locating their bicycles with difficulty. The rain became heavier still.

'Would it be safe to go to the teashop?' he asked.

'I think so. That's if it's open.'

It was. Much to their relief, it was also empty. They chose the table nearest to the welcoming fire and he had money enough to order bacon and eggs for them both, followed by cakes.

'This is luxury,' she enthused. 'How I pity the poor darlings back in the school enduring cocoa and dry bread, most likely.'

'Surely you do a little better than that.'

'Strictly speaking, I suppose we do. But it feels like that.'

'How did you manage to get out?' he wondered.

'By extreme cunning,' she boasted. 'Clever me.' She was scrutinizing the cake plate closely.

'These ones have marzipan and brazil nuts inside,' she remarked when her careful choice had been made. 'They're scrumptious.'

She was teasing him.

'Come on,' he insisted. 'Out with it. How was it done?'

'The aunt who hasn't as yet forgotten how to smile. I told you about her.'

'I remember. How does she come into it?'

'Two years ago she wrote to say she wished to take me into town to visit her dressmaker and have me fitted out for some clothes. She had also business in the village and asked that I should be given permission to meet her there to save time. When I presented the letter and was given permission they forgot to take it from me. My aunt hadn't put any date at the head of the letter, and in the body of it she only wrote the date she wished to meet me on, which was the 17th. The first clever thing I did was to keep the letter. I felt it might come in useful. And I was right. I just had to do a little fiddling about with it and present it again and it worked. So here I am. My friend Laura got my bicycle out earlier for me and left it against the wall under the entrance archway.'

'And what time must you be back?'

'That's the sad bit,' she said, her face clouding. 'I must be in by eight o'clock.'

He looked at his watch. It was seven already.

'I've been out since two o'clock,' she explained, 'but I couldn't see you any earlier because it had to be dark. In daylight it would have been too much of a chance.'

'From two to five-thirty – that was a long wait. What did you do?' he asked.

'Skulked in laneways and things and sheltered from the rain under hedges,' she admitted.

He was appalled.

'That must have been interminable.'

'It was worth it, Lem. I'd do it anytime.'

Her eyes were brimming with love and amusement.

The rain had eased when they went outside again. They were able to push their bikes alongside each other and walk and talk. They thought it wiser that he should leave her some distance from the school.

'The Christmas break is coming soon,' he told her. 'We won't notice until it's on top of us.'

'No,' she said.

They kissed and he watched her as she mounted and waved to her when she looked back. In a moment the darkness enveloped her and she had gone. He turned to the road.

It was pitch black. The rain became heavy again and the wind drove it against his face and through his overcoat and the collar of his shirt. The battle to keep moving against it occupied all his attention and threatened at times to overmaster him. But, when he was in bed at last and the long fight against the elements won, his thoughts returned to dwell on the long hours she had had to endure, waiting for him in lonely laneways without shelter from the rain and in the constant anxiety that she might be seen. He imagined her now awake in a dormitory of sleeping girls, high up in the darkness above the drenched hedges and sodden fields and listening to the steady drumming of the rain. He concentrated on her image and sent his love winging to her through the desolation and the darkness.

Chapter 12

Margaret strapped Paul into the basketwork carrier on the back of her bicycle and set off on the five miles to the village of Tallaght, where Teresa and her husband John lived with their four children. They found accommodation cheaper out there and they could make use of the large area of ground about the house to grow an appreciable part of the family diet.

In her handbag she had the three pound notes that were the reason for her visit, and in the shopping bag which dangled from the lampbracket in the centre of the handlebars, the shirt which Paul had now outgrown and a pair of his cast-off shoes.

The morning was pleasantly warm, the traffic on the Rathmines Road and along the gradual incline that led through Rathgar unusually light. After Terenure it reduced to almost nothing at all. The hedges spreading along either side of the road gleamed with the glossy sheen that lingered in the wake of the earlier morning mist. They made way at intervals for occasional homesteads and successive gateways to fields that awaited the harvesters.

At Templeogue bridge where the house of the poet Austin Clarke hid behind its trees, young boys with bathing togs wrapped about the handlebars of their bikes leaned over the parapet and strained to catch a glimpse of the trout lurking in the brown and gold of the waters. They were on their way to Pussy's Leap, the oddly named pool that had been popular back in her own childhood. In a month or so they would be wandering the same roads and laneways in search of blackberries or beech nuts. She had done so herself in her time. Paul, whose hands she could feel gripping the belt at the back of her jacket, would be doing the same thing in another few years. He was now past five and ready for school. School posed a difficulty which clouded over her enjoyment of the morning and then, after a little while, faded away. She could deal with it later. But pretty soon.

Teresa's house was a small one, solidly constructed by the county council with a generous parcel of ground about it and the needs of the rural labourer in mind. The toilet was an outdoor one but clean and efficient. There had been no bathroom but John had built on to the kitchenette to accommodate a hand basin and a shower which served almost as well. He cycled daily to the store in the city where his job as an assistant was respectable but not very well paid. The two eldest children cycled in to school. The other two were not yet old enough but when their turn came Teresa would take them in by bus and meet them again in the evening. She dreaded that because it seemed to absorb the whole day, and it cost money. Still, it was cheaper than living further in.

She had coffee for Margaret in the tiny sitting-room, and sweet biscuits which she shared with Paul and her second youngest who was with her.

'David,' she told him, 'take Paul out into the garden with you and have a picnic. The morning is beautiful.'

They already knew each other and went off contentedly together.

'You'd never guess they were the same age,' she remarked. 'Paul is a lot bigger than David.'

It was her habitual observation whenever she saw them together.

'I wouldn't worry,' Margaret assured her, as she always did. 'Children grow differently. They catch up.'

She opened her shopping bag and took out the shirt and shoes.

'I thought of David before I started and rooted around for these. They may do him. Paul has outgrown them.'

'Lovely. I'll try them when he comes in,' Teresa said, pleased. 'I put by some thing for you which the two older girls wore when they were Aoife's age. They might do her. I mustn't let you go without them.'

Margaret thanked her. She opened her handbag and took out the notes. 'And I got you the money. Three pounds you said?'

'If it isn't too much—'

Margaret handed the notes over.

'We've always helped one another, you, me, Maeve—'

They had. But usually with loans that were much smaller: five shillings perhaps, now and then ten shillings; in very dire times as little as half-a-crown. Three pounds was exceptional. When Teresa had broached the matter on the telephone she apologised at length. David was five and she felt he must go to school when the new term began at the end of August. It would be wrong to keep him at home any longer. Additional clothes were involved and a schoolbag and other odds and ends. She had put money away but it fell short of what was required.

'I'll have it to give back to you sometime in September,' she promised. 'Back-to-school time always brings in extra business and a bit of welcome overtime for John. Will that be all right?'

'Frank has done well for some time past. There's no hurry.'

'Have you thought of sending Paul to school this term? He's the age now.'

She had thought of it a year ago when he turned four. There was a problem.

'He should be at school already,' Margaret acknowledged, 'the problem is – where?'

Teresa looked puzzled.

'But surely Mother Splendiferous is the answer. You're a past pupil. Don't you want him to start his schooling where we all began?'

'Of course. The question is will Reverend Mother want it. Since I stopped being one of her Children of Mary she's been pestering me with messages through Maeve to go to see her. I don't wish to do so. And I don't intend to be browbeaten into doing so.'

'I'm sure she wouldn't penalize a little child—'

'I don't intend to give her that chance,' Margaret said.

But within a day or two she was consulting Maeve who knew the situation in more intimate detail than Teresa. It was also true that she wished him to start in the school where he would mix with the children of her friends.

'Write in and ask for an appointment to present him,' Maeve urged. 'You have to get his name put on the list.'

'I can't write to Reverend Mother.'

'You don't have to. Write to Mother Omniscient.'

'That's a new one. Who's she?'

'A senior nun who came some time ago to supervize the running of the school. The older girls christened her Omniscient.'

'But she won't know who I am.'

'Don't worry. I'll see that she does. And do it now or you'll miss the draft.'

Frank urged her too. There was little time left. The term for newcomers commenced a week or so later than the rest but that still meant within the month of September. In her application she explained who she was. That Reverend Mother was bound to read it she had no doubt. Reverend Mother would scrutinize every application that arrived, regardless of who was supposed to be the supervisor of the convent's educational affairs. But preferential treatment was given to applications on behalf of the children of past pupils. And she believed, as Teresa had done, that Reverend Mother would refrain from penalizing a little child.

The reply came quickly and offered her an appointment. She brought Paul along and sat with other parents and their children on the benches which had been arranged along the hallway to await her turn to be called into the parlour. Some of them she knew from her classroom days. It was pleasant to see them again after so long a time and they talked together with easy familiarity.

Then her name was called and she knocked at the parlour door. Inside she found the Teaching Superior seated with papers spread about the tasselled cover on the long table in front of her. A young novice was in attendance to pass the relevant documents and make entries in a heavy register. The Superior, angular and severe of face but kindly enough when she began to speak, was probably in her middle sixties. She asked Paul if he knew any prayers or anything at all about God or Heaven or his Guardian Angel and such matters. Paul told her that he knew about Baby Jesus being born in a stable and the Three Wise Men and he could bless himself, which must be with your right hand and he proceeded to show her and he also knew some prayers.

'Could you say a little one for me?' she asked.

Paul closed his eyes tightly and after some false starts and forgettings finally assembled what he wanted to say:

> Angel of God my guardian dear
> To whom God's love commits me here
> Ever this day be at my side
> To light, to guard, to rule and guide
>> Amen.

Margaret heard the handle of the door behind her being turned while he was reciting, but resisted the temptation to look around. The sound of hands being clapped very quickly when he finished surprised her. It was Reverend Mother. She came forward with Sister Loquacious and Sister Inconspicuous in faithful attendance.

First she smiled at Margaret and said formally but without coldness, 'Margaret my dear. How nice to see you.' And then she turned to Paul. 'So this is Paul? A very good boy. You spoke that prayer so perfectly that a little reward is surely called for.'

She rooted a while through a series of voluminous folds and

brought out three toffees in coloured wrappers. It was a lifelong habit of Reverend Mother's. However splendiferous, she took care always to be well equipped in her classroom inspections to distribute little prizes of fruit or sweets as rewards for brightness and good behaviour.

'And how old is Paul?' she asked him.

'Five, Miss,' he answered.

Sister Loquacious, with a quick smile about the room, prompted a correction. 'Reverend Mother, Paul; not Miss.'

'Paul will learn,' Reverend Mother admonished, 'don't confuse the child.'

She turned to the Reverend Superior.

'Forgive my intrusion, we were passing. Please see me when you have finished. I wish to hear your report and consider the admissions.'

'Certainly, Reverend Mother.'

Reverend Mother patted Paul on the head and nodded to Margaret before leaving.

'Come, Sisters,' she commanded.

Sister Inconspicuous held open the door for her.

The letter of acceptance was formal with details of the basic equipment required for the newcomer and it was signed by Reverend Mother. A week later Margaret had to run the gauntlet of Reverend Mother again when she took Paul to the convent for his first day of attendance. They queued first at the school shop which the nuns ran themselves and which sold copybooks with the convent crest on them, pens and pencils, colouring crayons and a book of morning and evening prayers for children which a nun of the Order had compiled. It was a slightly amended copy of the one which Margaret herself had been equipped with at the beginning of her own convent career. The nuns liked to keep the profit to be gathered from such small but essential purchases with the Order. While she waited in the queue, Reverend Mother came with her two attendants to walk slowly along the line of mothers, smiling at them, inspecting their children, pausing now and then for a brief word of exchange. She nodded pleasantly at Margaret but passed on without stopping. As she did so Margaret observed that age was now firmly in the ascendancy. Poor Mother Splendiferous had met her match.

The telephone on Frank's desk rang. He picked it up. Miss Downey was at the other end. She sounded anxious.

'Frank, there's someone on the line who wants to speak to you and I'm not sure whether to put him through or not.'

'Why so?'

'Well – he has a very low voice.'

'I can tell him to speak up, can't I?'

'I don't mean low like that. I mean vulgar, ignorant, low class – that kind of low.'

'Did you ask his name?'

'I think he said it was Peter Brady.'

'My dear, devoted protectress,' Frank reassured her, 'you have on the far end of that telephone line none other than Ballcock Brady, City Councillor and public representative. Switch him through.'

Miss Downey did so.

'I wanted to discuss something with you,' Ballcock explained, 'but I don't want to detain you on the phone and I wouldn't dream of disturbing you by entering within the printings of your office building, so I was hoping when next you're over this way you'd be kind enough to drop in to me.'

'Certainly,' Frank said.

'How soon, do you think?'

'This evening on my way home, if it suits.'

Ballcock expressed delight. 'You're a gentleman,' he said gratefully.

The office of the Construction Workers Co-operative Society was Ballcock's by virtue of his secretaryship. He attended regularly on Sunday mornings and on odd evenings after his ordinary working day. His job was to keep the books, and administer the Loans and Savings Scheme, which was regularly availed of not only by the members but by their thrifty wives as well. He also negotiated discount privileges for them in the city shops and provided smaller items such as cigarettes and boxes of toffees or biscuits at reduced rates. When Frank called he was dividing the weekly supply of football doubles for distribution to a corps of helpers who sold them in various factories and workplaces for a small commission. It was a dingy office with a clutter of ledgers that recorded the transactions of long past years, and out-of-date membership cards gathering dust on shelves and in boxes. The naked electric bulb which hung from the ceiling was a begrudging and inadequate source of light.

'You're good to come so soon,' Ballcock said, 'and I'll try not to detain you. It's an idea I have for a series for the *Bulletin* on the same lines as the couple of pieces you put together from your chats with

Bandmaster Fogarty. These would be about the memories of a long-standing corporation member regarding the people of his constituency and the work he does.'

Frank smiled to himself.

'What corporation member had you in mind?'

'Myself – who else.'

'I don't think I'd have time just now to ghost another series.'

'You wouldn't have to. I can do that myself,' Ballcock said.

Frank remained silent, thinking hard.

'If you have doubts about it,' Ballcock offered, 'maybe you'd come with me on one or two nights when I'm making the rounds of my constituency. There's a lot to be seen and heard.'

Frank hesitated. Ballcock's company at such close quarters would be trying. On the other hand it would be a contribution to the good-client-relations strategy so dear to the heart of P.J. He pushed his doubts aside.

'Very well,' he agreed. 'We'll give it a trial.'

Ballcock turned up for their meeting in his bowler hat and Sunday suit. The medals on his watch-chain jingled momentarily as he seated himself.

'Do you know,' he confessed, 'I'm delighted you brought the motor car. I don't think I've ever done the rounds in a motor car before. It'll make a great impression.'

He directed their journey through the labyrinth of streets that housed his constituents. They were for the most part the lowest paid, forgotten and without influence in society at large, but of prime importance to Ballcock. Their approval or otherwise could elect or reject him.

He made sure they noticed the car. When he presented himself on the doorsteps of their tiny cottages he deliberately left his briefcase behind so that his return to the car to collect it was in full sight of the householder awaiting his return at the open halldoor. On tenement landings he explained that a companion was waiting in his car below in the street and asked permission to bring him in. He made notes of all their needs. They required hospital treatment and were waiting for beds. He took the details and promised to use his influence. They had complaints about unemployment payments and disability allowances. He would look into it.

A young married daughter and her husband living with her parents wanted to be considered for a corporation flat. He explained how they should apply. In one area the houses had been condemned and whole communities were being shifted out to one of the new corporation estates. Many of them were unwilling to go.

'The missus here won't budge,' a husband told Ballcock.

'Wild horses couldn't drag me,' his wife confirmed. 'We went out there a couple of weeks ago to see Joe and Lottie Gibney. They're two months there now. Merciful God it was cruel. Houses on roads that are miles long and bang in the middle of nowhere. A wind that would skin you and no shelter. No matter what she does the house is always cold, Lottie told us. There's no buses and the shops are a day's walk away. No one knows anyone else. All the old neighbours are scattered. Poor Lottie and Joe are heartbroken.'

'I've been saying it at meeting after meeting,' Ballcock complained. 'Communities mustn't be broken up. Neighbours must be kept together. I might as well be talking to that china dog you have over there on your mantelpiece.'

At one point he suggested parking the car and exploring on foot for a while. The air in the streets was damp. A light fog trailed down narrow laneways. Tenements with wide-open doors raised their tiers of lighted windows high above the streets.

'Here's the worst of the tenements now and there's nothing to be done except knock them down, no matter what the people say,' he remarked. 'Otherwise they'll fall down unaided. Some of them have only one lavatory to serve the whole house. In a few you'll find two families sharing the one room. And T.B. is here, there and everywhere. It terrifies them. If they have to go to hospital for an X-ray they get in a panic as the day draws nearer. The dispensary doctor explained to me that it is spread by contaminated water and by the milk. It seems both of them are crawling with orgasms.'

A tall figure approached through the dusk and greeted Ballcock with familiarity. Ballcock returned the salutation. But when the figure was out of earshot he said to Frank, 'There goes one of the patrons and begetters of iniquity – a notorious bloody money-lender. The people around here are even more terrified of that particular party than they are of the T.B.'

They had a drink when their inspection came to an end.

'May I ask what you think of my suggestion now?' Ballcock said when they were seated.

'I agree with what you said. There's a lot to be seen and heard. How often do you make your rounds?'

'Once a month as a rule. Sometimes twice. I've been doing it for over twenty years now. It got me the seat on the corporation early on. But I've never been nominated for a governmental election. The party doesn't give me the backing.'

'But you keep at it?'

'I keep at it,' Ballcock said, 'because I have principles. Once I heard old Jim Larkin saying he wouldn't be content to put a loaf of bread on the table of a hungry man. He'd put a bowl of flowers there as well.'

'And you think you might do so too?'

'No,' Ballcock admitted, 'but I think I could help.'

On the drive home he asked again what Frank thought of his idea.

'Let me sleep on it,' Frank answered.

But his estimate of Ballcock had gone up a little.

They were together in Morrissey's office and had just concluded some business when Morrissey said quite unexpectedly:

'I've been thinking on and off about that night we went on the piss with Don Maguire, the night I let my hair down in quite a massive way.'

'You've been worrying about what you said?' Frank asked.

'No. I trust you.'

'I assure you.'

'In fact there is something I didn't tell which I'm going to offload on you now. I implied, I think, that my father's degradation all took place while I was away hospitalized. Most of it did. But not it all. I'd like you to have the whole truth. It began when I was at home and he was discovered to have committed some serious neglect of duty. Normally my father supervised the labour of others. On this occasion, as a punishment Old Bowden ordered him to clean up a great mound of dung from the cow byres and barrow it to the storage place where it was allowed to accumulate for later use as fertiliser. Old Bowden also ordered my mother to leave what she was doing in the house for five minutes of every hour and to take me with her so that we would stand together watching my father, while he worked until it was dusk, crossing and recrossing the courtyard under the eyes of all who came and went. After some hours, when sweat ran from his face and his legs were buckling under the weight of his barrow of dung, my mother came to him with a can of tea and some bread. They refused to allow her to give it to him. I think it was that which set him finally and irreversibly on the downward path.'

Morrissey stopped. Frank could think of nothing to say. Morrissey resumed.

'The strange thing is that whenever I thought about that

afterwards in hospital, a change had come about. Instead of watching it from the courtyard with my hand in my mother's, I was looking down at it from one of the windows high up in the big house. The bell above the stables was ringing for the morning assembly and the tenants were gathering in the courtyard to be allotted their tasks for the day. And then, when they were dismissed and parted to go their various ways, I would catch sight of this man crossing and recrossing as he refilled and pushed barrow after barrow of dung. There was a woman watching him but no child. The woman was not my mother and the man was not my father.'

Morrissey reflected deeply for some moments:

'I find that quite frightening whenever it returns,' he confessed. 'Nowadays, thank God, it seldom does.' Frank refrained from speech. For a long time they sat together in silence.

When Paul returned from school and handed her the letter, Margaret, believing it to be one of the customary notices of some forthcoming religious function or an appeal for funds for one or other of the convent's charitable causes, left it aside unopened while she put his meal before him and took tea for herself to keep him company. She tidied up after him and did several other small tasks before picking it up and sitting down to read it. The address on the envelope was in Reverend Mother's own hand. It had become spidery and uncertain but she could still recognize it.

Dear Margaret,

I have asked your dear friend Maeve not once but many, many times to let you know my earnest wish to have a visit from you so that I may talk to you. My knowledge of the long-standing friendship between the two of you encouraged me to hope that Maeve would be the most persuasive and influential source to employ in order to win your consent. Alas, this was not so. She assures me that she has conscientiously delivered all my many invitations but that your reluctance to respond seems to remain unshaken. This is not only hurtful to me as your childhood mentor and guardian in the practice of your religion and personal holiness, but distressing also because I am aware of the root cause of your reluctance through the letter of resignation you, in your honesty, sent me. I know our Very Reverend Chaplain, despite his deep study of such things, may not in this instance be the ideal person to offer to help you and I have been close to despair for some time. Then I thought of sending this note by your little Paul and I feel I may congratulate myself on hitting at last upon the perfect little courier, a veritable Angel Gabriel who, when he bears a request to you, cannot be refused. I hope you will recognise him as such.

Won't you come and see me? I am not going to preach either to you or at you, for I have taken counsel of one intimately familiar with the many stubborn and varied religious difficulties to be encountered, not only here at home but among the peoples of the many lands he has traversed in the course of his lifetime as a missionary. He is regarded as an expert guide on many present-day problems and I can also say that on several occasions he has been a most valued counsellor to me personally. Come, and I will tell you who he is and how to consult him. Please respond positively.

> *Yours in Jesus Christ*
> *Your old teacher and Rev. Mother*

Reverend Mother had all in readiness. She herself was seated in the easy chair on one side of the leaping fire. On the other its empty twin awaited Margaret's arrival. Between them on a low table the fine bone crockery, the plate of assorted biscuits, another of seedy cake and, resting for warmth on the brass fender, yet another of toasted scones beneath their silver dish cover conveyed their special welcome.

Sister Loquacious, escorting Margaret down the hall, begged her to be prepared for the change in Reverend Mother. She would find her considerably failed physically but, all things considered, still sharp enough in her mind, although eccentric at times in her utterance. There were occasions when it became very difficult to know what it was she wanted and there were times, indeed, when one would wonder – God forgive us – if she knew herself. But that was an inescapable consequence of advancing years. It was something which must be understood and accepted and cheerfully borne.

Sister Inconspicuous opened the door to their knock and let them in, then disappeared unnoticed but reappeared moments later with a silver teapot and attendant pieces on a silver salver. Reverend Mother indicated that she should leave the salver on the table and go. With a tremulous hand she invited Margaret to pour. A parabola of tea, well-bred in hue, emerged delicately. Margaret passed the sugar, which was silently declined.

'I am very pleased you have come at last, but not in the least surprised,' Reverend Mother announced when she had stirred the tea and returned the spoon to its saucer. 'I was certain I had found my Angel Gabriel. And you'll be so happy, I know, when I repeat that in addition to his propensities as a young Archangel he is doing very encouragingly as an aspiring scholar. He is punctual, attentive and highly articulate.'

Modesty prompted Margaret to suggest that Reverend Mother was being, perhaps, overkind. Reverend Mother rejected this and proceeded:

'You have another little one at home—'

'Yes indeed,' Margaret answered, 'a girl, Aoife. She's three and a half – almost.'

'So she'll soon be coming here, too. You won't feel the time passing. And your husband – he's in good health?'

'He is, thank God.'

'And,' with hesitation, 'in employment?'

'He's in advertising, Reverend Mother, an artist and designer.'

'Splendid. I hesitated to ask. So many nowadays are not so fortunate.'

Reverend Mother began to smile a little as she contemplated something that had entered her mind.

'I almost found myself in the ranks of the jobless a short while ago. They sent me a teaching superior, if you please, to run the school. They felt I was getting on in years and needed assistance.'

'I believe I met her,' Margaret recollected, 'when I brought Paul for his interview.'

'I found it necessary,' Reverend Mother continued, 'to make it clear who was Reverend Mother. My teaching superior and I get along splendidly together now.'

'I'm sure you do,' Margaret said, smiling.

'You will remember Father McDermot, my nephew. You would have seen him calling to visit me from time to time. He's been retired and back permanently from the missions now and I asked his advice about it. You are Reverend Mother, he told me, and don't let them forget it. Put your foot down at once. They won't want a battle with one of your standing and experience. If you act swiftly they'll think again. So I did. And he proved to be right.'

Margaret offered more tea. Reverend Mother accepted. Margaret then helped herself and waited in anticipation.

'I took the liberty of talking about your problem to him,' Reverend Mother said.

That was as Margaret had anticipated. A ripple of irritation caused her to straighten stiffly in her chair.

'We were both aware, of course, that it is something which troubles countless young parents throughout the Church. Father McDermot told me he has made a deep study of it and spoken to many young married people about it. His views are liberal, too liberal, I would have felt some years ago. I find I am not so certain now. I think he could help you and I would ask you to go to see him.'

Margaret expressed gratitude for Reverend Mother's concern. She would give it serious thought and make known her response. Reverend Mother nodded her satisfaction at this. She could furnish a note of introduction. Father McDermot, she said, had discussed in considerable depth the dilemma of faith which the teaching on family planning gave rise to. Not all authorities, he had emphasized, were unanimous in their conclusions.

'When I was young in religion I thought dissent of any kind must be condemned as sinful,' she confessed. 'Now it seems not to be so. You must pray for me, Margaret. I will not be here much longer and the old need the prayers of the young.'

Her eyes squeezed up into two narrow slits and her frame hunched and seemed to shrink as a sudden unbidden thought assailed her and swamped the whole of her mind. 'When I get up Above,' she added, with hatred in her voice, 'I'll have a thing or two to say about those who tried to foist that dreadful woman on me. I'll see they get their just desserts.'

She was referring, Margaret guessed, to the appointment of the Reverend School Superior. Her wish for revenge was far removed from the crowning holiness she had pursued with such heroic dedication throughout her long years in religion. It was the sudden, unreasoning malice of senility, Margaret concluded, unbecoming and mindless, but in all likelihood, blameless.

Father McDermot's courtesy set her at ease. He asked his questions with skill and experience and had the art of guiding her when she had difficulty in formulating her answers. It took him less than fifteen minutes to decide on his advice. There were moral determinants, he told her, that demanded consideration before the goodness or the evil of any act could be identified. There were three of these: the object of the act, the circumstances surrounding the act, the purpose that the one performing the act had in mind. He had been testing her answers against these elements even as she gave them. He had also in mind that the sexual act between husband and wife, over and above its procreative function, had the purpose of expressing and confirming their mutual love. He asked her if she wished to make her confession.

When she had finished he said, 'I am not asking you to refrain from sexual congress. You are a mature and responsible young woman and you alone have the charge of using your own body as common sense and reason dictates to you. It is not my prerogative, nor is it that of anyone else, to attempt to usurp that right. If, in consequence, a particular recourse seems necessary to prevent a threat to the stability of your marriage you may justifiably make use of it. Above all, continue to avail of the sacraments of confession and Holy Communion. If you are in doubt or anxiety at any time, come and talk to me and I will do my best to guide you. You may wish to suggest to your husband that he should do likewise. Now, make a good Act of Contrition: O my God I am heartily sorry . . .'

He left her to continue the formalised Act of Contrition while he blessed her and spoke the words of absolution over her.

Frank decided to accept the invitation to confess also, though he had already grown noncommittal and sceptical about the whole matter.

'I may as well,' he said at last, 'though whether it's sinful or not, sinful seems to depend nowadays on who you go to. They keep contradicting one another.'

'That's the part that makes me uneasy,' Margaret confessed, 'Supposing the Father McDermots are the ones who are wrong?'

'A matter for the Father McDermots. It doesn't affect us.' He smiled to think how it had come about and added, 'Poor Mother Splendiferous. If she only knew what she was playing her part in starting—'

But Margaret looked over at him and said in a puzzled tone, 'It's an odd thing. Thinking back over her conversation with me, I'm beginning to half-believe that Mother Splendiferous did.'

'Never,' he insisted. 'In the matter of sex a liberal priest may be a possibility. A liberal Reverend Mother is unthinkable.'

In the New Year Ballcock Brady's series of constituency sketches began to appear in the *Bulletin* and drew unexpected interest. Joe Dunne admired them and congratulated Frank for getting them underway. Members of Ballcock's political branch also took notice and began to remark on their propaganda value. They were simple reports on the lives of the cottagers and the tenement dwellers, their fierce attachment to the areas they had grown up in, and their

stubborn reluctance to exchange familiar surroundings and neighbours for a bewildering web of terraced houses in the middle of
greenery and farm animals. He pictured their dependence on the
pawn shop and the social life that surrounded it; he spoke of the
tolerance for petty crime and the hatred and fear of the money-
lenders. It was a world he could account for with authority and
humour. He reported to Frank that his standing in the party was
improving dramatically. How much so would have to await a
general election and the selection of party candidates.

'Perhaps you've made it at long last,' Frank suggested.

'If a general election is called within a year, or even two, I think
I'd stand a chance of being selected,' Ballcock predicted. 'And I owe
it to you.'

'You owe it to a lot of hard constituency work and a sound
knowledge of the people you're dealing with,' Frank suggested.

'That's true enough,' Ballcock agreed. 'I'm shrewd enough to be
sure always to keep my finger on the tempo of the people.' His tone
changed. 'Are you not interested in politics yourself at all?'

'Not in the slightest.'

'You should be. A smart, educated young chap like yourself
should go for politics. You look well and you talk well and if you
can do that it's half the battle won. There isn't much else to
it.'

Some time later, when he was delivering the last of his articles to
Frank for setting, he became suddenly conspiratorial.

'I've been following that series that's running in the *Review* this
while back. Joe Dunne gets it regularly.' Frank pretended
ignorance.

'What series is that?' he asked.

'They call it "On The Side Of The Angels". It's beginning to put a
flea in certain influential beds. I happen to know you do the
cartoons.'

'Do I?' Frank said with as little interest as he could manage.

'You do the cartoons and Simon Morrissey does the copy. I
admire your courage but as a friend I feel I should warn you that
taking on religion or politicians is a dangerous game in these parts. I
knew a man some years ago, and in the end they were tapping his
telephone and getting a gang to break into his house. Ramsacked it,
they did, looking for something to pin on him.'

'The series is anonymous. I'm wondering how you know?'

'Unanimous or not,' Ballcock said, 'I don't need to go far to find
these things out. I'm a long time on the road.'

Morrissey only found his suspicions confirmed. The leak was from the *Review* office.

'It's O'Halloran', he decided, 'I'm sure of it. He's after Con Andrews. He'd do anything in his power to get at Con Andrews.'

Chapter 13

For Christmas Lemuel badgered Stella until she consented to ask permission to have Margot for her guest for a few days during the season. Her parents were going to be away and she expected to find herself dumped down the country among a handful of elderly ladies.

Stella smiled. 'You're quite gone on Margot Penrose, aren't you?'

'And what about you and Johnny O'Grady?'

'I'm twenty. You're barely seventeen. Isn't that a bit precocious?'

But she was only teasing and asked their father who agreed without trouble. She wrote inviting Margot to come on Stephen's Day or on the day following, which would be Friday, for a short stay. Margot sent her sincerest thanks and said she had been given permission by her aunt and would be delighted to come on the Friday evening.

After that, Stella turned to the business of preparing their Lansdowne Road house for the festival and their friends who would call. He became her devoted helper. Under her direction he hung the usual large motto from the hallway ceiling. She had embroidered it a few years before and kept it since for annual re-use. It read:

A Hundred Thousand Welcomes
– Shakespeare, Coriolanus, Act II Scene I

He helped her to stretch the paper chains so that they radiated from the motto to the walls like spokes from the hub of a wheel. He transported large bundles of holly and ivy and advised on the most advantageous position for the mistletoe. She had acquired three lamps from the firm of Messrs Green Brothers at a cost of eight shillings and sixpence each. They were a recent invention, a type of candleholder with a delicately coloured shade fitted at the top, marketed by Green Brothers as a brand new model under the curious designation, The Arctic Lamp. These she arranged here and there in the hall to enhance its appearance and provide additional light for the arriving guests.

The first to admire them was Uncle Crispin. He examined them minutely on his arrival on Christmas Eve and pronounced them to be designed on the same principle as the old-style carriage lamp, with a spiral spring on the bottom which pushed up the candle as its length burned shorter.

'Very good,' he approved. 'You'll find there'll be no ugly guttering and no nasty fumes to be endured when you extinguish them. Not a scrap of candle will be wasted.'

His eyes wandered against his will towards the hallway motto. It had irritated him when he first saw it and it still did. But he had avoided comment in the past and he did so now.

'Has my luggage arrived, my dear?' he asked instead.

'It's in your room,' Stella confirmed.

'Could you tell Jenny or whoever's job it is, to bring me some extra clothes hangers?'

'I'll bring them myself,' she offered.

She found him spreading items of clothing on the bed. Among them, to her surprise, were a frock coat, striped trousers and a tall silk hat.

'My, oh my, Uncle Crispin,' she exclaimed, 'what brazen swank.'

'Seasonal activities may call for them,' he answered. 'I have spats here somewhere too, should the need arise.'

'Then don't hang them yet,' she advised. 'I'll take them to Mrs Bolger to be pressed.'

Jonathan, as usual, was observing strictly the fast and abstinence prescribed by the Church for Christmas Eve. He had them dine sparsely on omelettes and toast, and, although he had wine on the table to accompany it, he was unusually restrained when it came to pouring it out. Uncle Crispin, well acquainted by now with his brother-in-law's strict ways, had taken the precaution of eating secretly and fully beforehand to make sure there would be no danger of going hungry. While Jonathan said grace he projected his amusement across to Stella by pointing to his plate and turning his eyes heavenwards. She nodded her sympathy. After the meal Jonathan offered port in such a parsimonious measure that Uncle Crispin looked ruefully at Stella once again and tilted the barely half-filled glass from side to side to convey his feelings.

He said to her, 'I've been admiring your decorations, my dear.

I've always loved the hanging-up of green boughs at Christmas and the lavishing of holly and ivy.'

'Thank you,' she returned, knowing from the tone of his voice that he was up to something.

'Stella has always had great skill and taste in these matters,' Jonathan put in.

Uncle Crispin looked surprised.

'I'd have thought you'd disapprove,' he confessed.

'Disapprove?' Jonathan repeated. 'Why should I disapprove?'

'Because you are a Christian of deep conviction and stern observance. I thought that the pagan origins of festooning the place with all this leafery and greenery could only displease you.'

'Pagan origins. Are you sure?'

'Quite sure,' Uncle Crispin insisted. 'In December the ancient Romans decked out their houses in exactly the same fashion to commemorate the feast of Saturn. It symbolised his power to clothe the earth in green again and to bring about the re-growth of the crops in due season.'

Jonathan preened with self-satisfaction.

'In that case,' he announced, 'I am delighted our Christian information is more accurate than that of the Romans. We know the true identity of Him who ordains the annual miracle of renewal. As always the Church has been tolerant, abandoning the paganism, but retaining the greenery.'

'And that, you believe, is tolerance?'

'We are not puritans, to silence the bells. The greenery and the gaiety are from God.'

'Your observance of Christmas Eve isn't very gay,' Uncle Crispin remarked drily.

'We fast and abstain. Fasting and abstaining are for the vigils of all great feasts.'

'As I understand it,' Uncle Crispin suggested, 'the fasting and abstaining only apply to flesh meat and the quantity of the food allowed. I don't remember that these restrictions were intended to apply to the port.'

Jonathan looked down at the extended glass and then up at the rueful face. He made a sound of apologetic self-disapproval.

'Forgive me, Crispin. My custom is to curtail myself. But I claim no right to coerce others.'

He hastened to make amends and poured a lavish measure. Later as he rose to excuse himself, he pushed the decanter across the table for Uncle Crispin's convenience.

Uncle Crispin was used to the routine. Jonathan would now retire to his room and remain there until he was due to leave for Midnight Mass, which he would attend alone. When it was over he would return to spend the intervening hours in prayerful vigil until it was time to attend the six o'clock morning Mass, again on his own. On his return he would take three or four hours sleep before presenting himself for the simple domestic ceremonials of Christmas morning: the exchange of presents, the morning glass of sherry, the courtesy visits from old neighbours who exercised consideration by keeping them short. Young Jonathan was five this year, so to match his growing awareness there would be a little more emphasis on Santa Claus and the surprises he had brought.

Uncle Crispin, who genuinely admired his brother-in-law's steadfastness, regretted his deceit in having eaten twice, but fast or no fast, he was damned if he was to be forced into going hungry. He set about chasing his unease away by replenishing his glass. Rigorous spirituality held no allure for him. Brought face to face with it, he was content to skulk among the weaker vessels.

On the evening after St Stephen's Day Margot arrived at the station in the company of the aunt she had referred to as the one who hadn't yet forgotten how to smile. She was Aunt Amy, a small woman, kindly of manner and shy, who declined their invitation to tea so that she could join the friends with whom she was to spend the next few days the more quickly. They would be awaiting her arrival. Lemuel found a hansom for her and rejoined Stella and Margot at the cab which was already waiting for them.

'Lovely,' Margot said as she lay back into the darkness and the sheltering warmth of the upholstery. She was muffled voluminously against the cold.

'You're tired,' Stella sympathised.

'Not really,' she denied. 'I simply adore train journeys.'

'You'll have something to eat as soon as we get home.'

Lemuel took the heavy luggage in for her. She paused in the hallway to admire the Arctic lamps and remarked on the impressive size of the welcoming motto.

'Stella's handiwork,' Lemuel said. 'It took her weeks and weeks.'

'A Hundred Thousand Welcomes,' Margot read out. 'I know what that is in Irish. Céad Míle Failte.'

'Have you been attending the Gaelic League's Irish language classes?' Lemuel teased.

'No,' she said. 'But if I had the opportunity I would.'

'All the O'Gradys are in it,' Stella told her, 'including Johnny. He doesn't seem to care that it could jeopardise his prospects of promotion.'

'It could?'

'Young officers of the Curragh command are not supposed to favour home rule or harbour nationalist views.'

'Stop,' Margot begged. 'They've been dishing out loyalty lectures to us all through this term. I'm turning into a diehard Sinn Feiner as a result.'

Lemuel brought the luggage up to her room. A lamp had been lit in readiness on the dressing table and the fire in the grate was burning cheerfully. She was to dine in her room on her own because it would be more restful, and then she would join them downstairs. It was too late to think of doing anything except sitting and talking together. Lemuel took her hands in his.

'Happy Christmas, Margot.'

'Happy Christmas, Lem.'

They kissed.

'Sit down at the fire,' he suggested. 'I'll have them bring your meal.'

Lemuel and Godwin were already on either side of the sitting-room fire when she joined them. Stella was engaged in some solo card game or other.

'Nothing much to do tonight, Margot,' she apologized. 'Pity you weren't here yesterday. We had a box at the Gaiety pantomime. So had the O'Gradys. It was marvellous.' She took a note from the sidetable.

'Brighter news ahead, though. Look at this.' She handed the note over to Margot. It read:

Friday December 27th	Meet Margot evening train. Nothing special. Chat.
Saturday 28th	Party at the O'Gradys. Introductions, dine, then dance. Fortune teller.
Sunday 29th	Uncle Crispin to arrange tour around – weather permitting.
Monday 30th	Reception here, Lansdowne Road. Dinner. Impromptu concert. Magic lantern show (Uncle Crispin). Dancing.
Tuesday 31st	(New Year's Eve) Margot leaves, afternoon train.

Margot folded the note and put it away.

'The little bit at the bottom looks sad,' she remarked. 'Margot leaves. What is the magic lantern show?'

Godwin left down his book.

'Can't you guess,' he invited. 'A series of slides of the plan and elevation of the four-cylinder, chain-driven motor car with several dozen others illustrating in excruciating detail the workings of the four-cycle engine.'

'Godwin, please,' Stella protested. 'You mustn't be smart at your uncle's expense. He's a kind and most tolerant man and quite brilliantly clever.'

'Will this fortune teller at the O'Gradys tomorrow be a let's-pretend one or a real one?' Margot asked.

'They believe they'll be able to engage a professional.'

'I hope like anything they'll succeed.'

Margot's enthusiasm alarmed Stella.

'For God's sake,' she warned, 'be sure not to mention it in front of Father. It's condemned as a completely unacceptable superstitious practice by the Church and he wouldn't hear of it.'

The O'Grady party was for younger adults. Godwin, at 15, was still just a shade too young to be invited. Johnny O'Grady was among the oldest at not quite 24. He looked resplendent in his lieutenant's uniform and took over Stella completely. Margot enjoyed the same fate with Lemuel.

As they touched glasses together after the introductions, Margot whispered, 'Lem, will I tell you a secret?'

'I'm all agog.'

'I've never, ever before tasted champagne.'

'In that case you're entitled to a wish after your first sip. But you must take it immediately after tasting it. And you mustn't tell anyone what it was.'

'Not even you?'

'Not even me.'

She sipped. They touched glasses again. The babel of voices grew as the champagne was repeated again by attentive servants. Whispering was no longer practical.

They were seated side by side when it was time to dine, and applauded the two or three brief speeches which accompanied the coffee and the port. Then Johnny O'Grady, who was presiding, announced that numbered pieces of paper would be passed around the table and each guest who wished to visit the fortune teller, who was now installed in one of the upper rooms, should drop his or her numbered token into the bag which would also be passed around.

When the bag came to Margot she dropped her token in but Lemuel declined.

'Oh, go on,' she urged.

But he was adamant.

'I'd feel like a fool.'

'Lem dear, it's only for fun.'

'Yes. For the fortune teller.'

Most of the young men seemed to be of like mind. The young women were almost unanimously in favour.

Johnny announced a short entertainment before the dancing began. It started with a recitation from one of his military comrades with the seasonal title of 'The Mistletoe Bough'.

> The mistletoe hung in the castle hall
> The holly branch shone on the old oak wall
> And the baron's retainers were blythe and gay
> And keeping their Christmas holiday
> The baron beheld with a father's pride
> His beautiful child, young Lovell's bride
> While she with her bright eyes seemed to be
> The star of the goodly company.

But young Lovell's bride grew bored and demanded a change of entertainment:

> I'm weary of dancing now, she cried
> Here tarry a moment – I'll hide – I'll hide
> And, Lovell, be sure thou art first to trace
> The clue to my secret lurking place

So she ran off to hide and after an interval they set off to look for her, searching every tower and every nook and every cranny, scouring high up and low down, until foreboding seized on them all:

> And young Lovell cried 'Oh where dost thou hide?
> I'm lonesome without thee, my own dear bride'.

Margot, absorbed in every word, linked her arm through Lemuel's.

So they searched for the young bride all that night and the next day without success. A week passed, a month passed, and the years in turn went by, until young Lovell was no longer young and children who had been told his story would say to one another when he passed them by:

> 'See! the old man weeps for his fairy bride'.

But at long last the answer to the mystery was discovered:

> At length an oak chest, that had long lain hid
> Was found in the castle – they raised the lid –
> And a skeleton form lay mouldering there
> In the bridal wreath of that lady fair
>
> Oh! sad was her fate – in sportive jest
> She hid from her lord in the old oak chest.
> It closed with a spring – and, dreadful doom
> The bride lay clasped in her living tomb!

Margot removed her arm from Lemuel's to join in the exuberant applause. Stella was bringing someone over to introduce her.

'Margot,' she said. 'You haven't met Kitty, Johnny's sister.'

'How do you do,' Margot said pleasantly.

'I'll tell you how I do,' Kitty complained. 'I'm simply furious with that brother of mine. After all the trouble we went to he omitted to announce her name.'

Margot frowned.

'You won't believe it,' Stella explained to her. 'Johnny forgot to announce that the fortune teller is Princess Zeranova. She's all the fashion.'

'The cards she uses are from ancient China,' Kitty enthused. 'They're wafer thin and made of silver. People say she also has an Egyptian set made of gold which she uses, but extremely rarely.'

'Are you going to consult her?' Stella asked Lemuel.

'I don't believe the future can be foretold, so what's the use?' he answered. 'And even if I believed it could I'd rather not know.'

'I'm the opposite,' Margot confessed. 'I wouldn't miss it for the world.'

'What number did you draw?' Kitty asked.

'Number nine.'

'That means you'll be called quite early on during the dancing.'

For the dancing they moved into an adjoining room where the musicians – violin, violoncello, piano and drums – had set up their chairs and stands and were already limbering up by playing quietly as though to one another only. Shaded lamps and candles in their separate pools of light cast softly mingling colours on walls and ceilings. The dancing began and was becoming a dream-like trance of movement and melody when the summons for card number nine was announced. Margot jittered.

'Wish me luck,' she pleaded. Lemuel pressed both her hands as he released her.

The music recommenced. Couples began to move about her as she picked her way across the floor. In the hallway a servant curtseyed and led her up two flights of stairs to a landing where she stopped before an open door and, when she had indicated in silence to Margot that she should enter, left. Margot hesitated. The isolation after the crowded dance floor and the utter silence after the music unnerved her. A lamp on a table just inside the open door lit the room dimly. She stepped in. A large object which filled the whole centre of the room and reached almost to the ceiling was barely discernible except for another small lamp which glowed inside it. It was a fortune teller's tent. Margot stared in disbelief.

A low voice called from it in a clear but unfamiliar accent, 'Please come in.' The lamp Margot had seen through the fabric of the tent stood on one side of the table at which Princess Zeranova sat. She was dressed in silk from head to toe. A colourful kerchief adorned her head. She was festooned with bracelets and jewellery which rattled and flashed in the weak lamplight at every movement. The silver card pack was extended, and Margot was instructed to select one and then another and yet another until a small pile had grown beside her. When Princess Zeranova was satisfied she picked them up and scrutinized the individual cards as she spoke.

'You will appreciate,' she explained, 'that with so many people gathered here there is only limited time and this is but a mere glance – a sample as it were. We have but five minutes or so. Should you desire a full and deepfully explored scrutinization it will be necessary to appoint with me and attend at this destination.'

She handed Margot her card. It was headed:

> Princess Zeranova
> Clairvoyant, Mystic, Fortune telling,
> Horoscopes, Astrology, etc.

While Margot read she continued her scrutiny of the cards and said eventually, 'You are an only child, I think?'

'That is so,' Margot confirmed.

'And a lonely one?'

'Much of the time.'

'Your parents are dead?'

'No. They are alive.'

'But you do not see them so much. Or they are inattentive to you?'

'You might say so.'

'You are musical?'

'Not very.'

'An artist, then?'

Margot shook her head.

'You write poetry. If not you read it and collect for yourself those pieces which pleasurize you in the deep soul?'

'I do that — yes.'

'This is because such pieces become as friends and keep you to feel secure.' She looked closely at the cards before her. 'I cannot say if you are in love with somebody, but you may soon be.'

'I am very much in love already,' Margot said.

'Now it is clearer.' Princess Zeranova said, after consideration. 'You will find much happiness. You will have a journey with him. But if it is to be soon and if it is to be across the sea, be cautious. There is peril in water. That is all we have a little time for.'

Margot rose. 'You are very kind. Thank you.'

'Not so. It is a pleasure to speak with the young. I wish you to find deep happiness.'

Margot smiled her thanks and found her way out. She was high up in the house and could look down from the deserted landing into the deep well of the stairs. Nothing stirred about her, but remotely, and barely audible from behind closed doors, there came to her the alternating six-eight, two-four rhythms of the five successive episodes of a quadrille. She stood listening, alone in a way never before experienced. In the space of a few seconds she had lost the world and could only eavesdrop on it from an infinite distance. Her isolation frightened her. Her descent of the stairs took a million years.

In the morning, Lemuel left Margot reading at the breakfast room fire while he went with the rest of the family to Sunday Mass in their parish Church of St Mary's in Haddington Road. On his return the breakfast room was empty, but on the sidetable at the fire she had left the magazine she had been reading. It was a special Christmas number. Beside it lay her open notebook in which she had freshly written:

Thoughts at Christmas by Annie S. Swan. 'The older I grow the more strongly do I feel that it is not love that saddens the earth but the dearth of it. There is too much living for self among us all; we are too apt to regard the little world within our own four walls as the only spot of any consequence, and through such narrow vision we are bound to become selfish and circumscribed. Let us look beyond. The whole human brotherhood should concern us, even as it concerned our Master when He walked with men. We want more light, more wideness of vision, more sympathy towards the suffering and the sad.'

He turned the magazine over and looked at the title page.

> The Woman at Home
> Annie S. Swan's Magazine
> Profusely Illustrated
> London
> Hodder & Stoughton
> 27 Paternoster Row
> 1895

When he looked up again she was standing at the door.

'I decided to get dressed for Uncle Crispin's outing,' she told him.

'You look stunning.'

'Borrowed splendour. You should recognize it. Stella loaned it to me.'

He offered her her chair back. As she sat down she picked up the open notebook.

'I've been reading what you've just written in that,' he confessed.

'Well—'

'I found it very creditable and pious.'

'You all went off to Mass while I had no church to go to so I wrote out what Annie S. Swan had to say in her new "Over the Teacups" feature. It provided my own private Sunday morning service. I thought it suited very well.'

He turned the pages of the magazine, pausing from time to time to read a sample of the text or examine the pencil sketches which appeared as profusely as the title page had promised.

'You buy a lot of magazines, don't you. Surely it's expensive?'

'A group of us at school club together and pass them around. Of course they have to be ones that have been approved. Annie S. Swan is highly trusted.'

The door opened again and Stella appeared. She was followed by Godwin, then by her father and finally by Uncle Crispin who caused a mild sensation. He was resplendent in tall silk hat and frock coat. Stella looked down at his feet. He was wearing the spats as well. Protruding from them were the glossiest pair of boots she had ever seen.

'I ordered a second cab,' he grumbled, 'but it doesn't seem to have arrived yet. If I had bought a motorcar this kind of thing could not arise.'

'If you had bought a motorcar,' Jonathan pointed out, 'you'd have us all decked out in goggles and veils. I wouldn't fancy it. The weather is too inclement.'

They were wined and dined in the Shelbourne Hotel at Uncle Crispin's expense and strolled afterwards in St Stephen's Green to breathe the air and aid digestion. They thought they might make a trip to Howth, but decided against it because the day was very cold and it would be too exposed. A trip through the Phoenix Park to the Strawberry Beds was chosen as an alternative, but it too had to be abandoned. They were still jogging through the park when the world beyond the cab windows darkened and the skies grew menacing. A sudden gust of wind bombarded the glass with great blobs of rain.

'I think we should turn back,' Jonathan suggested.

'I'm afraid so,' Uncle Crispin said, disappointed.

They signalled the following cab to a halt. Uncle Crispin climbed out from his and went across to convey the decision.

'What a shame,' Margot said.

'Stop at my place on the way back,' Uncle Crispin requested. 'I have some things to collect.'

His house in Fitzwilliam Square had no staff, except for a caretaker and his wife who had permission to hire casual help as required. It was redbricked and tall, rising four storeys above a basement which was half hidden by massive railings. Granite steps mounted proudly to the halldoor. Wrought-iron balconies adorned the windows. A torch extinguisher with a large, cone-shaped head occupied the ornamental fanlight above the door.

'What can it be?' Margot wondered as they entered the hallway to help Uncle Crispin to carry out an outsize magic lantern and its necessary accessories.

'It was for putting out the torches which the link boys carried to light the gentry through the street at night when these houses were first built around sixty years ago,' Uncle Crispin explained. 'The torches were of pitch and tow. That extinguisher was still there in the fanlight when I bought the house, and I left it be because it had once seen the torches held aloft over the sedan chairs of fashion.'

The picture his words evoked thrilled Margot. She gazed up at the extinguisher in wonderment.

'How beautifully romantic,' she enthused.

'I thought so too,' Uncle Crispin agreed, grunting under the weight of the magic lantern.

On the way back to collect more bits and pieces he caught sight of

imself in the hall mirror and was rooted to the spot by his sartorial
plendour.

'What in God's name,' he demanded in astonishment, 'possessed
me to tog myself out like that. I look ridiculous'.

'Nonsense,' Margot assured him, 'you look most fiercesomely
mpressive.'

He stared at her with wide eyes and arched eyebrows. Their
udden laughter filled the hallway.

Most of the evening back at Lansdowne Road was spent helping
him to get his equipment into place: the lantern in the centre of the
loor, a table for the box of slides, a music-stand to support the
cript of his commentary. A white sheet had to be spread on a frame
and the frame moved forwards and backwards until the correct
distance for efficient projection had been established. His plan of
resentation required a piano and he had arranged to hire one
because the house piano would be needed downstairs for the
lancing and, anyway, was far too heavy to be moved. When it had
ot come by five o'clock he dragged Lemuel off to the house piano
o run over the music he had selected. Stella and Margot, sitting
ogether at the fire in the small family retiring room, could hear
emuel hammering and banging away at the keys in loud, military
tyle musical flourishes and occasionally, the voice of Uncle Crispin
ellowing raucous, out-of-tune snatches.

'I hope the singing isn't part of the magic lantern show,' Stella
emarked.

'I hope it is,' Margot confessed. 'It's so ghastly I find it irresistible.
hall I fetch the crackers I told you about?'

'Please do.'

Margot retired and returned after a few minutes with a parcel
vhich she handed to Stella to undo.

'Some of the girls at school saw them advertised in a magazine
nd sent for them. My friend Laura got these for me. They're called
Kiss And Tell crackers and they have paper hats in the shape of
earts inside them and special little romantic verses. There are only
welve in the box so you'll have to decide who's to get a Kiss And
ell cracker and who an ordinary one.'

'That won't be easy. How can we know what the verse says until
he cracker is pulled?'

'There's a booklet here which relates the verse to the colour of the
racker.'

Stella took it to examine. She smiled immediately at the first
ine:

Verse (Green and Yellow Cracker)
The sweet crimson rose with its beautiful hue
Is not half so deep as my passion for you
'Twill wither and fade, and no more will be seen
But whilst my heart lives you will still be its queen.

The second one pleased her even more:

Verse (Red and Blue Cracker)
My dearest heart please whisper low
That o'er my life your presence sweet
Will make my heaven here below
Where love its counterpart may meet

'These are marvellous,' Stella approved. 'Pity we've only ten among all the guests.'

'There are twelve,' Margot corrected.

'Ten,' Stella persisted. 'I insist on keeping one for Johnny and myself. And another, I presume, must be kept for you and Lemuel.'

Margot's face lit up with pleasure and she blushed deeply. In the next room Lemuel stormed the keyboard once more and again Uncle Crispin bellowed unmelodiously. Stella repeated her worst fears.

'I swear to God,' she complained to the ceiling, 'that uncle of mine is going to sing tomorrow and spoil the whole evening.'

But almost from the start it was clear even to Stella that nothing could do that. The reception went perfectly, the meal was greatly admired, the right verses from the Kiss And Tell crackers were got to the couples they were aimed at and sent already melting hearts beating faster. In the darkened room where they gathered for Uncle Crispin's magic lantern show, lovers moved close together and touched in secret with hands and cheeks.

His introductory item was a short sequence of scenes from the Zulu War. The main feature followed, a series of slides relating the tale of Ali Baba and the Forty Thieves while he read with unexpected competence from the accompanying script. He concluded with a blood-curdling sequence featuring the Afghan War. For its presentation Lemuel had to leave Margot's side to take his seat at the hired piano, from which he supplied various bugle calls and military effects, including a tumultuous cavalry charge. Uncle Crispin confined himself to two songs about soldiering: one of them told of the friend who had saved the singer – his boyhood comrade – from the attack of an enemy tribesman at the cost of his own life

The second was descriptive of the charge of the 9th Lancers during their victory at Kandahar. Stella recognized it as the one which had given rise to the furious bellowing during its rehearsal on the previous night. It was not quite so bad when you were actually looking at Uncle Crispin. Nobody seemed to mind and some even smiled in enjoyment. Stella, close to Johnny O'Grady in the darkened room, would have been content to let Uncle Crispin bawl all night. Margot, although she regretted that Lemuel had to leave her side to attend to the piano accompaniments, welcomed anything that prolonged the night. Tomorrow would separate them for an unpredictable stretch of time.

In the morning, while the rest of the house lingered longer abed than usual after the late night before, Lemuel and Margot, having breakfasted at the normal hour, were happy to gain a little more time to be alone together. After it they muffled up against the sharpness of the morning air and decided to go walking by the strand road at Sandymount and along the seafront to Blackrock.

At Irishtown they stopped to look at the old military barracks almost half a mile away. The ebbed strand spread its wrinkled surface all the way from their viewing point to its high lopeholed walls. An enormous bullseye with white circles on a black background rose in lonely isolation at the strand's centre. Behind them on the piece of wasteland which bordered the wall, a group of football-playing urchins filled the chilled and salt-laden air with excited cries. Almost all of them wore clothes that were the cast-offs of others. The ball, a home-made one, had been fashioned out of rags rolled tightly about each other and held together by twine. Beyond and to the right of the barracks the hill of Howth humped its blue back and spread itself on the metal-grey sea like a resting whale. When they turned to resume their walk again, the roofs and spires of Kingstown rose in thronging companionship under the protective mountains. They quickened their pace and the salt air brought a blush of pink to their cheeks.

'I've been wondering since the O'Grady's party,' he confessed as they walked, 'what Princess Zeranova had to say for herself.'

'I meant to tell you on Sunday. Then I thought it might be unlucky. Do you think it could?'

'I don't see why.'

'Last night I made a wish after seeing her, because that was my first time with a fortune teller.'

'I'm not curious about what your wish was. Only about the fortune teller. Was she any good?'

'I think so,' Margot decided. 'She guessed I was an only child and that I was often a lonely one. She thought my parents might be dead, which was wrong, but when I told her so she suggested I didn't see very much of them which was true. She told me I would soon find myself in love with somebody.'

'And so—?'

'I told her I was very much in love already,' Margot answered simply, 'and she said in that case I would find happiness. But she warned me against a journey across the sea with the one I loved if it was suggested for the near future, because for a while to come there would be peril in water.' Margot smiled. 'However, we are unlikely to go sailing the seas, aren't we?'

'Worse luck,' Lemuel agreed.

'And then she said she found great pleasure in talking to the young and she wished me well.'

They got back for an early lunch because there was the evening train to catch. Uncle Crispin, who was passing through the hallway as they entered, stopped for some kindly words.

'You are leaving us today, my dear?'

'Unfortunately, yes.'

'But you'll be with us again very soon, I sincerely hope. Lemuel does too. I know that. I've never seen him so cheerful.'

They both blushed.

'You are all so kind and hospitable,' Margot answered. She looked up at the motto. 'I think Stella has expressed it so beautifully. Don't you?'

Uncle Crispin looked up at the banner above his head:

A Hundred Thousand Welcomes
– Shakespeare, Coriolanus, Act II Scene I –

He winced as he read.

'Politeness should compel me to agree,' he answered eventually, 'but I can't bring myself to tell such a whopper. Between you and me, my dear, I think it hideously wrong. But I haven't ever told Stella, because she's a dear, sweet girl. I'd be grateful if you wouldn't mention it to her either.'

He put his index finger to his lips, enjoining silence, then went happily on his way. Lemuel looked after his retreating figure in amusement.

'I can't see anything funny about it,' Margot said. 'I think the embroidery is extremely skilful.'

'The embroidery may be skilful, but the attribution is ridiculous.

After all, 'A Hundred Thousand Welcomes' is a phrase of common speech. Would you stick up a banner in the hallway saying:

Well, Good Night
– Shakespeare, Hamlet, Prince of Denmark, Act I Scene I –

Margot thought for a while. 'I see what you mean,' she said eventually. 'No. I would not.'

When they met her aunt on the platform of the station, the winter's evening was already over the streets and the gas lamps hissed above their heads while they made their farewells.

Stella and Uncle Crispin came with them. Margot was glad. Their presence kept the worst of the loneliness at arm's length. Aunt Amy talked of her own friends and how warmly and hospitably she had been received. They had had so much to talk of, she said. There were so many, many Christmas seasons now to share memories about.

Then it was time to take their final farewells and to board the train. It pulled out of the station with a lurching of coaches and a hissing of steam. They had the carriage to themselves. At first she made conversation with Aunt Amy, telling her of the two parties and the abandoned outing and an assortment of trivial details. Then she fell silent. The carriage swayed gently and its gas lamps whispered to each other above their heads as the unseen countryside flowed past them in the outer darkness. All was rhythmic motion and hypnotic sound. Very soon Aunt Amy closed her eyes and drifted into sleep.

Chapter 14

The short Christmas season slipped away too quickly and left Lemuel with time once again to notice the dreary progression of January's days. Frost rimed the rooftops or icy fog drifted in from the sea. Rain sweeping the streets for hours on end soaked huddled carters and their sodden horses. Corporation binmen put sacks about their shoulders while they gathered the city's waste, and stuck it out because wives and children had to have food and shelter. There was no respite from winter's inclemency, no glimpse of the sun to hint of comfort or hope.

Or so it seemed to Lemuel. On damp and cheerless evenings he stood again by the sea wall at Sandymount staring in lonely recollection across a strand that was being obliterated in stealth and silence by the gathering dusk. The three Arctic lamps that burned in the evenings to add cheer to the hallway revealed only absence and loneliness.

For the rest of them life at Lansdowne Road was agreeable. The paper chains were removed after the feast of the Epiphany, the holly with its red berries was consigned to the fires, the motto was taken down from the hall and folded away for use in the future. Stella got out on her own every Tuesday afternoon to attend Miss Typhosa McPartland's Young Ladies Academy of Arts for drama and singing lessons. Whenever John O'Grady was at home he would meet her there to go walking together. Or he would bring her to his parents' house where she was now an accepted and welcome visitor. Godwin revelled in the early months of the year because they saw the rugby season getting under way and he was both an ardent spectator and an enthusiastic college league player. To young Jonathan the weeks and the months meant nothing at all. He was still only six and not yet of an age to fret about the weather.

Uncle Crispin continued to stay with them. His own house lacked its necessary compliment of domestic staff and he was tardy about recruiting them. But he was well content. At supper one evening he spoke with unqualified optimism of the year ahead:

'Do you know, Jonathan,' he declared, 'I have great expectations of 1896. The trams, for a start. You'll see electric tramcars in our streets for the first time. And the motor car – big developments are on the way for that too. Then there's this new free-wheeling bicycle. Take that in combination with the railway systems. You can easily cycle up to twenty miles to a railway station, put your bicycle aboard and use it again when you get to the station of your destination. That's going to mean a revolution in social communication, even for the most humble among us. There's a new world only a step or two down the road.'

'I don't think you're right about the electric tram,' Jonathan objected. 'The opposition is too general. The humble horse is at the centre of our economy. The whole city will jump to its protection. Not just the tramway workers, which is to be expected, but the coachbuilders, the blacksmiths, the harness makers, the stablemen, the veterinary profession, even the farmers who supply the fodder and the dealers who buy and distribute the manure. They're all predicting massive unemployment.'

Uncle Crispin was dismissive.

'Hullabaloo,' he declared with a wave of his hand.

'Answer me this. What about the fire brigade experts?' Jonathan challenged. 'They've reported that the trolley wires would make dealing with fires impossible by getting in the way of the firemen's ladders. Surely that's a serious consideration?'

'They've got over it elsewhere,' Uncle Crispin pointed out. 'There's money for electric transport among our crafty captains of business. There'll be powerful lobbying both here and in the Mother of Parliaments across the water, and no shortage of financial sweeteners. No. I have complete confidence. Whether it likes it or not, Dublin's going to bow to the electric tram.'

He was equally confident about the motor car and the successful introduction of The Locomotives On Highways Act, already long overdue.

'No more cretins with their ridiculous red flags hobbling along in front of the most revolutionary invention in the history of man, the mechanically propelled carriage,' he told them, not for the first time raising his voice over the matter. 'The flag waggers are doomed to go. And when that happens you'll be waving good luck to Uncle

Crispin as he hurtles past you in his horseless carriage.' He mulled the matter over. 'When I was across at the Tunbridge Wells motor exhibition last year, an acquaintance complained that on the Ashburnham and Totnes road the toll on his motor car had been two pounds, while for a coach and four horses it was only three shillings. How's that for prejudice and partisanship?'

A week or two later they discovered he had acquired yet another enthusiasm. He arrived back one evening with a cinematographic machine. He insisted on projecting, for the entertainment of Jonathan and Lemuel, a film loop of an artiste in a circus, swinging back and forth interminably on a trapeze and, when they wearied of that, as they very quickly did, he substituted a man with a golf club who did nothing else except strike ball after ball after ball.

'That's pretty tame stuff,' he admitted, 'but there are great possibilities ahead.'

He had been studying accounts of the demonstrations of cinematographic projection Edison had given back in 1890. He was convinced they had been highly professional and successful and proved beyond doubt that it would be possible to cope with far more complicated movement in the near future.

Jonathan was interested. He wondered if subjects such as horse racing or boatraces or even, for example, complete playlets might become possible in time.

'Undoubtedly,' Uncle Crispin said, as he dismantled the apparatus. He had learned that there was to be a demonstration of the latest technical standards of cinematographic projection by Lumière of Lyons and intended to go to London later in the year to attend it.

He paused in his dismantling to say, 'You seem to be interested, Jonathan?'

'Yes, indeed. Fascinated.'

'Then why not take the trip with me. You'll find it quite exciting.'

'Thank you, but no,' Jonathan answered. 'I have other more important plans. They concern Stella. I haven't talked to her as yet, so I'd ask you not to say anything to her until I've had the opportunity to do so.'

They assured him of their complete silence. He continued:

'Stella will be twenty-one years of age this year. It's time to let her see a little more of the world.'

'Why not come and take her as well?' Uncle Crispin suggested.

'What I have in mind is a little bit more comprehensive,' Jonathan revealed. 'I've thought of a week in Rome. Then to

Vienna. Paris certainly. And, of course, London on the way back. In August, preferably, because I understand young Henry Wood is likely to continue his new promenade concerts in August.'

'Will Lem here be going too?'

'His turn will come later,' Jonathan answered. 'In three years' time. When he's twenty-one. All right, Lemuel?'

'Perfectly all right,' Lemuel said. He was pleased for Stella. He himself would rather stay at home to be with Margot. It sounded like a trip that would take six to eight weeks, which would occupy the whole of the summer holidays. It was not until he was helping Uncle Crispin to move the equipment out that the consequences of Stella's absence for so long hit him like a blow between the eyes. He almost dropped what he was carrying.

Excitement sent Stella searching for him later in the evening. At first she thought he must be out. Then she knocked at his bedroom door and he called to her in response. He was sitting by the window, an open book in his lap.

'Lem, I had to find you – I'm so excited—'

'You're going on your travels.'

'How did you know?'

'Father mentioned it. Sit down,' he advised, 'or you'll explode.'

'It's to be Rome. Then Vienna. Then Paris and London. I wish you were to be with us.'

'My turn will come, Father says. In three years' time. When I'm twenty-one.'

'In Rome we'll be seeing the Pope, no doubt, and the basilicas and the Sistine Chapel and all that,' Stella assumed. 'But when we're there I'm going to persuade Father to take me to Naples as well.'

'Why Naples?'

'Because of that book by Bulwer Lytton that was among Mother's favourites. You and I used to read it together. Do you remember it?'

'I remember it well,' he confessed, 'it was called *The Last Days of Pompeii*.'

'I've been looking at the maps. Pompeii is right beside Naples.'

'So is Vesuvius. Take care it won't suddenly erupt all over again.'

'I don't give a fiddlestick. Ever since we read that book I've dreamed of walking, sometime, in the streets of Pompeii... Oh Lem—'

Her excitement touched him. He postponed mentioning his own dilemma. Instead he said gently, 'You'll have a lovely time.'

Dear Margot,

It is Saturday and I have been able to make use of the school half day to cycle out here to leave this in the hope that you will manage soon to slip out of custody (so to speak!) to see what I may have left. I have to make it short because already the light is going, especially in here among the trees, and the leaves underfoot are sodden and everything about me damp with wet. I even had some trouble locating our tree to leave this in it. I didn't dare to send it to you at the school. If they happened to read it there would be too many questions to be answered.

To get to the point: Stella is twenty-one this year and Father has decided to take her on a kind of coming-out, culture-vulture tour in Europe which will keep her away most of the summer. When he first announced it I was delighted for Stella's sake because it will be most exciting, with all its opportunities to see historic places and noble monuments and see great ballet companies, I suppose, and hear great music. Then I suddenly thought: if Stella is away all that time how can she invite Margot to stay with her during at least part of the school holidays? I have been racking my brains about this until I have myself in a panic of anxiety. It is beyond any possibility that they would allow you to spend your time in a house without either parent present and in the company of a group of young men. I have wondered could Kitty O'Grady ask you to stay, but that seems not feasible. Kitty hardly knows you as yet and it would require far too much explanation and downright falsehood to make it appear normal and convincing to her parents.

Can you think of anything? Please write to me the moment you can – even if you have no solution to offer at the time. I am in the very pit of gloom and need your comfort. It is starting to rain and I must finish before the paper is destroyed along with my spirits. As well as that I have to grope my way out from among these trees and find my bicycle again when I've done so. Dear Margot, I wish I were this letter to hide in the hollow of a secret tree and wait to be found by you.

All my love,
Lem

Dear Lem,

Yesterday, during our free afternoon, I managed to slip away unnoticed and went to Avonmore to see if you had been able to *leave anything for me that would cheer me up and when I found your note my heart gave a great jump of joy, so it had three times the normal distance to sink when I read the* appalling *news about Stella; appalling, that is, for us, not for her. I am writing this during our study hour and have envelopes and stamps and all the necessary things and will smuggle it out and post it as soon as I can.*

I have no idea what we can do, but surely there is something. It is bad enough to have so few opportunities to see each other for most of the year without the whole summer passing and not seeing one another. What is to happen to me I don't know, except that my doting parents are highly unlikely to have me around the Continent, although it is quite on the cards for them to confer the privilege on themselves. The likelihood is that Aunt Amy will be saddled with me, and I with her. Not that I mind that too much. It is not her fault that the goings-on in her corner of County Westmeath are short on excitement. She herself is a dear, kind person and I am glad to have her to be loved by and to love in return.

Lem, I will rack my brains to try to think what may be possible to do and please, you keep on doing the same thing. Please! As soon as I know where I am to be parked for the summer, I will find the earliest way to let you know. I am tempted to wish I had not gone near our tree, but that would be silly. Not knowing a thing doesn't make it go away, does it? We must both pray hard!

    All my love,
    Margot

By the time the final weeks of the school term were in sight they had managed to meet on three occasions: once at the hollow tree in Avonmore; then at the abandoned mill with its riverbank walks and secluded lanes; then in the small tearooms, which was the most pleasant meeting place but also the most exposed. They believed, however, that they had not been seen.

She found out she would be staying with Aunt Amy as she had guessed. Her parents were going abroad. Going abroad, she now knew, was only a front. Once they got abroad they went their separate ways.

'How can you know?' he questioned. 'You hardly see them even at home.'

But she had overheard talk between Aunt Amy and friends and had plucked up the courage to question her about it.

'You may as well know,' Aunt Amy had confessed. 'Your father and mother hardly speak to one another except when there is company. It is very sad, but it is a fact of life that marriages are like many another thing and can die out over the years without either one or the other being particularly to blame. They wished to keep the situation from you, at least until your schooling is complete. That, by now, will be soon enough, so you may as well be told.'

'Does it upset you to know?' he asked.

'Not really. In a way it helps a bit. It suggests a reason for their coldness which would not be entirely selfish or uncaring.'

'So it's Aunt Amy and Athlone for the duration—?'

'There may be a break. Laura's parents may have me for a week or two. I hope so. There are some young people among Laura's crowd so it's a bit livelier.'

'Is Aunt Amy's house in the town itself?'

'It's on the shores of Lough Ree, about four miles from Athlone town. It's quite pleasant, especially for sailing. It has its own private little jetty at the bottom of the back garden where you can tie up your boat.'

'That sounds tiptop—'

'Except that Aunt Amy doesn't have a boat.'

'Is Aunt Amy very stuffy?'

'Not really. No. She's not a bit stuffy. In fact, she's a trusting little woman. She's kindly. I can't really complain.'

His questions told her he had something in mind.

They left the tearooms to cycle further into the countryside together. The hedges bounding the road were alight with hawthorn blossom. On the higher ground beyond the hedges the undisciplined gorse flowered in yellow profusion, tinting the air about them with delicate odours.

'Lem, why did you ask me if Aunt Amy was stuffy?'

'I was wondering. If I got to stay for a few days somewhere near the house on some excuse or other, could we devise a way of meeting without it being known—?'

'Why don't we try?'

He became determined, 'Let me think about it,' he suggested, 'and write down the address for me. That will be the first step of the road.'

She did so as they were parting. He read it over silently before putting it away. Hope lightened the long journey home.

There was growing activity in Lansdowne Road. Jonathan was in and out of town arranging travel plans and bookings. Uncle Crispin, involved though he was in his motor enthusiasms and his exploration of the world of cinematography, found time to plague Jonathan with outlandish travel suggestions and had to be restrained from taking sole charge. Stella, having impressed on her father, after considerable difficulty, the critical nature of a young lady's wardrobe needs for continental travel, was kept busy with dressmakers who seemed to call to the house every other day, and with calls of her own to various outfitters in the city. Kitty O'Grady, her chief adviser, was hardly ever absent from her company.

Lemuel, planning ways of seeing Margot, found the islands of Lough Ree suggested certain possibilities. They had been extensively used as retreats from the world by the monks of the early monastic era, and were plentifully supplied with ruins of churches and habitations that dated back to the sixth century. His plan was to tell his father that he was keen to study the monastic movement in closer detail and wished for the opportunity to visit the islands during the summer holidays. Early Irish monasticism was near to his father's heart. He reckoned there was every chance the money to do so would be forthcoming. If he got to spending a week or so around Lough Ree he would be on Margot's doorstep. It should be easy to arrange an accidental meeting. He felt he was not being completely deceitful. Early monasticism commanded his mild interest.

His father approved the suggestion heartily. He himself had explored the islands of Lough Ree thoroughly.

'I'll fund the expedition with pleasure,' he agreed. 'But I want also to make you aware of some difficulties you'll encounter. For example, actually getting on to the islands. They're quite remote and you'll need boats and boatmen to carry you back and forth. It requires a deal of organisation.'

'I've thought about that,' Lemuel said. 'My solution would be to camp near the lake with Godwin and Eddie O'Grady. They've both agreed they'd love to come. There'd be three of us to handle a boat, so we could hire one for the week or so. We could bring a tent. In fact, that could prove unnecessary. Johnny O'Grady is bound to know some fellow officer in Athlone barracks who'd let us borrow one from the army stores.'

'Very good,' Jonathan agreed. 'Work out the cost. I'll be happy to know that you'll have something worthwhile to occupy you while your sister and I are away.'

Godwin and Eddie O'Grady were enthusiastic. Their interest in ancient monasteries was tepid, but camping and boating and fishing were a different matter. He wrote to Margot about his success. He promised firm details as soon as they were available. The presence of Godwin and Eddie O'Grady, he believed, was a shrewd ingredient of his plan. It would supply the necessary plausibility.

On the morning of May 16th, 1896, Uncle Crispin saw his faith in the inevitable victory of progress justified. To see the first electric tramcar emerging from its depot in Ballsbridge he led all the occupants of the Lansdowne Road house, including the servants, who left their domestic activities in abeyance with Jonathan's permission. They walked the short distance from the house to the tram depot together. Uncle Crispin donned his frock coat, striped trousers, tall silk hat and spats for the second time in five months in honour of the occasion. Stella and Kitty O'Grady, inseparable as ever, took the morning off from their unremitting survey of the niceties of fashion. Lemuel and Godwin attended as a matter of course. Even Jonathan, who always found difficulty in detaching himself from his set routines, went along with the rest of them and led his six-year-old son Jonathan by the hand to witness so momentous an occasion.

They joined the waiting crowd, which included the Lord Mayor and other municipal dignitaries, and cheered loudly when the tram emerged. It was being driven by one of the company's directors who stood on the open platform with his hands firmly grasping the controls, and a tall hat on his head as shining and as elegant at Uncle Crispin's own.

'His name is Cliften Robinson,' Uncle Crispen informed them when they asked if he knew who the director was. 'Thirteen years ago he was only a humble tram driver who got himself sacked when he punched an inspector who shouted at him for arriving late at his destination one evening. He went off to the United States to find work and did so well there that he was able to return and become a founding director of the Dublin and Southern District Tramway Company. Take a good look at the first electric tram to run in Dublin, and the best-paid tram driver in history.'

They cheered louder than ever and waved hats and handkerchiefs as the horseless tram trundled past them. They gaped in awe at its hissing trolley. A week later they all took a trip on it together from Haddington Road to Dalkey and back. They travelled on the open deck on top and marvelled from their elevated perch at the medley of pedestrians and horses and carts below them, and at the unfamiliar views of the great bay of Dublin on the one side and the mountains lifting in shapely sequence on the other.

After that they returned to address their everyday business once again. Uncle Crispin set off for London, discussing with himself whether he should invest in a motor car while there, or hold out for another twelve months in the certain expectation of further technical advances. Stella and Kitty resumed their pursuit of elegance. Lemuel and Godwin talked frequently of camping and camping equipment. Jonathan, in preparation for the unforeseeable hazards that might lie in the weeks of travel ahead, took himself off to the austerities of his study in Avonmore House, where he fasted and prayed and refrained from unnecessary contact with his fellow beings, overlooked at all times by the works of the Early Fathers which burdened the bookshelves in massive antiquity.

> *Pompeii*
> *June 29th, '96*
> *Feast of Saints Peter and Paul*

Dear Lem,

See what I've written at the top on the right-hand side! Yes. Pompeii! Where I'm writing from, or rather from the modern city beside it. But I have walked in the ruined streets and I've seen the ruined houses. Daddy was very agreeable to coming and said he would be very interested himself. So here we are.

The guidebook tells us that after behaving itself for centuries, Vesuvius suddenly erupted one morning and took everybody unawares. It says it happened in AD 79 (which I knew already) and that it poured cinders and ashes and God knows what on the people for three days (which I also knew – thanks to Bulwer Lytton). It buried everything so deeply that it was forgotten about until after nearly seventeen hundred years the archaeologists thought of digging it up again. So now you can see the drinking fountains and the ruts made in the stone surface of the roadways by the wear of countless chariot wheels. They have on display the remains of the charred nuts and fruits and loaves of bread that the volcanic dust clung to and preserved. It did the same to humans and animals. We saw the body of a sentry which was turned into a stone statue by the ashes and a dog also turned to stone and the poor animal is all twisted in agony. On the gateway to one of the houses was a sign which read: Cave Canem (Beware of the dog, even I could translate that). Anyway, it was one great thrill so when I get back I'm going to read The Last Days of Pompeii all over again.

I'm glad to be done with Rome. At first I thought Rome was going to be a deeply moving experience, but I got weary traipsing around an endless succession of shrines and churches and basilicas, never mind the pagan monuments etc, etc. the Romans left behind.

We attended a general audience with the Pope. He's Leo XIII Gioacchino Pecci Daddy says, and that around five years ago he wrote an encyclical called The Condition of Labour *which was not very popular with businessmen and has been quietly buried since. He was carried in on an ornamental chair – his* sedia gestatoria *it's called – on the shoulders of six attendants, and Father was very moved and I heard him praying to himself and I could swear when the Pope was passing he looked straight at me. Daddy says he thought the same.*

That's all for now. In a few days we'll be setting off for Vienna and I'm looking forward to that. And to the train journey, which I find exciting. Margot, who I know loves trains, would adore travelling in them here on the continent.

> *Your loving sister,*
> *Stella*

He sat above the pebbled beach which ringed the lake's edge, fixed to the grassy bank by the noonday langour and the weight of the sun's rays on his neck and head. He wished he had thought of keeping back his bathing towel when the others had left to go fishing, and had draped his pocket handkerchief over his head as a not very adequate shield instead. Margot was somewhere about. When they had finished inspecting the little monastery which the tutor of Saint Ciaran of Clonmacnoise had founded on the island in the beginning of the sixth century, and the remains of the five churches that had been erected in the stretch of another six hundred years, she had wandered off on her own to explore the maze of little tracks that gave access to the island's stretch of woodland.

Nothing stirred about him. The lake in front of him lay like a mirror, its sheen of sunlight unrippling beneath a light pall of evaporating water. On the grassy stretches behind him a group of cows had seated themselves in a rough circle. Further away a few sheep and their lambs lay side by side. He was well pleased with the manner in which everything had worked out. When Johnny O'Grady's friend in Athlone barracks learned that they intended to hire a yacht and sail it themselves, he suggested they should get one with sleeping accommodation and not bother about a tent. He could arrange one with a three-berth cabin and a small cooking galley for very little extra outlay, and they would be a great deal freer to regulate their comings and goings. That was five days' ago.

It had worked out very successfully. So had his contact with Margot. They staged a meeting and Margot in turn reported the matter to Aunt Amy who invited them to call. The studious objective of their trip impressed and edified Aunt Amy. She was delighted to accept their reciprocal invitation to spend an afternoon with them visiting one of the islands to inspect some of the monastic antiquities. Lemuel outlined their history and she listened with interest and good manners and admirable tolerance (as she thought), because she knew enough about the matter to know there were no Protestants knocking around in the sixth century. She was set entirely at ease and, being a trustful little woman by nature, saw no reason to prevent Margot from going off with them on her own. The weather helped. The days had been made so agreeable by the sunshine that everyone was unfailingly pleasant.

'Where did you get to?' he asked Margot when she returned.

'Right through the wood to the shore on the far side. There's a lot of fern on the way and the midges would eat you alive.'

She sat down beside him. 'And you?' she asked.

'I just sat here,' he answered, 'pinned to the ground by the heat. I stared at the world and the world stared back at me through a sunny haze; fields, hillocks, trees, the blue sky and the sun itself all transfixed by the heat. The cows behind you there stopped chewing for want of dribble and that sheep over there looked as though it was ready to swap its lamb for a handkerchief to mop its forehead. I think a swim is the answer.'

'A swim would be frantic,' she enthused.

'We'll have one when they get back.'

'And something to eat. I'm starving.'

'Hang on. Rescue is at hand.' He got to his feet.

The yacht had rounded the bend of the shore and was creeping forward with snail-like motion. Godwin was steering. Eddie O'Grady was sculling at the stern. After several minutes he left down the oar and dropped anchor. They hailed him and waved. He undid the dinghy and rowed across.

'I was wondering would you make it,' Lemuel remarked as they got into the dinghy. 'Is there any wind at all?'

'Not much. That's why we're late. But it's better out of the lee of the land.'

'Any luck with the fishing?'

'Not a hope. The water is so clear you can count the stones at the bottom. Any trout with a bit of sense is in hiding.'

They boarded the yacht and after twenty minutes or so found enough wind to supply a slow but steady motion.

'Margot is starving,' Lemuel told them. 'And so am I, but a quick swim before we eat is a must.'

They turned the cabin over to Margot for undressing and used the deck area themselves. The water was warm to swim in and unseen insects droned in chorus as though the monks were still near at hand, reciting their litanies. They made their meal in the little galley and despatched it sitting around on the deck. It was a world of wide skies and wide waters, a place full of light. In the early centuries, when the monks became pilgrims for the sake of Christ, Lemuel reminded himself, lakes like Lough Ree and waterways like the Shannon were their thoroughfare to exile. They would stow away their books in their leather bags and the bread of Christ in its Chrismal, and carry it before them to frighten off demons and robbers and wild beasts when they were traversing the great forests of the continent. They would leave their island settlement on such a day as this, perhaps, sailing downstream in their currachs with the blue skies and the small, fat clouds high above their assortment of tonsured heads. And they would recall it all later in far foreign lands with longing recollection:

Scant of breath the burdened bees
Carry home the flowery spoil
To the mountains go the cows
The ant is glutted with his meal

The wind awakes the woodland's harp
The sail falls and the world's at rest
A mist of heat upon the hills
And the water full of mist

When he recited it to Margot and told her his thoughts, she wrote it down to add to her chapbook collection. In the evening the breeze freshened a little and they began a leisurely return under skies that were now on fire with the declining sun and waters that mirrored in more muted tones the colours of its setting. Eddie O'Grady played his mouth organ as they sailed, and the fire in the sky melted gradually away and the light on the waters became a dappled silver. The trees crowding along the shoreline lost their colours, too, and reached upwards in dark silhouette.

Aunt Amy, standing in the shadow of the trees that ringed the little harbour and its jetty heard the distant notes of the mouth organ and knew they were coming. She was relieved. They were later than expected and she had begun to wonder if anything had gone wrong. But now the sound of mouth organ music stopped, and their yacht appeared as a ghostly presence out of the silvery dusk and grew in bulk and glided with a muted creaking of timber and ropes until the jetty was close enough for Godwin to drop on to it and begin tying-up. Eddie O'Grady apologized for their lateness.

'For quite a while we were becalmed,' he explained. Aunt Amy understood. She pressed them to come in for cocoa and biscuits.

'I expect you're all starving.'

So they sat in a pleasant room with a massive but ornate lamp set in the middle of the table and two more, but smaller ones, at each corner of the mantelpiece. A window looked out over the garden and its jetty which by now was barely visible. A fire burned in the grate.

'However warm the day may have been,' Aunt Amy confessed, 'I always light the fire in the evening time. I find it cheering and companionable.'

While they were sitting around having their cocoa and biscuits she examined each of them curiously.

'I'm trying to guess who is the harmonica player,' she explained.

'Eddie here,' Lemuel told her, 'we call him Our Minstrel Boy.'

The drollery pleased her. She smiled.

'You must play it for me when you've finished supper,' she suggested. 'I never hear music at my own little fireside.'

When the cups were cleared away Eddie O'Grady obliged as requested. He played a couple of popular tunes for her. He played 'The Last Rose of Summer' and they joined in. Then he left down the instrument and sang 'Shake Hands With Your Uncle Dan, Me Boy'. Everyone applauded. He played more tunes and Aunt Amy joined in the singing. At last he left down the mouth organ and remarked that they were keeping her up too long. It was also too dark now to think of moving the yacht.

'You must stay where you are and leave the moving until the morning,' she insisted.

They slept aboard, and in the morning were invited in for breakfast. After that the days flew. They fished with some success and pleased Aunt Amy by bringing her the trout as a gift. The weather remained perfect except for some hours of one afternoon when a storm broke suddenly from nowhere and the wind whipped up great waves. The yacht pitched and tossed. Lightning ripped the sky and thunder echoed from shore to shore. Margot, who was with them, became pale and frightened. Lemuel made her lie down in the cabin.

'I'm a great coward,' she apologized. 'Thunder and lightning terrify me.'

'You'll be safe here. Just lie still. It won't last long.'

He went out again to help the others and in twenty minutes or so it was all over. The wind died down. The thunder and lightning moved away into the distance. Steam rose from the drenched deckboards as the sun took command once again in a clear blue sky.

A few evenings later it was time to say their farewells and leave the yacht back again at its berth upriver. Athlone railway station smelled of steam and hot metal. They put their bicycles in the guard's van and boarded the train. It carried them eastwards to Dublin across the central plain while Eddie O'Grady entertained them on the mouth organ from time to time with airs that were predominantly melancholy, and the sun in their wake went down the sky, once again blending colour with colour in unbridled virtuosity.

Dear Lem,

Although it's not yet a week since we parted at Aunt Amy's house I thought I'd write to you because in no time at all I'll be back in Edmundscourt, gracing its venerable halls of learning in my school uniform and wondering what you are doing and if we can contrive in some way or another to meet and how soon. My only consolation this time is that it will be my last year and that this time next year I'll be free for ever of the drudgery of being educated. How lucky you are to be finished as of now. Do you think your father will change his mind about private tuition for you and pack you off to university after all? Have you yet decided whether you yourself would prefer private tuition or university? I think university should be more interesting. I imagine you'll take a while to yourself before deciding.

It was a dismal business the day the three of you left. I stood watching as you sailed upriver away from the little jetty, getting smaller and smaller, and I wondered not for the first time why all nice things have to come to an end (of course so do not-nice things, too, thanks be to goodness). I think Aunt Amy was sorry to see you go, too. In fact she as much as said so that night at the fire because she said to me, 'It's going to be very quiet now without the boys asking if they might tie up their boat at the jetty and borrowing drinking water and young O'Grady playing his harmonica.' (She thought that really lovely).

I loved every moment of it – well not quite every moment, I still think of the bit of a storm which happened, though it was over very quickly. I told you an untruth when I said I was terrified of thunder and lightning. I don't like it but I'm not terrified of it. What terrified me was I suddenly remembered what that fortune teller told me about going on sea journeys with you, and perils by water, and I thought My God This Is It. Perhaps your father is justified in his disapproval of fortune tellers, if what they say can make you behave in such a silly way. Anyway I've confessed to the truth and I feel the better for it.

Could we meet somewhere on the way on the day I go back to Edmundscourt? You are very likely to be free and I could perhaps break my journey at some point. If I do nobody will be the wiser because they won't know at the school what time I set out. Please write. I'll be at Aunt Amy's until then.

> *With all my love,*
> *Margot*

They managed to meet as she suggested. It was a strange coming together. For him school was finished with forever. The thought was much present in his mind. For her it would be its final year. They spoke about it and wondered what new paths would open before them. What was ahead would be different, they both knew. But in what way? And would it be better? More satisfactory? They thought so. It would be better, much better, yes. They swore to ensure that it was. How was not yet clear. But somehow or other.

Chapter 15

It turned out to be a year which stayed with Lemuel Cox for the rest of his life. He pondered it over and over again at all stages and at all the twists and turns of fortune, from the closing years of his teens through the years of active manhood and into those that were pacing the slow decline of his powers. It was with him even now, hovering over his seventy-five-year-old figure as he sat by the fireside in the company of even older Stella.

She was seated at the opposite side. She was knitting. Hardly a night would go by but she would have her workbox on the small table beside her and the ball of wool in her lap and the needles in both hands perpetually in motion. It had not been her loss of interest in his piano playing and the favourite works he selected for performance that finally turned him against her. It was not her refusal to endorse the unmistakable similarities between Margaret McDonagh and Margot Penrose, or even her reluctance to concede that she had any memory at all of Margot Penrose, or that Margot Penrose ever existed, infuriating as that was. No. It was the almost ceaseless clicking of needles.

There were times when he thought it would be better to get rid of her. Carefully regulated doses of arsenic could eventually do the trick. An even simpler method, and one which ought readily to pass for an accident, would be to take the manhole cover off the stretch of garden path down which it was his custom to push her chair when she had a wish to sample the fresh air. It was deep and ample enough to swallow chair, Stella, knitting needles and all. The explanation would be that he had been checking if the drains needed repairs and had left the cover off while he returned to the house for something or other. In the meanwhile she had been operating the chair herself and, unable to halt it in time, she had toppled into it and broken her neck, or whatever. But his plotting was not really in earnest. His religious beliefs taught him that love must be extended to fellow beings no matter what justification for withholding it might be advanced. Besides, time would eventually put a stop to the needles. The punishment to be endured in the flames of hell if you were despatched to it for fratricide would go on for eternity. So his church taught and so he was obliged in faith to believe.

She was speaking to him.

'I believe young Frank McDonagh was telephoning you today.'

'Was he? What had he to say?'

'I don't know. Mrs Holohan took the call.'

'And she didn't tell you?'

'No.'

'Did it not occur to you to ask her?'

'I don't care to pry into other people's affairs.'

Not half you don't.

It had become too hard to love Stella. Even in the cold fulfilment of duty. She went out of her way to make it so. As he walked across to the cabinet to fetch his glass and the bottle, the floorboard in front of it creaked as it always did. She looked up. She disapproved of his drinking. She could disapprove as much as she liked. He tilted the glass from side to side to admire the whiskey's radiant glow. He returned to his earlier reverie.

That year had been spent purposelessly for the most part, because although they had agreed on private tuition his father had been so tardy in pursuing the arrangements that time slipped over with nothing finalized. It had been the year 1897, the year of Queen Victoria's Diamond Jubilee, when disaffection flowed over into the streets of Dublin and caught him up in its hullabaloo for a brief hour or so. It was the year of the little country town circus, where they watched in suspense as a local volunteer of spunk and spirit bearded the lion in its den for a bet of a five-pound note. It promised to be a madcap kind of a year but it let them down badly. It was the year of hope's end.

Margot would be at Aunt Amy's once again that year for most of the summer vacation. He decided to try to get down to see her by persuading his father to advance the money once again for him to pursue his studies of the early monastic movement, this time exploring the ancient site of Clonmacnoise. It was on the east bank of the River Shannon about fifteen miles or so from Athlone. No yacht would be required. It was easily accessible by road. The train would bring him to Athlone and his bicycle would look after all the local travel involved. To ensure success in securing his father's agreement he decided to hold off from approaching him until he had a detailed proposal written out for his scrutiny. In preparation for it he embarked on a programme of specialized reading. Stella, deprived of his company for much of the time because of it, objected strenuously.

'Between Father with his self-imposed fasts and his personally devised and conducted novenas and retreats,' she complained, 'and you with your abbeys and round towers and high crosses, and all those inscribed gravestones begging without a stop for over a thousand years: A Prayer for Uallach the Abbess; A Prayer For Conn The Almoner; A Prayer For Nessan The Navigator, I'm beginning to feel I'm trapped in some kind of bloody monastery myself.'

Stella's use of strong language was so unusual that it startled him. Uncle Crispin approved. He was just back from yet another motor exhibition and had called unexpectedly. As usual he was agog with enthusiasm.

'You're far too young to be burying yourself in the past,' he admonished, 'you should have your eyes fixed on the exciting developments that are waiting for all of us just around the corner.'

He had met a fellow enthusiast from County Meath at the exhibition who kept a car of his own at his residence near the village of Slane and had been invited to come there on a visit to see it and try it out. His new friend was to stay the night in Fitzwilliam Place in a few days' time, so they could travel down together the next morning.

'Why don't you come with us,' he said to Lemuel, 'have a spin in one of the most revolutionary of modern miracles? I can quite easily get him to invite you.'

Lemuel hesitated, then let himself be persuaded. Richard De Courcy, Uncle Crispin's new friend, was a grey haired, well-set-up man in his early forties. In addition to their mutual interest in motorcars they shared a common enthusiasm for whiskey. Lemuel joined them in Fitzwilliam Place on the night before setting off for Slane and found them indulging both predilections in Uncle Crispin's study, which was welcoming and comfortable, despite its clutter of metal and wooden models of machinery and vehicles made by Uncle Crispin or invented by him for obscure purposes. He had managed to recruit enough extra staff to attend to the needs of his visitors for their overnight stay. Having poured liberally for Mr De Courcy, he turned his attention to Lemuel.

'My boy,' he questioned, 'what's this you are – twenty by now, is it?'

'Nineteen,' Lemuel corrected.

'Nineteen is near enough. You're qualified to join us in a glass or two of whiskey.' Uncle Crispin put down another glass.

'I think I'd prefer sherry, Uncle Crispin.'

'Sherry? By all means.'

Uncle Crispin fetched a sherry glass and searched the cabinet for the appropriate bottle. He remarked to Mr De Courcy over his shoulder as he poured, 'The young fellows of today don't measure up to the bold boyos of our time, Richard. They settle for sherry and such. At nineteen, whiskey still intimidates them. Begod I can tell you it didn't us.'

'Perhaps they are wiser,' Mr De Courcy responded. 'It leads to gout, I believe, if indulged in too early in life.'

Uncle Crispin brushed this aside. 'In the matter of gout,' he asserted firmly, 'I'd exonerate whiskey. It's the damn sherries and the port wines are the villains. However, Lemuel, every man to his taste, as the farmer said when he kissed the cow. Here's your sherry. And here's your health.'

They raised their glasses in cheerful amity. The assorted objects on the shelves about him stirred Mr De Courcy's curiosity. He left down his glass.

'Forgive me if it sounds impolite,' he remarked, 'but you have a mysterious conglomeration of objects strewn about the place and I'm at a loss to put a name on even one of them.'

'They are models of some inventions I attempted when I was a lot younger than I am now,' Uncle Crispin confessed. 'I thought I had something of a flair for it. The trouble was I kept finding the things I was inventing had been invented already. I've been meaning to get rid of them.'

Mr De Courcy smiled and turned to Lemuel. 'And you,' he asked, 'do you share your uncle's enthusiasm for the worlds of science and engineering?'

'Lemuel is a philosopher and a man of intellect,' Uncle Crispin put in. 'He believes with the ancient Greeks that in the perfect society The Wise Men are the golden ones and come first; the warriors are the silver race and come second. And below them are the ragtag and bobtail who are not worthy of intellectual or spiritual pursuits: the bronze nonentities, the artisans and the engineers and the riff-raff; in other words, Richard, you and me.' He turned to Lemuel. 'Am I right?'

'That would be my understanding of the Greek concept,' Lemuel agreed.

'And you are likely to make philosophy your study?'

'My father has suggested it.'

'A degree in Thomastic philosophy, no doubt?'

'That could well be what he has in mind.'

'Lemuel's father is an estimable man,' Uncle Crispin said to their guest. 'But he has religion on the brain.'

'I've read recently,' Lemuel remarked, smiling, 'that St Augustine was furious when the monks of his time began to adopt Greek ideas. He complained that all of them were engaged in contemplation and prayer and there was no one at all doing the day-to-day work in the monasteries.'

'My understanding of the character of Augustine,' Mr De Courcy suggested in a very low voice, as though people might be listening, 'is that he had not always been very good at the prayers himself.'

'Give me chastity and continence, but not yet,' Uncle Crispin quoted. 'That was the burden of Augustine's prayers for long enough.'

'I've heard that said,' Mr De Courcy confessed in a conspiratorial tone. He turned to Lemuel. 'Yours is a deeply religious home. I hope we don't embarrass you?'

'My father informed me about the early life of Augustine before giving me *The City Of God*, to read,' Lemuel answered simply.

By their third glass of whiskey they had begun a discussion on the Oscar Wilde trial and his pending release after two years in prison. They were very conscious of his presence, Lemuel knew, but very determined to accord him adulthood by treating him as a man among men. He did not mind. It was the penalty that had to be paid for being a mere nineteen years of age. Besides, his father had always spoken quite freely of such matters to all of them, without rousing any sense of embarrassment among them. His father, Lemuel realized, was in fact more liberal than either of them.

Richard De Courcy's property near Slane was a substantial residence surrounded by an estate which spread its wide and fertile acres across the loveliest stretches of the Boyne valley. Like Uncle Crispin he seemed content for the present to remain a bachelor. The life he lived was that of a country gentleman, fishing for salmon and trout in the abundant waters of the royal and historic river, shooting in the extensive woodlands, exercising on horseback or exploring on foot in the mazy lanes that wound in secrecy and concealment between dense and luxuriant hedges.

But for the duration of their visit these activities were suspended. Uncle Crispin and Mr De Courcy gave their all to the new motorcar. They both had enough professional instruction, most of it learned in England, to be able to get it started and to attend to its basic needs. They were both reasonably qualified to handle it on the open road once they had a few refresher runs on the private roadways of the estate.

It was a small vehicle designed to accommodate three, though often enough there were four squeezed into it. These, Lemuel noted, were most likely to be young ladies from the neighbouring estates that stretched successively across the breadth of the country. Uncle Crispin was extremely gallant in their presence. The more flighty among them never hesitated to consent when invited to share a lone drive into the countryside with him. It became commonplace to see a begoggled Uncle Crispin at the wheel with gamey-looking young things by his side dressed up in large hats with chin-ribbons and heavy veils, and tightly modelled coats and rugs wrapped voluminously about their knees. Perhaps, Lemuel thought, that was why they accepted the invitations so unhesitatingly. Uncle Crispin's moral character was no longer a factor. The number and complexity of the garments they decked themselves out in, even on the most temperate of days, made their virtue practically unassailable.

Lemuel himself made a number of trips with his host along the winding, heavily hedged roads where the blossoming radiance of the May bushes was becoming a challenge to the sun. Oak and elm, chestnut and sycamore towered in leafy abundance above the greystoned and embattled tops of demesne walls. The novelty of the motorcar was exciting and the countryside charming. But what delighted him was the unexpected discovery that Richard De Courcy was a keen antiquarian with a competent knowledge of the history of the county and the monuments that the passing centuries had spread so liberally across its landscape. His enthusiasm was re-awakened by Lemuel's response. Together they consulted the antiquarian works in the De Courcy library, including Sir William Wilde's *Beauties And Antiquities Of The Boyne* which Lemuel specially admired. After trips to inspect the monuments they had decided mutually to investigate, he would spend a couple of hours transcribing information from the Wilde book and adding it to his own observations for presentation to his father along with the Clonmacnoise material.

On the last evening of their stay when they were talking and drinking about the fire, Richard De Courcy insisted he should take the Wilde book home with him. He expressed polite reluctance but it was brushed aside.

'I'm hoping you'll agree to join me soon again for some further fieldwork,' he was told. 'You can bring it back with you then.'

Lemuel put it among his baggage with gratitude. He would study it further and the fruits of it would add substantially to the material on Clonmacnoise. He felt certain it would put the question of his father's consent beyond all shadow of doubt.

At breakfast next morning Uncle Crispin consulted his diary for some reason and began to chuckle to himself. He closed it and returned it to his pocket.

'Today is a most important day and I do believe the three of us had forgotten all about it. Can you remember, Lemuel?'

'Not the foggiest,' Lemuel admitted, when he had reflected on it.

'Richard?'

'I do. It is the 22nd of June and the Diamond Jubilee of our Gracious Sovereign, Queen Victoria.'

'Good for you,' Uncle Crispin said.

'I was so reminded because a few days ago I had a request from a group of my neighbours to instruct the tenantry here to light bonfires tonight in her honour.'

'Indeed,' Uncle Crispin asked. 'And have you done so?'

'I have not. They would have refused. And a refusal *en masse* is to be avoided. It undermines one's authority.'

'Quite.'

'The entertaining part is that Her Majesty has missed out by a squeak. Tomorrow night Meath will be ablaze with bonfires. It's St John's Eve.'

He drove them to Drogheda and the trip went off without mishap. On the train Uncle Crispin debated once again whether to invest in a motorcar now or to hold off yet a while longer. When they arrived in Dublin he found himself facing a more immediate concern. The usual overcrowded cab ranks were deserted. They hung around with other passengers until it became plain that something was very much amiss.

'We'll start walking,' Uncle Crispin decided.

It was growing dark. Their handbaggage was cumbersome and they had to rest it from time to time.

'What the devil is going on?' Uncle Crispin wondered.

He brightened up suddenly at the sound of hooves. An outside car approached and drew in when he flagged it down.

'Are you for hire?' he asked.

'It depends on where you're going, sir,' the jarvey answered.

Uncle Crispin was displeased. 'Are you being uncivil?'

'Not a bit, sir. Some parts of the city isn't safe at present. There's protests against the Queen's Jubilee and ferocious baton charges. I can't afford to have the car smashed up and me horse maybe killed on me.'

Uncle Crispin was mollified. 'We wish to get to Fitzwilliam Place.'

'I'd have to avoid the city centre, sir.'

'Do so. We'll pay for whatever extra travel is necessary.'

They handed up their baggage and climbed aboard. Crossing the river was the principle difficulty. Sackville Street and Capel Street bridges were impassable. They were forced to divert upstream to find one that was clear. Wild cheering drifted faintly to them, and the sound of crashing glass.

'That's the shop windows getting a bit of a doing up,' the jarvey explained. 'It started when a procession of the demonstrators appeared pushing a handcart with a coffin on it with *The British Empire* painted on it. The first baton charge came when they dumped it in the river. Then an old woman was killed by the police up around Rutland Square and the crowd ran amok. That's them breaking the windows.'

'I hope they stay away from 39 Fitzwilliam Place,' Uncle Crispin remarked when they came to a halt outside the halldoor.

'I don't think they'd harm a respectable neighbourhood like this,' the jarvey said. 'One of the leaders is Miss Gonne, a well-born and highly educated young lady. The other is Mr Yeats, the poet. I wouldn't imagine a poet like Mr Yeats would act the blackguard.'

'I believe you're right,' Uncle Crispin agreed solemnly. 'I can't see Mr Yeats acting the blackguard at all.'

He paid the fare and added his tip. It was an exceptionally generous one.

In the morning over breakfast he remarked that he would be staying on in Fitzwilliam Place for a few days, and invited Lemuel to keep him company.

'You could carry on with your work on your Boyne Valley project,' he suggested. 'In the evening we might get to a meal and a theatre.'

Lemuel decided he would. There were sources he could consult that would be difficult to get to from Avonmore.

In the mornings he did his research and in the afternoons he put shape on his proposals. It was becoming a substantial piece of work which deepened its hold on him as it progressed. Even Uncle Crispin displayed a mild interest. The valley had been a vast pagan burial ground before history began. Christianity took its first step towards its ultimate conquest with a fire that was kindled on the Hill of Slane on an Easter Saturday night in the early years of the fifth century. It was the fire St Patrick had himself kindled.

'If there are fairies and leprechauns still to be found in parts of Ireland,' he declared, 'and idols with malevolent powers and crones who can sour the milk in the churns of their neighbours and wizards masquerading as fowls of the air when up to no good and blacksmiths who's trade includes the casting of spells, then its around Tara and Slane I'd start looking for them.'

'Do you believe in such things?' Lemuel asked.

'I try to. It makes life more interesting,' Uncle Crispin said. He considered the matter further.

'There was a lot of belief in that kind of thing around our estate in Galway when I was growing up. I used to sit about the fires in the cottages with neighbours' children and listen to the stories that were told there nightly, and I'd be terrified to venture home alone.'

'I've wondered often why you sold the estate.'

'For the same reason that your father sold his. We both knew that feudalism in Ireland was coming to an end. We got out just before the Land League was formed and before it became the sport of the tenant to hide in a ditch and shoot his landlord as he rode past.'

'Have you ever regretted selling it?'

'No. Your father may have. He doesn't say. But not me. I came into it on my father's death and I hated it. I'd never cared for the idea of running an estate in the first place. All that cattle breeding and buying and selling. I had no interest in planting things and watching them grow. I wanted things that were capable on their own volition of moving about from place to place. To interest me in estate management they'd have to develop plants and trees and cabbages that have locomotive powers of their own. Cabbage plants that can move and have their performance enhanced by reducing their wind resistance, or can be equipped with a better carburetter. That's where my interest begins to quicken. Until that day comes I'll leave farming to others.'

He stopped to reflect on what he had said and beamed his satisfaction.

'I think I owe myself a drink,' he decided, 'be a dutiful nephew and fetch the whiskey bottle.'

The time passed pleasantly: research in the mornings, desk work in the afternoons, meals or theatre or music hall in the evenings. Uncle Crispin was a generous host and an entertaining companion. Then, on the fifth evening it was time to pack and make ready: Uncle Crispin to visit London once again, he to return to Avonmore. The next day they journeyed together by train as far as Kingstown Station where Uncle Crispin bid farewell and left to board the boat for Holyhead. Lemuel continued on to Greystones.

He was glad to be alone. The coastline and its beaches, though now, as it happened, deserted, reminded him of journeys as a child with his mother, when the smoke curled up from countless picnic fires and the sea was full of bobbing heads. He had the carriage to himself and his memory of her filled it for a brief while with her presence. She had told him little stories on those journeys, she had recited poems to him. He remembered it with tender affection and focused closely on his memories in an effort to make her presence abide. But it weakened in spite of him and over the seconds melted imperceptibly away. He thought of Margot instead. He would be in Athlone in three days time, all going well. He had written already to tell her so. She would have told Aunt Amy of his coming to Athlone to extend his last year's survey of the monastic era. Telling Aunt Amy in advance would help to pave the way.

At Greystones he was able to treat himself to high tea in the hotel with extra money which Uncle Crispin had pressed on him, and to engage transport for the remainder of the journey. In Edmunds-court he passed the ponderous bulk of Margot's school, now empty and silent. On the outskirts of the town the small tearooms which had given them sanctuary reminded him of precious meetings. He began to feel three days too long a wait.

At Avonmore the young servant who welcomed him at the door asked him if he would require food to be prepared and went off again when he told her he had already eaten. There was no sign of Stella. He left his hat and coat on their customary hanger in the hall and mounted the stairs to his bedroom. As he did so the air of quietness which seemed to have settled over the house puzzled him. Except for occasional, remote sounds from the kitchen area, silence reigned. As soon as he had finished unpacking he went to see if his father was in his study and, in anticipation of finding him there, took his listed proposals on the monastic project with him. There was no response to his knock. After some moments of indecision he turned the door handle and looked in. There was no one there. He entered and decided to leave his proposal notes on the desk. He returned again to his bedroom. The day's journeying had tired him. He stretched out on the bed. After a while he dozed off.

He awoke when someone shook his shoulder. It was Stella.

'I saw your hat and coat hanging in the hall,' she said. 'Welcome back.'

'Where has everybody got to?'

'It's been very warm. We all went down to the Pooka's Pool for a swim. Godwin stayed on there. He's teaching little Jonathan.'

'And Father?'

'Father's away. You were longer gone than we expected.'

'I stayed on with Uncle Crispin for the extra few days.'

'How is he?'

'Off to another exhibition. He'll turn into a motorcar. Is Father in town?'

'No. He's gone off to London—'

'London?'

'Mr Martyn wrote to him. It's some music festival, I think. They both went off together. They may spend a week on the continent as well.'

The news took a while to sink in.

'Did he leave an address?'

'Did you ever know Daddy to leave an address? But he's gone four days now so I expect we'll have a letter soon.'

He watched out anxiously for the post. After three days a letter arrived from their father which had an English address. But it also carried the news that he and Mr Martyn were leaving there for a visit to the continent for more music and religious ceremonies. There was no information as to its duration or their precise destination. Very likely it had not yet been decided. Stella was instructed to use the money in his desk to meet the domestic requirements temporarily. She knew where the key was kept. Meanwhile he would arrange for the housekeeper to receive the weekly allowance through the bank. He was sorry to have missed Lemuel's return and hoped he had enjoyed County Meath.

No further letter came by the time he was due to go to Athlone. To miss doing so and to disappoint Margot was unthinkable. He told Stella he was going to take the money from the cash in the study.

'I reckon I need ten pounds,' he said.

The suggestion frightened her. 'You can't,' she pleaded. 'You haven't his permission. What happens if he comes back while you're still away?'

'I'll leave a note in the drawer explaining why I've borrowed it.'

'But you're not borrowing it, Lemuel. You can't pay it back.'

'Yes I can,' he insisted. 'I can sell Uncle Crispin's watch.'

The idea had come to him too late to be acted on before he left for Athlone, but it could be arranged on his return.

He wrote the letter and left it in the desk. He explained how important the trip had become for him and pointed to his detailed proposals which he left in the drawer also, as proof of it. He also explained how he intended to replace the money. His father was likely to disapprove of the means but he had made up his mind. After all, Uncle Crispin had pointed precisely to such an advantage in having an item like the watch with its fall-back value if one hit on hard times. As a student, for instance. Besides, the watch was his. He showed Stella what he had written in the letter to his father. She felt more easy about it. He set off for Athlone with the ten pounds in his pocket and a peaceful mind.

Chapter 16

He called formally to Aunt Amy's house on the evening after his arrival in Athlone to let his presence in the town be known. He named the hotel he was staying in and explained that he was extending the scope of his studies of last year. He expressed the hope that he would be permitted to visit them during his stay. Aunt Amy said she insisted that he must certainly do so. He would be more than welcome. His sister Stella had invited Margot once again to be her guest at Avonmore later in the season and this was most kind. Margot, she well knew, enjoyed companions nearer her own age with the activities and interests appropriate to it, so she was delighted for Margot's sake. He must come to lunch the following day.

'Will your friends be joining you later?' she inquired. He told her he was sorry to say that they would not.

'What a pity,' Aunt Amy said. 'Especially Eddie O'Grady. He sings so nicely and can play the harmonica with such artistry.'

In return he had Aunt Amy and Margot to lunch in the hotel. He also took them to Clonmanoise to explore the antiquities and its surroundings, a couple of times with Margot and Aunt Amy together, when they picnicked by the river, and a number of times with Margot on her own. On one occasion the three of them, at his suggestion, went to a performance of a circus which was spending a week near the town. Aunt Amy was very excited but unsure that she wished to look at animals going through a repertoire of tricks because she had read that teaching these tricks sometimes involved an element of cruelty. On the other hand, as a child she had adored the circus clowns and felt she would enjoy their activities as much as ever.

In the course of the performance a bizarre piece of drama was played out which mesmerized Aunt Amy and Margot and left Lemuel wondering if some cunning piece of collusion behind the scenes had made it possible.

It involved a challenge from the lion tamer to anyone from the audience to spend a couple of minutes alone with the lion in his cage. The reward for an act of such foolhardy heroism would be a five-pound note. To their astonishment, amid a wild medley of appeals of dissuasion from the audience, the challenge was accepted.

Lemuel remembered it and puzzled over it at odd moments throughout his life. In old age he repeated it once again to Stella. She had no interest in these recollections of his any longer and habitually dismissed them.

'You have told me all this before,' she remarked. 'And the more I hear it, the more I suspect it to be a figment of the imagination.'

'It may have been a piece of blatant trickery,' he conceded, 'it possibly was. But it took place. After more than fifty years I can still recall it distinctly.'

'You probably dreamed it, Lemuel. You tend to invent things – quite unwittingly, of course, I don't accuse you of falsehood – but your imagination is at fault. It is disordered.'

Because the recollection, however slightly, involved Margot Penrose, Stella resented it. For some reason, he believed, she had come to begrudge them their brief and youthful encounter with happiness.

'I'll prove it to you,' he declared.

It meant fetching his walking stick and donning hat and coat. It involved a long walk down the puddle-strewn driveway where a chilling wind threatened his sense of balance and triggered off his now almost habitual terror of falling. In spite of it he pushed on until he reached the copse and picked his footsteps among the perils of its muddy and uneven floor. Among the accumulated envelopes and yellowing paper in the bole of the tree he eventually found the newspaper clipping he had come to retrieve. He faced the rigours of the return journey with triumphant heart and thrust the clipping under her nose.

'Read that,' he demanded.

'Have I read it before?'

'No. Read it,' he insisted.

She held the discoloured piece of paper at a distance and began to go through its fading print with distaste.

The Midland Democrat
Daring Feat by Mr John J. Joyce

On Thursday night, during the visit of Buffalo Bill's Circus to
Ballymore, a most wonderful feat was performed by a local
gentleman, Mr John J. Joyce, Ballymore, in bearding a lion in his
cage. Mr Joyce, who possesses extraordinary nerve and exceptional willpower, entered the cage after making a gracious bow to
the spectators. The latter raised cries of: 'Joyce, don't enter,' but
Mr Joyce was determined and without much ado performed the
feat with the greatest of coolness. To the utter amazement of the
spectators, Mr Joyce closed the gate after him and held the lion,
whose eyes flared, at bay for a considerable time. The lion
remained unmoving, notwithstanding that the same animal had
done away with two keepers previously, a fact which Buff Bill
conveyed to Mr Joyce before he performed the feat. The latter,
however, entered at the peril of his life, on a wager of £5 with the
proprietor. He was vociferously applauded on his re-appearance
before the public. The feat will form an interesting chapter in the
history of Ballymore and a standing monument to the in-
domitable courage of Mr John J. Joyce.

'Well—?' he questioned when she had returned the clipping to him.

'It's very clear to me,' she answered, determined to concede
nothing. 'You read this and were so struck with it that you cut it out.
When you had thought it over long enough and kept it by you you
began to believe you had actually been present. Illusions of that
kind are not uncommon.'

She was crouched in her wheelchair, her back curved rheumatic-
ally, her knitting resting on the side table, her hands tremulous as
they always were when unoccupied. He thought again of leaving the
cover off the manhole on the garden path and offering to wheel her
out for air. But she had only to set her face outside the door to reject
any notion of an outing on so inclement an evening.

As he replaced the clipping in his pocket his thoughts unbidden
winged back through the years to that circus of long ago: the busy
field, the bright caravans, the sweet, heavy odour of trampled grass.
He remembered again the great Marquee, the flaring lamps and the
heat; the sweat smell of packed human bodies, the even more
unpleasant ones of the circus animals. He remembered a conversation that had passed between himself and the man in the seat
next to his when he had expressed to him his puzzled admiration of

what had occurred. The man acknowledged his remarks with a non-committal nod.

Then he said, 'Of course you can guess the truth of the matter?'

'Yes,' Lemuel admitted, knowing from the man's tone that his suspicions were right. 'I think I can.'

'I've known John Joe Joyce a long time,' the man confirmed. 'He's blind drunk.'

All so long ago.

A few days after the circus he had returned to Avonmore to find that his father was still absent on his unpredictable wanderings. But Stella was there with Godwin and young Jonathan and she had taken advantage of their father's absence to have Johnny and Eddie O'Grady come earlier than originally planned. Stella was so young then, so full of love and generosity and of life. And Margot was to begin her visit in a few days. Fortune seemed in its friendliest mood and to be firmly on their side.

On the day before Margot was due they decided to inspect a tiny shooting lodge which they used occasionally for overnight stops when they wanted to penetrate further than usual into the mountains. Its two small rooms were equipped with rough bunk beds and heavy chests in which enough blankets to meet their average overnight needs were stored. Stella stayed behind and waved to them half an hour later when she spotted them still climbing on the lower slopes.

The four-hour journey was completed by nightfall. They gathered wood that lay about the woodland path and built up a fire in the large fireplace to cook supper. Then they piled it up high to dry out the must-smelling blankets.

Johnny O'Grady had two half pint bottles of Power's whiskey which he opened when the rough beds had been made-up and they were seated about the fire. Godwin was despatched to draw fresh water from the spring well which was always clear and icy cold.

When Godwin returned and they had diluted their whiskies, Johnny pronounced with all his authority as an officer and a connoisseur, 'Whiskey should be taken neat. But if one must dilute it then pure, cold spring water only should be used. Things like soda water or ginger beer and the rest are barbaric.'

'It tastes very good,' Lemuel agreed, 'but are two bottles not a bit spendthrift?'

'He won them at a game of cards in the officers' mess,' Eddie declared.

'Poker,' Johnny said. 'It's safer than the rival attraction. You don't get a dose of the clap from the Queen of Hearts.'

'I've often wondered about that,' Lemuel said. 'It's such a huge military encampment. Are there lots of ,' he hesitated, searching for a comfortable euphemism, 'lots of, well, camp followers?'

'You mean whores, don't you?' Johnny said coolly, lighting his pipe with studied care. 'Of course there are. On a weekend in any of the nearby towns, you're falling over them.'

'If you're not falling on top of them,' Eddie offered.

'You'd want to be mad,' Johnny said, 'and yet there are those who do. The worst enemy of the soldiers of the Queen is the clap. Especially rank and file. The officers can afford to patronize the better class kips in Dublin.'

'And the better class pawn shops, I've heard you say,' Lemuel added, seizing an opportunity.

'Every so often an officer and a gentleman who is also into gambling finds them indispensible. But why introduce that?'

'I'll speak to you later,' Lemuel said.

They sat a long time about the fire, talking or listening while Eddie played the mouth organ and they contentedly polished off the whiskey. As they rose for bed Lemuel beckoned to Johnny.

'Could I have a quick word with you?' he asked. They stepped outside.

'I have a problem,' Lemuel confessed. 'I'd like your advice.'

He told him about the money he had borrowed from his father's desk in his absence and the circumstances which had prompted him to do so. He also spoke of his decision to pawn or sell his watch in order to pay it back.

'I brought it with me,' he said, taking the watch from his pocket.

'I know it well,' Johnny said, examining it. 'I've seen you wearing it from time to time.'

'Would I raise ten pounds on it?' Lemuel asked. He waited anxiously. Johnny handed it back.

'More, I should think,' he advised. 'Certainly more than ten if you decide to sell it instead of pawning it.'

'I'm asking you in the hope that you may be able to recommend some reputable and acceptable dealer.'

'No problem,' Johnny answered. 'Take the watch and yourself to Mangan & Bassington, Valuers and Antique Advisers, 6 Cecilia Street, behind the Empire Theatre in Dame Street. Ask for Mister Gustav Samstag, the proprietor, and give him my name.'

'He's discreet?'

'A man of unexcelled discretion,' Johnny assured him. 'Trusted without reserve by every hard pressed officer on the Curragh.'

Lemuel sighed with relief.

'You've lifted a great weight off my mind,' he said gratefully.

They awoke next morning to a day of heavy mist and incessant rain which kept them in the lodge awaiting a clearance for most of the morning. In the afternoon they decided it was useless and began their descent. Johnny O'Grady led the way. He took regular compass readings as they went. The groundsheets which they had wrapped about themselves like cloaks hampered their movements and gave little protection, the mountain terrain under the pressure of their feet squirted water back up at them like a great sponge. Rain lodged about their eyes and had to be constantly wiped away. When they reached the house Lemuel's calf muscles had grown stiff from effort and the sweat on his back cold. The smell of canvas and rubber rising from his cape and haversack clung about his chilled body. Margot had already arrived. She was keeping vigil at the window with Stella.

'You poor famished things,' she cried out when Stella opened the door to them. 'You're destroyed.'

They were despatched without delay to their rooms to dry and change, and returned to a blazing fire and the aroma of sizzling bacon. When they had fed voraciously, Stella began to clear up. Margot went over to help but she declined it.

'I had the fire lit in the breakfast room,' she said. 'Why don't you and Lem sit in there for a while and talk. You haven't had the opportunity for ages.'

In the breakfast room firelight played on the walls and rain still pattered incessantly on the window. Lemuel lit the lamp and drew the curtains. They embraced.

'Stella's awfully good,' Margot said.

'A brick,' he agreed.

They sat down.

'From the moment I came until you all returned,' Margot said, 'she was at the window.'

'Stella worries.'

'Me too. I could see the four of you blundering over a cliff.'

'Not with Johnny O'Grady up front,' he assured her.

'Lem, I've something to tell you. I told Stella while we were watching out for you. Mother and Father are going ahead with their divorce.'

'Does it upset you?'

189

'No. I'll be going permanently to Aunt Amy, which will be a million times better. But I'm glad I don't have to go back to school.'

He wondered what that could have to do with it.

'The gossip. The whispering,' she explained. 'A couple of years ago it happened to the parents of one of the girls there and it was dreadful. The school barred all newspapers from us. But of course we got them and all the lurid details. The parents have to get spies to give evidence about each other indulging in all sorts of quite unsavoury behaviour. They confess to utterly unspeakable things. The parents of the other girls complained and threatened to remove their own children if the girl was allowed to stay on. The school didn't want her either so they kept after the girl until she begged her people to remove her. She was a lovely girl. What she was made to go through was shameful.'

'Never mind. You'll be much happier to be settled properly with Aunt Amy.'

'I know,' she agreed. 'Aunt Amy's will be a real home. I'll be able to have my friends visiting me. I'll have a Christmas tree at Christmas like everybody else. Aunt Amy is a Christmas tree person.'

She was excited and happy. Her happiness moved him. She had known too much loneliness.

'Aunt Amy is great,' he encouraged. 'I thoroughly approve of Aunt Amy.'

They fell easily into the now well-established routines. They climbed the surrounding hills, they swam in the Pooka's Pool, they played tennis, both at Avonmore and at neighbours' houses. They made cycling expeditions into Edmundscourt to have tea and cakes in the little teashop and to discover what popular magazines, if any, might have survived the hazards of the journey from Dublin to the shelves of the local newsagent's shop. As they did so Lemuel noted with approval a change that was beginning in Margot. She was shedding a little of her underlying timidity and uncertainty and acquiring, however marginally, some of the confident and adventurous ways of the rest. She was a degree more assertive, a shade bolder. He put it down to the prospect of the divorce bringing years of uncertainty and frequent hurt and loneliness to an end. It had to do with her belief that, in becoming part of Aunt Amy's household on a permanent footing, she would be stepping at last into affection and approval in a stable world.

He fostered the change wherever he could. He pushed her into expressing her own opinions and in the discussions that arose among themselves. He praised her skill on the tennis court. During their mountain trips he helped her to prove to herself that she was just as capable as any of them of surmounting whatever difficult situations presented themselves. At the pool he had her practising their ritual of the dive from the central rock and swimming underwater for longer and longer distances. She hung from the supple, overhanging branch like the rest and allowed herself to be pushed back and forwards like a pendulum until she was swinging far enough out over the water to release her hold and drop with a gigantic splash and a sound which to her seemed like thunder. Eddie O'Grady told her if she completed their routine by sitting on the underwater ledge she would be qualified to be admitted as a full member of The Fellowship Of The Pooka Club, but she still hesitated.

'I'm too much of a coward,' she said. 'Haven't I told you time and again.'

Johnny O'Grady suggested she should be admitted just the same. It was unanimously agreed. That night they drank to the health of their new member and Stella produced from somewhere or other a cake with five candles representing themselves to which they added a sixth to mark her election and inclusion.

The days slipped by with stealth and speed, so unnoticed that when there were only four more of them left he still had made no move to dispose of the watch. It involved the long journey into the city and he kept putting it off. She spoke to him about it on a number of occasions.

'If you replace the money before your father returns you can tear up the note you left in his desk and you don't have to tell him about getting rid of the watch,' she urged. 'The fact that he's still away is a golden opportunity.'

'There are only four days left,' he pointed out. 'I don't want to waste one of them.'

'But it will solve so much, Lem. It's well worth while.' He knew she was talking good sense and gave in. He could start very early in the morning to cycle to Greystones and take his bicycle with him on the train. By using it to get around town he could have his business done much more quickly and be back with her by teatime.

He had sandwiches and a flask of tea prepared for himself and was up at dawn. Even at that early hour it was warm. He could feel the heat increasing as he cycled to the station. In the train he travelled with his collar loosened and the window open. Much of the journey ran parallel with the coast, along which family parties had already settled with their picnic parcels and shopping bags. The sea spread its glittering mirror the length of the journey and stretched in calm and cool invitation to the limits of the horizon.

The streets of the city stifled. Heat struck at him from the walls of the houses and rose from cobbles strewn with the dust of horse dung and scattered debris. In the web of lanes behind the Empire Theatre he dismounted in his search for 6 Cecilia Street, locating it at last when he spotted the three brass balls which hung above its entrance. The door beneath them was locked. He wondered if there might be a second entrance but could find none. He examined the large plate-glass window and discovered among its conglomeration of bracelets, rings, binoculars, silver and gold cigarette cases, watches and jewellery of every kind, a black-bordered paste board which conveyed the necessary information:

> Mangan and Bassington
> Valuers and Antique Experts
>
> As a mark of respect to the late
> Annalisa Samstag, mother of our
> Proprietor and Managing Director,
> Gustav Samstag, these premises will
> remain closed until Thursday next, when
> they will reopen again at two o'clock p.m.

There was nothing to be done except return home. He had his flask of tea and his sandwiches on a bench in the railway station where it was a little cooler than the streets. The first available train, he discovered, went only as far as Bray but he took it and cycled the extra distance by narrow roads where the air hung without motion and the evening heat, undisturbed, was more stifling than ever.

She was in the garden, her arms full of flowers that Stella had asked her to gather for the house. When she turned and saw him she gave a little cry of pleasure and came forward to greet him.

'How lovely,' she said, 'you're back so much earlier than I thought. I'll organize some tea.'

'What I want before anything else is a swim,' he confessed. 'Will you come?'

'I'd love to. Let me leave these flowers inside and fetch my togs.'

He went in with her. They set off together with towels and togs a few minutes later. While he undressed on the bank by the water's edge she retreated to her usual spot among the trees. He was already splashing about when she re-emerged. She joined him in the pool and, after crossing it from side to side several times, swam to the central rock and climbed on it to rest. She waved to him.

'Isn't it just heavenly,' she shouted, out of breath after her exertion.

Later they dried off and sat together on the bank to let the sun complete the job. Behind them the gnarled beech trees encircled the clearing that stretched from the earthen pathway to the river. In front a little rainbow had formed where sunlight struck at an angle through the web of spume that hung above the miniature waterfall. The sound of cascading water was muted and soothing. Around and about them the world was sleeping.

'You haven't told me what the verdict was on the watch?'

'None at all,' he answered. 'It's still reposing in my pocket over there.' He pointed to the trousers lying discarded on the grass.

'Whatever happened?'

He explained that the premises had been closed and the reason why.

'Annalisa Samstag,' he concluded wryly, 'aged parent of Gustav, chose to intervene.'

'Never mind,' she sympathized. 'You know where it is now and can call in again.' Then she said, sadly, 'I'll be leaving on Friday, won't I. So don't go in on Thursday. It's our last day.'

'No,' he promised.

'That's how time flies.'

'Have you enjoyed your stay?'

'Need you ask? Still, I don't mind leaving quite as much as I did last time. I know I'm going to be with Aunt Amy for keeps. I'll have no school any more and she's fond of you and easygoing, so we'll be able to meet much more frequently. And that will be very nice indeed, because I love you, Lemuel Cox, very, very much.'

She put her cheek against his. It was soft and cool and held the subtle freshness of the river. After a moment she added, 'And now, there's something else I must attend to. I've been bracing myself for it for days past.' She stood up and began to descend the slope.

'Where are you off to?' he called.

'To sit on that damned ledge,' she answered. 'If I'm to be a member of the Pooka Club I want to be a proper one – not just admitted by grace of Johnny O'Grady's goodness of heart.' He rose to follow but she waved him back.

'Please, Lem,' she asked. 'Let me go on my own. I'm not a bit nervous any longer.'

He shrugged and sat down. Some moments later, when he heard the splash of her dive, he became uneasy and rose again. He walked down slowly to the bank's edge, confident now that if by some extraordinary chance she got into trouble he could be beside her in a few moments to fish her out. She was several yards upstream, swimming purposefully but close to the bank, unaware that he was watching. He saw her circling in the area about the ledge, carefully positioning herself as the rest of them always did. When she was fully satisfied she went under water and out of sight so quietly that the water above the ledge resumed its smooth and unbroken surface almost immediately. Nevertheless he quickened his pace along the bank. As he did so, the water above where she had submerged suddenly became broken and violently agitated. He panicked and raced along the bank until he reached the spot. He could see her struggling frantically just below the surface. He dived to reach her. She was trying to break away from the ledge and had one foot freed. The other, trapped in the fissure she had inserted it in to keep her steady while she seated herself on the ledge, was holding her firmly. He grasped her by the shoulders and pulled upwards but failed to get her head above the surface. He gave up and dived down to try to release her trapped foot but it had twisted and become more firmly wedged than before. In her struggle she had torn a deep gash along the side which was bleeding heavily. He tried again to raise her head clear of the water but had to surface for some seconds to breathe himself. He submerged again and tried desperately to manoeuvre her foot but without success. By now she had ceased to struggle and was quite still, her body sprawling outwards at an angle from the ledge, the water supporting her but still immersing her, the foot still firmly trapped. He left the water and, pausing only to pull on his shoes, raced for help.

It took some hours to organize. Eddie O'Grady was sent off on his bicycle to go directly to Edmundscourt to alert ambulance and police. Godwin was despatched to search among the houses in the neighbourhood to see if one of them contained a telephone, though it was thought unlikely. Stella remained on watch in case help of some kind presented itself unexpectedly. Johnny got togs and towel and went with Lemuel back to the pool. They took with them an iron bar and a small sledge hammer which Johnny thought might serve to widen the fissure which was holding the body.

He changed and went in to investigate as soon as they arrived. They spelled one another as they worked individually under water. It took them over an hour to widen the hole sufficiently to release its hold. They dragged Margot's dead body from the water and laid it on the bank. The clothes Lemuel had taken off earlier, before they had gone for their swim together, were still on the bank some distance away. He fetched his jacket from the bundle and used it to cover her face.

Two long hours passed before the ambulance came. They heard the creaking and jolting of wheels and the jangling of harness as it struggled with the uneven surface and the narrow dimensions of the woodland path. The police van, with its two outsized horses, followed close behind it, causing congestion and confusion as they tried to accommodate themselves to the confined space and the deepening dusk. Lemuel and Johnny gave their brief statements. The police signalled their consent to the ambulance crew. Margot's body, concealed now in an uncouth covering of tarpaulin, was lifted into the ambulance. They got back down the pathway with renewed difficulty and stopped at the house for consultation. Lemuel decided he would accompany Margot to Edmundscourt and spend the night in the hotel. He was known there. They would hold the account for his father's attention.

'How do you propose to get there?' Johnny asked.

'My bicycle, I suppose.'

'I'll keep you company,' Johnny offered.

'I'd be most grateful,' Lemuel said. 'Can we start right away?'

'Aren't you going to put some clothes on?' Johnny suggested gently.

Lemuel, confused, looked down at himself. He was wearing only his swimming togs and his shoes. The rest of his clothes were still lying on the river bank.

'I'll go upstairs and change,' he said.

When over twenty minutes had elapsed and he had still not returned Johnny went upstairs to check. He found him sitting helplessly on the bed in trousers and singlet only.

'Lem,' he asked quietly, 'what's the matter?'

'I can't seem to get my shirt on,' he said.

It was lying on the bed beside him. Johnny picked it up and managed to manoeuvre it gently over his head. He did up the buttons and knotted the tie for him. He put on his shoes and tied up the laces.

'I've managed to arrange that we will travel in the police van,' he told Lemuel. 'I thought it would be more fitting than using bicycles.'

'Of course.' Lemuel said.

When he had regained his control Johnny led him downstairs, watching over him carefully.

The police van followed behind the ambulance all the way into

Edmundscourt. The wheels of both rumbled and jolted in unison on the rough country road. Dusk deepened while they travelled. Candles flickered in their carriage lamps as night settled over them.

Johnny O'Grady accompanied him to Aunt Amy's and the interment in Athlone and shared the hotel room with him. He was present to minister to him as best he could when his control again deserted him. It happened in a devastating way twice: on each occasion in an onslaught of uncontrollable shuddering which lasted for several minutes and was profoundly frightening to witness. But for the most part he remained withdrawn, speaking very little but grateful, Johnny knew, to have his company. They parted reluctantly at Mullingar station on their way back because Johnny had commitments at the Curragh which he was unable to postpone for longer.

Lemuel sat behind McGinty on the outside car and remained silent the whole way home. McGinty, with rare sensibility, left him be. The side roads as they passed them, the gateways, the fields with their stacked and marshalled sheaves, had changed their meaning. He recognized but no longer understood them. They were the left-behind furniture of a world that had melted away. When they turned in through the always open gateway of Avonmore and swayed the last few hundred yards of the carriageway, it too had lost its meaning. It had withdrawn from him. It existed only at a distance. He broke his silence to tell McGinty to send his account to his father, as was his usual habit. McGinty touched his hat in acknowledgement.

A young servant came to the door to admit him.

'If you please, sir,' she said as she did so, 'Miss Stella instructed me to tell you that your father is at home. She is in the drawing-room and would like to see you immediately.'

He found her standing by the window.

'I had been watching for you,' she told him. 'Father is in his study and wishes to speak to you.'

'When did he get back?'

'Just two days ago. He was appalled to hear what had happened and isn't in any way put out about the money. You would have had it without hesitation had he been here. He says on no account are you to get rid of your watch.'

Her mention of the watch startled him. It had slipped altogether from his mind.

'The watch,' he repeated. 'I'd forgotten it completely. I've no idea where I may have left it.'

He sat down, groping back in panic through the days that had passed.

'When did you last have it?'

He tried to remember. He had had it, of course, on his trip in to Mangan & Bassington, Valuers and Antique Dealers. He had had it when Margot asked him what had been the outcome of his trip. That was the same day as her death. Then he remembered.

'I had it on the day of the accident. I was carrying it in one of my pockets. It was among the clothes I left lying on the river bank. They should still be there.' He stood up. 'I'll go at once and look.'

The area where the ambulance and the police van had halted still bore the marks of their activity. Bushes were broken, the grass was trodden flat and marked with the crisscrossing imprints of their wheel tracks. His clothes, which he had left in a neatly arranged bundle, were scattered widely. He went through the pockets of his jacket without success. He searched around for his trousers and found them at last half concealed by a bush where a passing wheel had probably dragged them. He picked them up and found what was left of the watch in the first pocket he tried. The glass of the face had been splintered and cut his fingers, the hands had been wrenched off, the case crushed and bent. As he removed it bit by bit it became obvious that it was beyond repair. He folded the trousers and gathered up the rest of his clothes to take them home.

Going straight to his room to avoid Stella, he made a parcel of the watch pieces to leave for his father. He wrote a note to leave with it.

My dear father,

I had intended to return the money I borrowed without your permission by selling the watch that Uncle Crispin gave me as a birthday present many years ago. As a result of an accident these bits and pieces are all that are left of it, so I cannot now honour my promise to make good what is due. In the ordinary way I would make a point of seeing you to explain in person and express my shame and regret. But the tragedy that happened such a short time ago has left me unable to face up to doing so. My heart is weighed down with more grief than I think I will be able to go on bearing. It will be best to take myself away somewhere, not with any hope to escape the pain and loss, for that will follow wherever I go, but to hide away from the presence of much-loved people who remind me

of what has been lost and from places so associated with those
happy days that they are now well nigh intolerable.

 With, as ever, my deepest love and respect,
 Your son, Lemuel

He left a note for Stella also, telling her that she must not worry on his account. He intended to find employment of some kind. After that he packed spare clothes, awaited an opportunity to slip away unseen and cycled in to the Lansdowne Road house where his father retained a small staff and he would at least be able to eat. He searched for some days without success until one morning, while he was exploring along the quays, his luck changed suddenly for the better. He had stopped at one of the barrows outside a line of bookshops to examine the second-hand fare that it had to offer when a notice on display behind the glass in the window caught his eye. It read:

Help wanted
Inquire inside

He stood back to take in the general set-up. It was one of four bookshops standing side-by-side, smaller than the other three but, apart from its outside barrows where the books and magazines were very much the worse for wear, cleaner and tidier in its window display and, from what he could see from outside, more neat and orderly in the books on the shelves. Its exterior was finished in faded brown paint which was peeling here and there, and bore the name in gold letters above the plate glass of the window:

Norris Curtis: Bookseller

He stood for some minutes wishing to go in to enquire but shrinking from doing so. He tried to review what he might have to offer but had no notion what would be desired. He decided he had no hope of being successful and continued on his journey until the absolute need to find some kind of livelihood made him turn on his heel and go back again.

 A man in his early thirties climbed down from the short ladder which was used for reaching the higher shelves and said, in a friendly manner, 'Well. What can I do for you?'

 Lemuel felt embarrassed.

 'I wish to enquire about your Help Wanted notice,' he managed after a moment of blushing hesitation.

 'I guessed you might be back,' the man said, smiling. 'I was watching you through the window some time ago and reading your thoughts. You're interested in books generally?'

'I have been. I'm also urgently interested in earning a livelihood.'

'And I'm urgently interested in getting the right kind of help. What schooling?'

'I've finished at C.U.S. but I haven't yet made up my mind about university. In addition I've had some private tuition. I've Latin fairly well. Greek less so. And workable German.'

The man looked impressed. He went to the glass-panelled door that gave access to the office and held it open.

'Step in here and we'll talk,' he invited. 'We'll shove on a pot of tea while we're at it.'

He introduced himself as the proprietor, Norris B. Curtis. The job would not be permanent, but it would last some months. He would be required to serve in the shop while Norris Curtis addressed his whole attention to sorting and cataloguing his stock of books, and valuing the several rare volumes that he had been accumulating for over two years. If Lemuel wished he could have the use of a small, furnished room for sleeping and eating in return for a nominal rent. He was prepared to offer a month's trial. Lemuel opted for renting the room. The kettle boiled and they clinched the bargain over tea and biscuits. Norris Curtis was a talkative, companionable man.

He wrote to Stella to let her know he had found work and accommodation, but did not tell her where. For some weeks he stayed in or about the shop to prevent the risk of encounter. When he began to venture further afield he avoided the city centre and explored instead the meaner and unfashionable streets.

Chapter 17

Frank picked up the telephone on his desk and found Miss Downey at the other end. Her voice was anxious.

'Frank, I have that peculiar man with the low accent on the line again and I never know whether you want me to put him through to you or not. He's that Councillor Brady. Are you in?'

'Why not?'

'He has such a vulgar, low-class accent. I thought he might be making a nuisance of himself.'

'He's a public representative and by no means the worst of them. Please put him through.'

'Very well,' she agreed reluctantly.

Ballcock sounded mysterious.

'Hello, Frank?'

'Yes.'

'I've an important piece of information to pass on to you. It closely affects you. And a piece of news about myself as well which you may feel is of urgent interest to the *Bulletin*. It concerns this general election that's been suddenly sprung on us. Could we meet somewhere? I don't want to talk about it over the telephone.'

Frank decided it would be as well to get it over with.

'As it happens,' he said, 'I've to see Joe Dunne at half seven tonight. Will you be there around eight to half eight?'

'I'll be in the Co-op Society office,' Ballcock confirmed.

Frank found him there when the meeting with Joe Dunne had finished. He was bent over a ledger which lay on the desk in front of him, engrossed in adding up a long column of figures, his lips moving silently as he did so, the naked electric light bulb hanging directly above his head. He beckoned Frank to a chair and continued for some seconds until the tot was complete.

'Thank you for calling,' he said as he left down his pen. 'I want to give you the good news about myself and the general election. I've been selected as a candidate. Joe Dunne knows, of course. Did he mention it to you?'

'Not a word.'

'I want to thank you, Frank. I owe it to those articles you published in the *Bulletin*. The party was very impressed by the propaganda value of them.' He rubbed his hands smartly together. 'Do you find it a bit cold in here? Would you rather move over to the pub?'

'It feels quite all right,' Frank said.

'You're sure? I turned off the central heating. I always turn off the central heating. Do you know what I'm going to tell you. That bloody central heating has people destroyed. Especially the Yanks. Every one of them looks dried-up and emancipated.'

'Would you prefer the pub yourself?'

'To tell the truth, I wouldn't say no to a drop of something.'

They moved across to Ryan's. For all his absurdities, Frank thought, there was a worthy side to Ballcock. He worked hard. He performed a multitude of small but important services for the lowly. He understood their needs.

'The other matter concerns yourself and Simon Morrissey,' Ballcock said when their drinks had come. 'That series in the *Review* – 'On The Side Of The Angels' – is coming in for very close scrutiny indeed from a dangerous quarter, the executive of the Sept of St Malachy. They've been building up a file on the *Review* this long time as an anti-National and anti-Catholic propaganda organ, and they're looking for an opportunity to pounce. O'Halloran in the *Review* office is feeding information all the time to Sylvester Kennedy.'

'Sylvester Kennedy?'

'The Chief Ullamh of the Sept, they call him.'

'How did you come by all this?'

'Because the same O'Halloran is a bit of a thick and told me himself.' Ballcock answered. 'He's not trying to harm either yourself or Morrissey, but he hates Con Andrews and if he can harm him he won't worry about who else may suffer in the process.'

'I don't think I'd worry unduly about the views of the executive of the Sept,' Frank said, but with less confidence than he sought to convey. He remembered that Morrissey had felt Con Andrews was biting off more than they could chew when he decided to run the series.

'Don't underestimate the Sept,' Ballcock warned. 'I've seen them ruin careers or manipulate matters until some poor bugger gets the push from his job. And all in the name of Jesus Christ or Mother Ireland. Every one of them is a frenatic.'

There was not much that could be done. The articles had already appeared. The attempt at anonymity had been a failure. His own and Morrissey's identities had been known almost from the start. Ballcock went up to the counter to call his round. On his return he moved closer to Frank and adopted a confidential and slightly diffident tone.

'I've a small favour to ask—'

'Yes?'

'During the election campaign most of the others will have cars at their disposal and loudhailers for cruising around getting their message across to the electorate. I myself can get a loudhailer on hire but I've no way of getting a car. I was wondering if, in the last week before polling day, you'd let me have the use of yours for – say – just two afternoons and evenings?'

Frank hesitated.

'Can you drive a car?' he asked.

'No. But I can get a fully experienced man who can,' Ballcock assured him.

Frank was uncertain. It dawned on him that the tip-off about the *Review* had been a deliberate preliminary to the plea for the use of the car. It had been carefully planted. At the same time the request was modest enough. And Ballcock, he fully accepted, could never afford to hire a car out of his own resources. He gave it no further thought.

'Very well,' he conceded, 'you can have the use of it. Two afternoons and evenings, if you get someone competent to drive it.'

Some weeks later Miss Downey got what she described to Ernie Jackson as the greatest shock of her life. She was returning home in the evening from work when a loudhailer in an approaching car began to blare out its election message to the street. The voice, a little distorted by the level of amplification, puzzled her for a moment. Then she identified it beyond shadow of doubt. It was the voice of Councillor Peter Brady; its vulgarity, to Miss Downey's sensitive ears, magnified by several degrees. She could see neither Councillor Brady nor his driver through the windscreen but she recognized the number plate immediately. The car was Frank's. The driver, she assumed, deeply shocked, must also be Frank.

First thing next morning she confided in Ernie Jackson. She had begun to confide in him quite a lot of late. He listened always with sympathy and attention and in return entrusted her with little confidences of his own. Their relationship was developing steadily and pleasantly.

He felt exactly as she did about it. Frank was behaving imprudently.

'Not a word to P.J.,' he warned her, 'I'll speak to Simon and get him to talk sense into him.'

Before he talked to Frank, Morrissey consulted Penny.

'What's wrong with Frank driving his own car?' she questioned.

'He's using it in an election campaign and aligning himself too publicly with one political party. That's not good for business. P.J. is already making noises about the *Review* articles.'

'The prime target there will be you, my love, not Frank.'

'The prime target there,' he said, 'will be both of us.'

Frank in turn passed on Ballcock's tip-off to Morrissey, who manifested no surprise at all. He had expressed his reservations about 'On The Side Of The Angels' to Con Andrews when it had first been suggested. He had been sceptical from the start of the practicability of anonymity. The methods of the Sept of St Malachy and the thought processes of Priomh Ullamhs such as Sylvester Kennedy were knitted inextricably into daily living.

'Bugger Sylvester Kennedy for the present,' he decided, 'there's something more serious I've to talk to you about. You've been electioneering for that trick-o'-the-loop Ballcock Brady.'

'Certainly not,' Frank denied.

'But you've been seen driving him around his constituency, canvassing for him. That will mean big trouble with P.J. if he finds out.'

'I've done nothing of the sort,' Frank said. 'I lent Ballcock my car on a couple of occasions. He got someone else to drive.'

'Whether you drove it yourself or not doesn't greatly matter, from P.J.'s point of view. He'll say you're jeopardizing the firm's business.'

Frank was suddenly angry. He raised his voice.

'Then bugger P.J. as well.'

'My sentiments also,' Morrissey said. 'Bugger all the cowardly, craw-thumping time servers of bigotry and prudery and obscurantism that crawl like ants in and out of every layer of the society we're doomed to live in.'

'At some stage,' Frank said, no longer angry, 'there may be no alternative but to stand up to them.'

'That's what I fear,' Morrissey answered. He did so without relish.

Ballcock was elected. To celebrate the victory his followers lit a bonfire for him in the centre court of Napper Tandy Flats and were furnished with barrels of porter by the local publicans. There was a night of dancing and singing during which a line of washing went up in flames, two small children suffered minor burns and the caretaker's storehouse was reduced accidently to ashes.

Ballcock made a speech in which he congratulated the participants on their good sense in electing him. He scarified unnamed enemies who, in the course of the campaign, had tried to encompass his defeat by spreading lies and slanderous stories about him. These, he said, could all be entirely discounted and dismissed. They held no visage of truth. They were all – as the Latin tab had it – 'ad infinitum'. The applause echoed back thunderously from the towering walls of the flats, and the sparks from the bonfire sped skywards as the breeze lifted them.

Ballcock took his seat on the back benches in due course and continued to attend to the needs and difficulties of his constituents. Among them and on the hustings he spoke with eloquence and deep feeling. In the House he listened carefully to what was said and kept his mouth shut.

Chapter 18

In the evenings, when work in the shop had finished and he had prepared and dispatched his meal, Lemuel sat at times in his window on the top floor overlooking the river and the street and watched the seasons change. Under his gaze late summer turned to autumn with its soft twilight hours and its share of rich evening skies. Then the winter nights took over, and the paraffin stove became necessary to take the edge off the chilled air while the coals in the newly lit fire reddened and built up sufficient heat to take over.

The activity below offered some mild interest. Brewery barges on the river chugged up and down with their barrels of porter and stout. Important visitors on their way to the vice-regal lodge in the park passed by in their elegant coaches with uniformed escorts and a flurry of hooves. Troops, sometimes mounted, sometimes on foot, trotted out regularly from Richmond Barracks to attend to duties and ceremonies, and trotted back again in due course. Occasionally a new regiment would disembark at the North Wall and pass beneath the window with a great blaring of brass and pounding of drums and the rhythmic tramp of feet. Dublin Castle, only a block away, added its glittering influx for the occasional ball or banquet.

He got on well with Norris Curtis and in time was invited to Sunday lunch. They lived with their three children in the top floor flat of one of the tall Georgian houses near St Stephen's Green. It was a modest apartment, but comfortably furnished and adequate, they told him, to their needs.

'Martha would prefer a larger kitchen,' Norris explained 'and a large room for a study would be my own dearest wish. But the book trade, as I think you are beginning to find out, provides very modest returns.'

'We do well enough,' Martha said, contented. She was a pretty woman, not yet in her thirties. As she was about to retire into her kitchen she suggested they should have something to drink while they were waiting.

'A sherry perhaps? Everything will be ready in ten or fifteen minutes.'

Norris was thirty-two. He had taken over the bookshop a few years before on the death of his father.

'I've collected books since I first began to read,' he confessed. 'It started as a hobby. Now it's an addiction.'

'Books and rugby football,' Martha put in.

Lemuel looked across at the group photograph on the wall of young men togged out for the field, the back row standing, the front seated, the captain in the middle holding the oval ball in his lap.

'That's five or six years ago,' Norris, said, glancing over at it himself. 'The fellow in the front row, third from the left, is yours truly. I've dropped out since then and joined the ranks of the spectators.'

Martha smiled. They had been married for seven years and were still, Lemuel could see, very much in love. Their three children had been presented to him with obvious parental pride immediately upon his arrival. He became acutely aware of the happiness that was theirs and the years of companionship that stretched out before them. It would never be his. A tide of pain and loss gathered inside him as it still continued to do, time after time. To hide it behind general conversation he seized on rugby as a topic and remarked that the opening match of the 1898 Triple Crown season must be due to be played soon.

'Next month,' Norris said. 'Ireland meet England at Richmond. Why don't we go over together to see it?'

'Are tickets not difficult to come by?'

'I have my contacts,' Norris assured him, smiling.

He had expected the suggestion would be forgotten but Norris persisted and brought it up again. In the end they travelled over together and enjoyed it so much that they went to Belfast for the Scotland-Ireland match and to Limerick for the game against Wales. They saw Ireland beaten on each occasion but Lemuel did not mind. It established his friendship with Norris and helped to fill the loneliness in a way that made it easier to bear. It also shortened the winter. He watched from his window while the days lengthened and his thoughts were drawn back to summer evenings at Avonmore. They would never again be as they had been. Margot's death had quenched the sun of the world he had once known there. But he longed at times for another, earlier little world, which still existed there and which was peopled by his father, by Stella and Godwin, even little Jonathan. Above all he longed for reconciliation with his father. He knew he had only to put his feelings of guilt to one side and face the ordeal of a meeting. His father was compassionate and would readily forgive. On a number of occasions he had almost set his mind to it. But shame always intervened to persuade him otherwise. He confined his movements to the anonymity of the back streets and the wide spaces of the park which offered summer evening strolls, cricket and polo to look at, and occasional brass-band concerts in the bandstand area.

He said nothing to Norris about the background to his arrival in the city in quest of work, except to let it be understood that a family disagreement of one kind or another had been the cause. It remained so until the new rugby season was about to start with the Ireland-England match to be played at Lansdowne Road, and his point-blank refusal to go to it. Norris was puzzled at first, then deeply hurt.

'What have I done wrong?' he asked.

'Nothing at all,' Lemuel assured him. 'The explanation is simple. My family have a house beside the ground and on no account am I going to risk an accidental meeting.'

'I see,' Norris acknowledged. He hesitated, then decided to put the question which troubled him, 'May I ask what caused such a bitter falling out?'

'It wasn't really a falling out. It was something much more complicated and dreadful.'

He spoke about Margot's death and the events that had attended it.

'You may wish to tell something of this to Martha,' he said when he had finished. 'If you do I don't mind.'

After that the invitations to Sunday lunch became a regular affair. They indicated, he knew, that Martha had been told and was expressing her silent sympathy. It was a further extension of their friendship which he valued. Their flat became a welcoming haven. He could visit when he wished and come and go as he pleased. With Martha's active encouragement the rugby trips with Norris became a ritual. At the end of the 1899 season they were together at Cardiff on the March 18th to see Ireland beat Wales to win the Triple Crown. It was an unforgettable experience which became an unbreakable bond between them throughout the years that were to come. They celebrated it in fitting style on the boat home.

As he grew to know them the conversation and eccentricities of the regular patrons of the shop and its barrows became highly agreeable too. They were a mixture of scholars and men of letters, a sprinkling of elegant young women, booksmitten clerks and navvies, and even a few ardent schoolboys. Norris drew his attention to one young man of about his own age.

'He's James Starkey and he's been coming here almost every Saturday since he was a schoolboy of twelve with his few pence pocket money,' Norris told him. 'My father used to put the books away for him while he saved his pennies weekly until he had the price required. He grew very fond of the youngster and charged him half nothing.'

On Saturdays especially, necks were bent over the barrows in an unbroken line and fingers searched ceaselessly through the wares on display. Mondays generally were slack and gave time for filling the gaps left in the barrows after the brisk business of Saturday, and for restocking the side shelves. These were reserved for second-hand magazines which sold for a penny or twopence and were very popular, however ancient they might be.

On one such Monday morning at the beginning of September, while he was sorting a mixed bundle of magazines preparatory to putting them on display, a regular customer called looking for material on the prolonged negotiations between the Boers and the British Government on the tensions that had arisen in the Transvaal. He needed historic background for a report. While they searched together the customer spoke of his fears that the outcome would be war between the two sides. Lemuel doubted that a place as unsophisticated as the Transvaal Republic could take on the British Empire, but the customer insisted there were reasons to believe they could and would. There was evidence that the Boers had been arming heavily since the Jameson raid three years before and even as far back as the huge gold discovery near Johannesburg of over a decade ago. Gold, he declared, was a powerful recipe for trouble. They talked about it at length until it became clear that the search would yield nothing and the customer left to try elsewhere.

Lemuel returned to the magazines. Those he had already sorted he put out on the penny and twopenny shelves respectively outside the shop. The rest he left aside while he switched his attention to books.

Monday was a short day. Norris left at lunchtime and Lemuel

locked up behind him as usual. When he returned to the shop he noticed the unsorted magazines still sitting on the counter. As he lifted them up to tidy them away he grasped the bundle insecurely and felt the one at the bottom slipping through his fingers and falling to the floor. He put the rest away before returning to retrieve it. As he bent to do so the instantly recognisable cover drew his startled attention and transfixed it:

> The
> Woman at Home
>
> Annie S. Swan's Magazine
> Profusely Illustrated
> London
> Hodder & Stoughton
> 27 Paternoster Row
> 1895

It was the Christmas number. He remembered at once Margot reading it at the breakfast-room fire on that Sunday morning four years ago when he returned from Mass.

He took it up to his room and laid it on the table. She had copied a passage from one of Annie S. Swan's articles into her notebook. He flicked through the pages of the magazine and found it.

> OVER THE TEACUPS by Annie S. Swan.
> The older I grow the more strongly do I feel
> that it is not love that saddens the earth but
> the dearth of it. There is too much living for
> self among us all . . .

Margot, he remembered, had marked the passage with two lines drawn vertically down the margin at the side. The passage before him was unmarked so it was not the actual copy that Margot had been reading. Nevertheless, it evoked with blinding clarity her presence and that vanished week of Christmas.

To prepare his usual midday meal was out of the question. Instead he let himself out into the street and ate in one of the quayside pubs. After that he walked street after street, hardly aware of the lunch-hour bustle, images from that Christmas season thronging his mind. When he let himself into his room again and looked at the magazine still resting on the table, he knew he must attempt at once to communicate with her. He saw in his mind's eye the old beech tree in the greenlit silence and the wavelets glinting as they rose and receded along the edge of the shoreline. He saw the

driveway meandering on its easygoing way to Avonmore House.
He sat down and wrote:

My darling Margot,

*Today, while attending to the ordinary routines of the bookshop
where I now work and live, I came suddenly and unexpectedly
across an old magazine which evoked with almost savage clarity a
morning when you and I were together in the happiest Christmas
season of my life. I regarded it as more than an extraordinary
coincidence and I have walked the streets exploring the circumstances attending it. Why should it have been the bottom magazine
of the bundle? Why should it have been that Christmas issue with its
unique potency, evoking your beloved presence so palpably and a
longing to burst a way back to that day through the impregnable
barriers of time. I came to recognize it for what it was: no mere
accident or coincidence but a deliberate sign from you to me that, as
Tom Moore once put it, 'Our love is remembered, even in the
sky . . .'*

He continued for several minutes, then folded the paper and put it in
an envelope which he inscribed simply: Margot.

Dusk was fading rapidly into night by the time he reached
Avonmore. The deserted driveway was barely visible, nothing
stirred in the familiar fields. To pick his steps to the beech tree he
had to take the lamp off his bicycle to light the way. When he had
put the letter in the box and returned it to its hiding place in the bole
of the tree, he moved on further until he was standing by the edge of
the river. The last of the light had faded from the sky. The stillness
was deep and broken only occasionally by the faint slap of a wavelet
against a stone.

Someone had set out night lines. He chanced to see them in the
light of the lamp and bent down to discover four in a row. They
were illegal, which meant poachers had been around. As he stood
upright once more, his senses sharpened by the discovery, he
detected a faint, sweet odour that he had failed to notice before.
There was a dead animal somewhere. He moved from place to place
until the smell hung more heavily and became sickly and unpleasant. In the beam of the lamp he at last located the source: a
dead fox in a trap. It was a well built, mature animal. Its bush had
been removed. He knew now for certain that it was the work of
poachers.

He picked his way cautiously back to his bicycle and had his
foresight confirmed when two men emerged from the cover of the

driveway bushes and accosted him. One had a shotgun. The other carried a lamp which he switched on and shone directly into Lemuel's face.

'Leave the bike where it is,' the one with the shotgun said. 'You're coming for a walk with us instead.'

'Why should I do that?'

'Because you're a bloody poacher and we've caught you red-handed. That's why.'

'And not a very clever one,' the other commented, 'leaving your bike by the roadside for the world and his wife to see.'

'You're completely mistaken,' Lemuel told them.

'We've been keeping a look-out for yourself and your mates for over a month. You've planted so many of your traps around the place that you have it like a bloody minefield. Come on – march.'

'Where are you taking me?'

'To Mister Cox. He'll be delighted to make your acquaintance.'

'Thrilled skinny,' the one with the lamp said. 'He's the gentleman who happens to own this estate.'

'And I happen to be his son,' Lemuel told them.

They found this hilarious and laughed together.

'We'll soon find out,' Shotgun said. 'March.'

There was no option. He took up his position between them as directed and proceeded up the driveway. The situation was nonsensical. But worse than that was the prospect of having to meet his father face to face after avoiding him for nearly two years. His hope was that the girl who answered the door would recognize him or, failing that, that his father would not be at home. But the girl was new and had no knowledge of him, and his father was in his study.

'Tell Mister Cox,' Shotgun said, 'we've caught one of the poachers and have him here with us.'

She returned to conduct them to Jonathan. He was at his desk writing by the light of a lamp that was sitting on it. It left the rest of the room so dimly lit that he rose to receive them without realizing who it was they had brought with them.

But recognition dawned on him as he came across to them and he called out in disbelief, 'Lemuel! What is this?'

'These two gentlemen found me in the grounds and decided I was poaching,' Lemuel said.

'But this is my son,' Jonathan told them. 'How could you make such an outlandish mistake.'

'We watched him leaving his bicycle at the side of the driveway

211

and going in among the trees with a lamp to light the way,' Shotgun explained. 'We happened to have found that traps had been set there earlier on and were hiding to watch developments. We were doing what you had paid us to do, sir, or so we thought. It turns out we were wrong. We're terrible sorry, I'm sure.' They were extremely embarrassed.

'It was an understandable mistake, when you think about it,' Lemuel said to Jonathan. 'I'm not upset.'

After repeated explanations they withdrew with the affair patched up.

The door closed behind them. Lemuel stood in silence. Jonathan took the initiative.

'Were you coming to see me at last after so long an absence?'

'Not to see you,' Lemuel answered. 'But to visit a place where I was once so happy.' It told the truth. It also protected his secret.

'Sit down,' Jonathan invited. 'Let us talk.'

They sat, Jonathan behind his desk, Lemuel facing him.

'Why did you stay so long away?'

'For the reasons I offered in the note I left for you. I had taken your money and found myself unable to pay it back.'

'You explained that,' Jonathan said. 'It was sufficient.'

'I was deeply ashamed,' Lemuel confessed. 'In addition, the death of Margot Penrose and the unbearable nature of it . . .' He broke off. It was not possible to go on.

'Stella told me. It was dreadful. It was dreadful beyond words. It gave me all the more reason to long to see you and to comfort you.'

'I'm sorry,' Lemuel said. 'I think the truth is I wasn't in my right mind.'

'I've no doubt about it,' Jonathan said. 'You went through more than could be borne. Come downstairs to the sitting-room. Stella is there and will be overjoyed. And we'll have something to drink while you tell me what you have been occupied with for two long years.'

Stella threw her arms about him and cried and said over and over again that she simply couldn't believe it. When they had settled down and Jonathan had provided them with their drinks, he began to tell them of Norris Curtis and the bookshop and the room he had over it.

'Now that we understand each other once again,' Jonathan suggested, 'you must come back to stay here. There's the question of your studying. We can arrange to have someone stay here in a tutorial capacity. We can discuss it in detail later.'

But Lemuel felt he must remain with Norris for the present.

'He's been generous. Besides, the understanding was I would remain until he has himself and the business sorted out.'

'You'll stay tonight anyway,' Jonathan insisted. 'There'll be no further trains until morning and you can't face such a bicycle journey at this hour.'

'Yes. I'll stay tonight.'

Jonathan was satisfied. He lingered a while and then went off to bed. When he had gone Stella suggested, 'You could stay in town during the week and stay here on Saturdays and Sundays.'

He thought he might do that.

'At least promise to come out on Saturday week,' she pressed.

'Is it special?'

'Very special. Johnny is calling to see Father. We're becoming engaged. Of course, it's just a formality. Father has agreed already. And Uncle Crispin is coming to wish us good luck.'

'I do the same,' Lemuel said. 'I'm delighted for you both.'

'Johnny would like it if we could be married at Christmas. There are rumours about the Boer situation and the British demands and it's thought the regiment may be drafted. Do you think there will be trouble?'

'There is talk of it, certainly,' Lemuel admitted. He promised to do as she had asked.

He had breakfast very early next morning and stepped out into a world which had returned in a moment of witchery to its lost and primal innocence. The mountains raised themselves about him in delicate outline, their distant blue shining like the bloom on a plum. A light mist over the surrounding fields deepened the sunlight to a richer yellow and clung in tiny globules to the seeding grasses. The silence all about him was holy, an exquisite presence. He retrieved his bicycle and turned his face to the journey with, for however briefly, tranquillity and happiness of heart.

Uncle Crispin kept his promise. So, too, did Lemuel. It was not the formal gathering – that would come later. With Stella and Johnny were his brother Eddie, who was to be best man, Jonathan, Uncle Crispin, Lemuel and Godwin. Little Jonathan was there too, but at nine he hardly counted as a participant.

They were convinced that war was on the way. Uncle Crispin had it on good authority that the leading British newspapers were already in competition with one another to contract the services of the most outstanding of the war correspondents. He was thinking of applying for such a job himself. Had he not a good pair of eyes, a good pair of ears and as accomplished a prose style as the next? He was also an expert in the bicycle saddle, almost certainly as good as the renowned Frederick Villiers who, in the several conflicts he had covered in the course of his career as a war correspondent, had been seen invariably to use his green roadster.

He had also written to the War Office suggesting the setting up of a bicycle corps, or even a whole battalion on an experimental basis. It could be nominally an adjunct of the cavalry, although the whole tactical superiority of the bicycle lay in the fact that it required neither fodder nor water nor expensive and complicated harness. If it fell in battle it involved no laborious and time-consuming burial procedures. A dead bicycle did not decay and spread corruption all around. However, he entertained little hope of a reply. To most of the ancients in command, strategy was what you had done the last time. When the machine gun – as it would – advanced sufficiently in technical efficiency to decimate a cavalry charge, their solution would be to get more horses.

Johnny said the generally held belief in the army was that if war did begin shortly it would be over by Christmas. If it was not, then if their marriage had already been arranged he felt he would be granted a minimum amount of compassionate leave for the ceremony to take place. Uncle Crispin said come hell or high water, war or no war, he was off to London to examine the Daimler 1898–1899 at first hand to fulfil his ambition to own a motor car at long last.

Then Lemuel played for them and Stella sang. Eddie also sang but kept the mouth organ in his jacket pocket out of respect for Mr Cox's rather conservative tastes. The health of the espoused couple was drunk in decorous fashion and wine passed about, but in moderation. Sorrow and gladness alternated for Jonathan as the night went on: sorrow that Stella would shortly be leaving her home, sorrow as he looked back through the years to his own and his beloved Cecilia's betrothal; gladness that Stella had selected an upright young man from a much respected and comfortably placed family and, of course, that he was of the same church and faith. Uncle Crispin gave them a humorous recitation which he had composed himself. It concerned a scheming widow-woman and a miserly farmer, and caused much hilarity. All were staying over-night and retired to bed at a reasonable hour.

On the day after the arrival of Uncle Crispin in London, the eleventh day of October 1899, the war began. It was a Wednesday, and as day succeeded day he was the astonished observer of the sudden outbreak of patriotic fervour and public hysteria. He wrote back to Jonathan of crowds lining the routes of departing troops; the wild waving of thousands of hats and handkerchiefs and walking sticks; the countless wives and sweethearts and relatives either cheering or weeping or contriving to do both simultaneously with quite un-British abandonment, and the endless repetition by brass bands and singing spectators of the song that was suddenly all the rage: 'Good-Bye Dolly Grey'. He complained of the trouble he had finding anyone with any interest whatsoever in showing him, let alone selling him, a Daimler 1898–1899.

Although the war was far from being over before Christmas as had been generally predicted, for Johnny O'Grady the necessity to apply for compassionate leave did not arise. He was numbered among the many fallen on the battlefield at Colenso on December 15th 1899. When the news reached Lemuel he spoke to Norris Curtis and hastened immediately to Avonmore to be with Stella. He found her need pathetic and his company essential. At first he lingered indefinitely, but eventually decided to remain. Although he never worked in the bookshop again he visited it with regularity throughout the years. Norris Curtis understood perfectly. They continued always to be the closest of friends.

Part Three

Chapter 19

Success in the general election changed everything for Ballcock. He was no longer a mere city councillor but a member of the government of his country, credited by his constituents and the general membership of the Union with all the authority and influence they believed to go with it. He was granted leave of absence (unpaid) by the plumbing firm he worked for. The daily press interviewed him as a newcomer and added an outline of his career and a current photograph of him to their files. Don Maguire of the broadcasting service sought whatever information Frank could furnish about him, and when he thought it over arranged for Frank to introduce him. Joe Dunne thought Ballcock's new status could be an asset to the Union and decided it should be exploited. He had the office of the Co-operative Society on the ground floor cleaned up and completely redecorated with Ballcock's name and status displayed in bold letters on its newly painted entrance door:

> Peter A. Brady T.D.
> Hon. Secretary
> Construction and Allied Workers
> Co-operative Society

The change took Frank by surprise when he and Don Maguire arrived for their informal meeting. There was a small but significant change of style in Ballcock too, a departure from his habitual attachment to the dark suit and bowler hat. The bowler remained and so did the dark jacket. The dark waistcoat was still spanned by the two strands of the silver watchchain. But the plain dark trousers had given way to a pair of pinstripes. Ballcock was now the complete public man.

He shook hands vigorously, waved them to chairs and offered a genial glass of whiskey when they were seated. In an opening piece which sounded prepared, he confessed to a deep personal respect for the professionalism and integrity of the national broadcasting service of which the country could be proud. It was a privilege to meet someone who commanded so eminent and influential a position within it. He then launched into an account of his own career.

He intended to use his enhanced political influence, he said, in several ways. In particular, however, he was determined to keep a sharp eye on the national territory and the seas about it. He rooted among the papers on his desk and produced as an example the copy of a letter he had sent to the Minister for Defence.

'It's about the situation regarding our coastal waters,' he explained, passing the letter to Maguire for his scrutiny. 'I've been told on good authority that it's deplorable. They've become a deathtrap.'

'In what way?' Maguire asked.

'Sumbarines.'

'I beg your pardon?'

'Sumbarines. Russian sumbarines. They're loaded from stem to stern with automic weapons. Enough, I'm told, in the event of an accident, to blow ourselves and our poor unfortunate bloody country clean out of the water.'

'This is very interesting,' Maguire responded. 'I must inquire further into it.'

'Anything you may uncover,' Ballcock assured him, 'I'd be obliged to be made aware of.'

They left after half an hour shaking hands cordially as they did so.

When they had reached the street Frank said, smiling broadly 'You'll have to come up with something of consequence about those sumbarines.'

'Russian sumbarines,' Maguire qualified. 'That man's capacity for mangling the English language is unmatchable.'

'And inexhaustible,' Frank agreed. 'He phoned me some days ago to apologize for postponing an appointment. His explanation was that he had to attend a funeral which required his presence at a Mass in the church of the Passionate Fathers in Mount Argus.'

'The Passionate Fathers?' Maguire repeated. 'That's an Order I'd be tempted to join myself.'

'He was referring, of course,' Frank explained, 'to the Congregation of Discalced Clerics of the Most Holy Cross and Passion of

Our Lord Jesus Christ, founded early in the eighteenth century in Tuscany by St Peter of the Cross and known ever since as Passionists. They're great men to give a Lenten Retreat.'

'You seem to have studied these Passionate Clerics in the greatest depth,' Maguire said, feigning astonishment.

'I looked it up a few days ago,' Frank confessed. 'Ballcock affects me that way at times.'

They had reached the shop which the Communist League struggled to maintain in Pearse Street. Large white letters above the windows spelled out their purpose: The Left Book Shop. But beneath the letters the windows were boarded up. Slivers of glass which had escaped the brushes of the corporation sweepers lay scattered along the path close up against the wall.

'More trouble in our native land,' Frank quoted, coming to a standstill.

'The fruits of another outburst of public piety,' Maguire informed him. 'I was a fascinated observer of this one myself.'

'What caused it?'

'The appearance of the actor Orson Welles on the stage of the Gate. They denounced him as a divorcee and an ardent communist and picketed the theatre. Then, to relieve their ardour further, they marched down here to heave a few bricks through the windows.'

'Our homegrown McCarthyists,' Frank commented.

'Precisely. To preserve democracy and freedom of speech they would forbid us to listen to the Communists' point of view. In the same spirit they design the Censorship of Publications Act to protect us from the corrupting influence of practically all our own writers and most of the internationally acclaimed ones: Gide, Sartre, Hemingway, Steinbeck – the list goes on and on—' He broke off. His tone changed. 'I've been hearing that yourself and Simon Morrissey are qualifying for attention from the same quarters. I refer to your *Review* series: "On The Side Of The Angels".'

'How do you know Simon and I are involved?'

'It would be hard not to. It's the general gossip in all the best circles. Seriously, I'd worry that it might threaten Simon's freelance radio work.'

'You mean you might be forced to drop him?'

'If a public outcry develops I could be ordered to.'

'On what grounds?'

'On the grounds that public service broadcasting must not appear to be taking sides.'

'That's a funny bloody view of the matter,' Frank said in sudden anger. 'I'd regard depriving a person of the work he's been doing successfully for a number of years as taking sides with a vengeance.'

'So would I,' Maguire conceded, 'but add a dollop of imported McCarthyism to our home-grown variety and I wouldn't give much for our chances.'

P.J. was beginning to make noises too. He had been a member of the Sept for some years, not for reasons of piety, but for shrewd business ones. In the unceasing battle to determine who-got-what, he saw the Sept as catering for the Catholic side, just as the Masons existed to push for the other crowd. That, in P.J.'s uncomplicated view, was in the nature of things. When Sylvester Kennedy spoke to him (in confidence, as was the habit in the Sept) advising him that his junior partner was the author of the offensive material and the cartoonist was an employee of his, and added that this would not go down well with the Sept, P.J. had no need to be told. It did not go down well with P.J. either. He said as much to Simon Morrissey and asked him to give it up, like a sensible bloody man. He called Frank McDonagh in and ordered him to do so. If he refused then he'd be shown the door. The Kenny Morrissey agency employed him and would regard his sketching for anyone else as a breach of contract. He advised Frank McDonagh to show he was a sensible as well as a talented young man by doing what he was told.

Frank talked it over with Margaret. To his surprise she felt that he should see P.J. to hell first. It was how he felt himself. But the prospect of losing his job was a chilling one, especially in circumstances which of their nature would make it doubly difficult to get another.

With Morrissey he met Con Andrews to consider what might confront them. Morrissey recognized that his freelance radio work could very well be put in jeopardy by the continuation of the *Review* series, but said he was prepared to put up with that should it come about. He felt reasonably confident of holding on to his agency position. His status as junior partner would make it difficult for P.J. to get rid of him should he wish to do so, unless he took legal steps to bring the partnership to an end, which was unlikely. But Frank's situation was different. P.J., as the senior partner, held the right to dismiss him if he so decided. He could not be prevented. That, Morrissey said, was what caused him to hesitate. Persisting with the series could involve a considerable risk in Frank's case.

'If it came to actual dismissal,' Con Andrews offered, 'I think I could do something about finding alternative employment for

Frank. I'm a member of neither the Sept or the Freemasons but I'm not altogether devoid of influential friends.'

'I'm aware of that,' Morrisey agreed, 'but in the present state of things I'm not at all confident that even Con Andrews could put matters to right.'

Nor was Frank. He had never bothered very deeply about the political and religious tensions of the society he lived in. But now the pressures were no longer vague and distant. They were beginning to focus in a very personal way on his association with radical views which the *Review* had the temerity to express. He felt suddenly and for the first time under threat. The menace behind P.J.'s manner during their interview had not been lost on him. It had shown in the unfamiliar cast of P.J.'s face. It was the inflexible face of the Sept. He had a fleeting glimpse of the features of the opposing side some days later. They were essentially the same.

He had gone back into town around nine at night to meet Morrisey who was still trying to make up his mind whether to keep the series going or to drop it. He wanted to talk it over further. They chose a pub well away from their usual haunts. Frank, as a precaution against a heavy session, left the car behind and went in by bus. He found Morrissey there ahead of him, glooming over his drink.

'Sorry to drag you in,' Morrissey said. 'I've been agonising over whether to discontinue the series or not and I don't want to discuss it either in the office or at home. It's easier over a drink in a pub.'

'It suits me better too,' Frank agreed. 'The office atmosphere is all wrong and home makes the whole set-up seem ridiculous and unreal. What we must do is decide to resist as firmly as we can but within some kind of reasonable limits. What these limits are we've got to define for ourselves.'

'Exactly. Let me get you a drink.'

They spent nearly two hours going over ground which had already been explored more than once. It led back again to what had been obvious from the beginning. The decision to continue with the series or drop it lay entirely with Morrissey. If there were no articles from Morrissey, there was nothing for Frank to illustrate. If Morrissey continued with the articles Frank intended to continue supplying the accompanying cartoons.

'That means P.J. will dismiss you.'

'I know. He has said so.'

'You realise,' Morrissey said, 'that if he does I've no power to stop him?'

'I wouldn't wish you to try,' Frank said. 'To go on working for the agency in those circumstances simply wouldn't be possible.'

Morrissey left his glass down with deliberate firmness and said, 'Let me ask you this for the last time. Do you want me to discontinue the series?'

'Let me tell you for the last time,' Frank answered with equal emphasis, 'I am making no answer to that one way or the other. I am not going to influence your decision.'

'Very well,' Morrissey conceded. 'I'll take one more night to sleep on it.'

They walked a little of the way together and spoke of other things. They walked in friendship. Then they came to the parting point where Morrissey continued on his way to his flat which was nearby and Frank, crossing from the railings of Trinity College into Dawson Street, went on to pick up his bus. The hour was late and it might well be the last. One passed him, full, as he made his way. There were no other pedestrians and hardly any traffic. Shuttered shops and darkened offices rose silently above parallel strands of street lamps. He joined a queue of four or five others and waited, as they did, in silence until he became aware of a form huddled on the ground in the shadow of a doorway. He stared over without moving any nearer and gradually became aware of what it was. It was the figure of a man, well-dressed, elderly, whose hat, a bowler, had fallen off his head and lay on the doorstep beside him. He touched the shoulder of the man in front of him in the queue and pointed to the recumbent figure.

'What goes on over there?' he asked. 'There's someone lying in the doorway.'

'Some old toff,' the man said. 'The smell of brandy and soda would knock you over. He came tottering across the road about twenty minutes ago and fell out of his standing where you see him lying.'

'Perhaps we should do something,' Frank said.

'I went over to him when it happened,' the man said. 'I spoke to him and asked would I call him a taxi but I couldn't make out a word he was saying. Very posh accent, right enough, but too plastered to talk properly.'

'Is he hurt?'

'Bit of a cut on the forehead but it's superficial.'

'We could call the police or an ambulance,' Frank thought.

'We could,' the man said, 'and miss the last bus. There's four others in the queue here and not one of them took a damn bit of notice. He'll sleep it off where he is. Leave him to it.'

'He may be hurt,' Frank said, 'I'll have a look.'

224

He went over to the doorway which was only a few yards away. He raised the man's head, cushioning it in the crook of his arm. The eyes were closed, the face thin and blotched, the tight, trim moustache above the lip still fair, the hair on the head, in contrast, muddy grey and meagre. Blood from the wound on his forehead was leaving a track down his cheek and staining the white collar deeply. But when Frank took out his handkerchief to wipe some of the blood from about the wound it was, as the man in the queue had reported, superficial.

The eyes opened while Frank was examining the wound and stared uncomprehendingly at him for some time.

'You've had a fall and cut your forehead,' Frank said. 'But it's a light wound and nothing to worry about.'

The eyes focused as the words began to sink in.

'If you give me your address I can call you a taxi.'

The eyes narrowed as the injured man tried to concentrate, but in the end he shook his head.

'Perhaps I should get an ambulance?'

The head shook again. He tried to speak. The accent was unmistakably Protestant-Ascendancy but unintelligible. The man was silent for a while. Then he spoke again, repeating a phrase which seemed to be limited to two or three words. Frank bent down closer to hear.

'I don't understand,' he said. 'Speak more slowly.'

The repetitions were becoming less incoherent. Frank suddenly grasped it.

'The Commonwealth Club?' he asked.

The head nodded. It was only a couple of yards away, an impressive mansion overlooking the green and a surviving bastion of the old supremacy. It fitted in to the picture. The injured man had been coming from there, Frank guessed, after an evening of wining and dining with his peers. The face, the accent, the sartorial style, even the heavy brandy-and-soda smell added up to an exclusive lifestyle, an inbred disdain. Tonight it had taken a tumble. But only briefly. His station was above blemish.

'If you can get on your feet,' Frank said, 'I can help you to get there. It's quite near.'

The head nodded again.

'I take it you're a member. They'll have accommodation for you for the night?'

The head nodded again.

'Very well,' Frank said, 'let's see what we can manage.'

The man lay still for a while longer, gathering his forces together, bracing himself. At last he raised both arms towards Frank, who grasped him and struggled until the man was on his feet with one arm about his shoulder.

As they moved from the doorway a bus pulled up at the stop and the small queue moved aboard. It was the last one for the night. Frank resigned himself to a walk home. The man, after a faltering start, gained a little in control and got along reasonably well. He made no further attempt at speech until they reached the flight of massive granite steps which led up to the doors of the club. He came to a standstill and, still dependent on Frank for support, said in an indistinct voice, 'Here.'

'I know,' Frank said. 'We'll take the steps slowly.' He had some difficulty getting to the bell while still supporting the weight of the other, and then had to press it several times before it attracted a response. The halldoor was opened with deliberate slowness by a rotund functionary in the regalia of a butler, who stood in impassive silence and waited for Frank to speak.

'This gentleman has had a slight accident,' Frank said. 'You probably know him. He asked to be taken here.'

The eyes moved away from Frank and fixed on the other with the barest flicker of recognition. Then the arms reached forward to take hold of him. He was assisted gingerly across to a winged porter's chair which adorned the hall and was put sitting down. He made a sign to the butler who bent over to hear what was being said and in doing so masked him from view. After a brief delay the portly, bending form straightened and returned to the halldoor. One hand grasped the doorknob, the other was extended slowly towards Frank. It was proferring a five-pound note. Frank glanced briefly at the money before transferring his full attention to the heap of rotund impassivity and its inscrutable face.

'No, thank you,' Frank said, smiling a little. 'Keep it for yourself.'

Immediately he turned to go the door closed behind him, cutting off the faint odours of carefully prepared food, well-tended fires, fine wines and expensive cigars which were the permanent ghosts of the hallway.

It was after midnight. He walked by the railings of St Stephen's Green, recalling as he so often did the little altar server who had rung the bell of Newman's church on Sunday mornings, now long swallowed up in the past. In Harcourt Street he wondered how he would present the butler if he ever decided to do a caricature of him. He reckoned the face had a range of expressions which was limited to three: the one condescending, the other fawning and a third which consisted of no expression at all. At Portobello Bridge he remembered the little group that used to assemble there on Sunday afternoons in their Salvation Army uniforms, and heard faintly in some inner ear the whisper of their hymn tunes sounding on ghostly instruments.

Margaret came quickly to the door the moment his key turned in the lock.

'Frank, you're home,' she said, her voice full of relief. 'What on earth delayed you? Simon Morrissey phoned nearly two hours ago and was surprised that you still hadn't arrived home. When he left you you were heading straight for your bus.'

'I had a bit of an adventure after I left him,' Frank explained. 'I missed the last bus on the head of it.' Over cups of cocoa he told her of his role as good Samaritan and the frigid reception which was his reward at the Commonwealth Club. She was furious.

'The crowd in that place are well known for what they are,' she said angrily, 'a bigoted, loveless Protestant lot. I wouldn't lift a little finger for them.'

He smiled and said, 'The moment I opened my mouth the flunkey who answered the door knew I was one of the natives and a Catholic. In fact he knew it before, simply by the way I was dressed. His displeasure and disdain were incredible.'

'Bigots,' she said, still furious, 'stupid, insufferable bloody bigots.' Then she cast the matter aside. 'But never mind them. Simon Morrissey had news which I was glad to hear. He's decided to discontinue the series.'

'Is that what he phoned about?'

'He said he wanted you to know immediately and not prolong the uncertainty. He's phoned Con Andrews about his decision already and Con doesn't seem to mind very much. He's going to let P.J. know first thing in the morning.'

'Well,' Frank responded with relief, 'that leaves me in the clear I suppose. Are you glad?'

'Naturally I'm glad you're in the clear, Frank,' she said, 'but I'm not at all glad that the series should be dropped. There's something very wrong when things like that can occur. It shouldn't happen.'

'No. It should not,' he agreed. 'You begin to wonder who or what is in control.'

Still, it was a relief for the moment that confrontation would be avoided. If it had to come, it should come on some graver issue.

Chapter 20

Lemuel Cox sat on late and brooded over the companionable fire. A couple of hours earlier Margaret and Frank had completed one of their regular visits and had left for home. Stella, having sat on with him as she occasionally did when in a nostalgic mood, to talk over memories they shared of times gone by, had gone into a huff over something he said and demanded abruptly to be helped to her bedroom. Their fireside conversations, once so intimate and affectionate, tended more and more frequently to end in such behaviour on her part. Mention by him of Margot Penrose triggered it off. He was discovering that it almost invariably did. He had begun to talk of Frank and Margaret's visit and remarked in passing on Margaret's always pleasing manners and on how well and attractive she had looked. Stella acknowledged that she was a most agreeable companion.

'For me,' he confessed, 'her resemblance to Margot Penrose grows more and more striking.'

He knew at once he had done it again. He saw Stella as usual making ready to refuse to be interested. Her face became expressionless, her eyes without lustre.

'I am quite convinced there is some element of reincarnation,' he added. 'Today, when I complimented her on her pretty appearance, she made fun of it by quoting some lines that were very familiar to me indeed. She said:

> Love not me for comely grace
> Nor for my pleasing eye or face
> Nor for any outward part
> No, nor for my constant heart . . .

'Margot, I remembered, had the same playful habit. Quite often her response to a compliment was to recite those self-same lines.'

'They are lines that many young ladies have been much taken by, even in my own time,' Stella told him. 'I certainly wouldn't let them set my mind alight with ridiculous notions of reincarnation.'

'There is nothing ridiculous about reincarnation,' he insisted. 'Plato taught it. Today's Theosophists propagate it. The ancient Celts believed in it. So do most Eastern religions.'

'I'm very sure our own Catholic religion does not,' she said, flatly dismissing the matter.

'Any time I speak of her,' Lemuel remarked quietly, 'you become angry. Yet she was your close friend.'

'Who, pray, was my close friend?'

'Margot Penrose, of course.'

She looked uncomprehending. 'Margot Penrose?' she repeated. Her face wore a puzzled look.

He wondered if it was her deliberate intent to foster doubt in his mind, or if the sudden puzzlement was real and these lapses of hers were signs of the approach of senility, with its interludes of forgetfulness afflicting her in fitful spasms? When she had succeeded in planting similar doubts in the past the simple answer had been to go to the tree and look at Margot's letters that had yellowed and faded with the rest but were there to affirm the reality. He had done so on a couple of occasions, and although they had exorcised the demon of doubt, they had also penetrated to unhealable depths of grief and loss which he had no desire to disturb all over again. Showing her the letters had been useless anyway. She had suggested he had probably written them himself in some act of unconscious fantasy. He said no more but wheeled her to her bedroom and returned to the fireplace to sit on his own and let his thoughts dwell on an incident of the afternoon which it pleased him better to contemplate.

A copy of the current issue of the *Review* had been lying on his desk in his study while he and Frank were talking together. Frank had reached out his hand to pick it up.

'May I?' Frank asked. 'I haven't seen this month's issue as yet.'

'Certainly,' Lemuel said. Frank turned the pages.

'They've discontinued their "On The Side Of The Angels" series,' Lemuel added. 'The editor announces it in characteristic fashion inside.'

Frank searched for the announcement and found it:

There are several different ways of weathering a storm. The ass turns his rump to it and abides its discomfitures in patience. The man of courage meets it straight on and overcomes it. This *Review* has run into a storm over its series 'On The Side Of Angels' and must emulate the ass. But only briefly and for temporary respite. When we have delved more thoroughly into the identity and true motives of the various forces at work we will regroup and resume our exposures of the ills and idiocies that beset the plain people of this nation.

The Editor

Frank closed the magazine then and said, 'I expect you found the series offensive?'

'Ocassionally, but not generally,' Lemuel answered.

'Still, some of it must have offended,' Frank said. 'And I feel obliged to own up to some personal involvement. I was the person who supplied the cartoons.'

'I know that already,' Lemuel told him. 'I also know who the author of the articles was. Simon Morrissey. My father held membership with a number of religious groups and I have inherited his contacts with a few of the more militant. One of them is the Sept of St Malachy.'

'There is a Mr Sylvester Kennedy in the Sept, I'm told,' Frank admitted, 'who has been taking a close interest in Simon and myself.'

Lemuel smiled but added nothing further. After a pause Frank asked, 'Do you feel that there was an element of deceit in my not revealing my part in it until now?'

'You had no occasion to do so. Now that it has arisen you have been open and honest about it. I find that highly admirable. There was no obligation whatever to disclose your connection either to me or to anyone else.'

'Thank you,' Frank said. He was relieved.

'In fact, should you encounter trouble at any time,' Lemuel added, 'remember that I may be able to help.'

Frank nodded. 'Thank you,' he repeated.

The fire was sinking and required re-fuelling. Lemuel noted the total silence of the house about him. It betokened the lateness of the hour. Nevertheless his mood was to sit on. A small pyramid of logs stood in readiness as it always did at the left-hand side of the hearth. He rose briefly to transfer fresh wood from it to the fire to set it flaming. Some lines of a much quoted Yeats poem came of their own accord as he settled back again in his chair:

> When you are old and gray and full of sleep
> And nodding by the fire, take down this book
> And slowly read, and dream of the soft look
> Your eyes had once, and of their shadows deep . . .

She whom they brought so easily to mind had slipped away so young. She would never nod beside the fire under the weight of years nor doze under their burden in its heat. She would never comb grey hairs.

He had begun to try his hand at poetry on his own account, though the themes that suggested themselves were far from novel and puzzled him greatly at times. In one of them he mourned over the demise of many boon companions in such grieving lines as: Sadly, sadly they slipped away/ James who was grave and Jack who was gay . . . In another he lamented for the death of a child, and there was yet another he had called The Fairy Bush in which he described the nocturnal goings-on of the Little People who danced about it to the music of a fairy fiddle. Yet when he reflected on these themes afterwards he had to admit that, with the probable exception of Norris Curtis, he had never in his life had companions that could be described as boon. He had avoided children for the most part and had no experience whatever of having grieved for the death of a single one of them. Fairy bushes and peasant super-stitions about them appalled him. But in one of the less disastrous of his efforts he had discerned, in the broken arch of an abandoned bridge near the old mill they used to play about in childhood, a symbol of time suspended and brooding. This, he felt, was getting a bit nearer the mark. And in one of the poems, a mere four lines in extent, he had by some lucky fluke hit on the expression of an idea which pleased him:

> I do not know that God is good
> I do not know that God is wise
> I only know he gathers in
> My homing multiplicities

When he read it to Stella she found the first two lines blasphemous and the second two meaningless. He was unperturbed. It had a glimmer of style. It had a faint echo of the real thing. He allowed it a place among the yellowing hoard in the bole of his tree. It also implanted the idea that he had been a poet in some previous existence, and it set him searching through the poems attributed to Anon in several anthologies in a quest for anything among them that stirred a personal memory or suggested a style or mode of inspired thought that sounded as though it could, in some earlier existence, have been his own.

Before her fit of the huffs Stella had spoken with appreciation of a trip to the church in Edmundscourt which Frank and Margaret had taken them on earlier in the evening. It had been a great treat to see it again, she told him, now that she was unable to get there unaided. It had so many deep associations.

'When I stopped to look at the old, brass-framed notice board in the porch,' she reported with sudden emotion, 'I saw for a very brief moment, but very clearly, the notice that hung there when Godwin's death was reported to them.'

Lemuel remembered. They had offered Mass for him. Private Godwin Cox, Dublin Fusilier, killed in action on the Somme on the first day of July, 1916.

'That would have been his Month's Mind,' Lemuel said.

'A year later,' she added, her voice still echoing unbelief, 'it bore Jonathan's name.'

Month's Mind
Pray for Jonathan Cox, Enniskillin Fusiliers,
killed in battle, Flanders, July 27th, 1917.
The Holy Sacrifice of the Mass will be offered
in this church for the repose of his soul on
Tuesday morning next, 27th day of August
1917 at ten o'clock. Requiescat in Pace.

'Poor Jonathan,' Lemuel reflected aloud. 'I used to blame him for Mother's death. Do you remember what Father said when he stopped for a moment on going into the church to read the announcement,' he asked her gently.

She shook her head.

'He quoted that disconsolate question which Francis Thompson flings at God in The Hound of Heaven: "Why must Thy harvest fields be dunged with rotten death?" No doubt Father had poor Johnny O'Grady in mind as well.'

'We won't speak of that,' she answered. 'Not now.'

A moth had emerged from beneath the small pyramid of logs by the fire. Lemuel watched it. It made a series of attempts to approach the flames but on each occasion found the kerb of the fireplace too hot to endure and was forced back. Eventually it abandoned the attempt altogether and took off in search of more approachable suns. Had the kerb not stood in its way, Lemuel wondered, would it have immolated itself? The bulb of the tablelamp could never deter it. In summer the hissing Tilley lamp with its twin incandescent mantles and its white-hot globe which he used sometimes in the abandoned stables, drew them irresistibly to it and scorched them to death in scores. He considered the ancient expression about the love of the moth for the flame. How could so fatal a fascination persist in a species throughout countless generations? Had God omitted some essential protective mechanism?

Lemuel Cox pitied all living things. In spite of his Church's clear thinking to the contrary, he found it difficult to put aside a belief that the souls of animals and even insects were immortal. But he tried not to set his puny wisdom against the omnipotence of the Creator. Old Jonathan's stern injunction he had taken to heart at an early age: 'Before God the Father bend the knee.' He had ever obeyed it.

A tapping on the door startled him and scattered his thoughts.

'Come in,' he responded, raising his voice.

It was the housekeeper, Mrs Holohan. She was frightened.

'Sir, it's Miss Stella,' she said. 'There was a thump on the floor of her bedroom and when I raced up she had fallen out of bed and was stretched on the floor. I couldn't lift her.'

They hurried to the bedroom together. Stella's eyes were closed and her body without movement. But when he leaned closer he could detect breathing.

'We'll lift her together,' he said.

They got her on to the bed and propped her head and shoulders with pillows. She opened her eyes, and when he saw that she was trying to speak he took his hands from her shoulders to change his position. She immediately slid off the pillow and lay helplessly on her side. Her eyes when she opened them were filled with terror. Her left arm and left leg hung shapelessly.

He lowered his voice and said to Mrs Holohan, 'Telephone Dr Slattery to come at once. Tell him I believe it to be a stroke.'

Dr Slattery confirmed it. 'We must get her to hospital,' he decided. 'I'll summon the ambulance and follow behind in my car.'

'Can you take me also?'

'Of course. And bring you home again.'

'I may wish to stay in town to be near at hand. I'll phone my young friend Frank McDonagh. They'll have a bed for the night and in the course of tomorrow I can arrange a hotel.'

'As you wish.'

It was long after midnight when they reached the hospital. Stella's condition appeared stable but he kept vigil in the ward until morning came and an hour at which it seemed reasonable to phone Margaret. She insisted he should stay at least for that night. The hospital would have their telephone number to contact in case of necessity. It would be a sensible arrangement. In the end he stayed for over a week, visiting the hospital every day until Stella was reckoned to have recovered sufficiently to be allowed out. Frank drove them both home.

'I'm deeply grateful,' Lemuel said. 'Being able to call to the hospital every day did more than I would have hoped. It may have helped to stop a rift that has been growing between Stella and myself for a long time now. She thinks I've become subject to hallucinations of one kind and another. It made me very angry. Now I'm beginning to wonder if she may not have been right.'

'Most unlikely,' Frank said, reassuringly.

'Strange things seem to happen,' Lemuel said. 'A few days ago I believed I saw Norris Curtis again. He passed me by in the street. He was quite close to me but ignored me. When I turned to follow him he had gone.'

'Some look-alike,' Frank offered in an attempt to play it down.

'Probably so,' Lemeul answered, anxious to be convinced. 'How could it be otherwise?' But his face was clouded with doubt.

O'Halloran was suspicious. Something was afoot in the *Review* office and in the devious mind of Con Andrews, his one-time Brigade Commander in the War for Independence and now the best hated of the great multitude of his fellowmen that roused his ever volatile gorge. He recognized all the signs: the frequent telephone calls both incoming and outgoing, sometimes of marathon length; the flurry of letters with their parade of exotic stamps (Andrews, he had noted, no longer left them lying around after having opened them, so a surreptitious read of their contents had ceased to be possible); the unannounced absences of up to four or five days at a time. It provided O'Halloran with material for his habit of sustained solitary monologue and, when company offered that welcomed information about what the editor seemed to be up to, provided fodder for disclosure and scandal.

'He's gone missing again,' he told Simon Morrissey when he called in search of Con Andrews, 'where to or on what errand not disclosed. But of one thing you can be sure. He's up to his oul' tricks.'

'And what are they?'

'I don't know precisely because he's locking away the correspondence and telephoning only from his own office and waving me out if I venture to stick my head around his door. But I know what sparked it off. The fact that he had to put in that piece about discontinuing the series you and young McDonagh were doing for him.'

'That wasn't Con's decision,' Morrissey corrected. 'It was mine. I decided it looked like being disastrous for Frank.'

'You're wrong,' O'Halloran insisted. 'Some crowd got at the printers and he had no option but to back down. He swore to hit back. I'd take an oath that's what's engaging him now.'

'And you've no hint what he has in mind?'

'Nor what shape it will take,' O'Halloran acknowledged, 'but I know this about the oul' bollocks: he has the pride of Lucifer and that pride has been wounded. It'll be something spectacular.'

Ballcock's view was simple and unclouded.

'You're very wise to drop it,' he assured Frank. 'In this country you're not supposed to say things straight out.'

'Then how are you supposed to say them?'

'Be surruptious. Work away on the quiet. I've been clobbered myself often enough, usually for something Joe Dunne has been holding forth about, not me at all.'

He confessed to troubles of his own. His constituents were beginning to feel he was not being active enough in the House. They expected his voice to be heard more often.

'My trouble is that the few times I've got up to talk in there I've been laughed at,' he confessed.

'Why so?' Frank asked.

'You know bloody well why so,' Ballcock answered. 'I make a balls of the words. I've been doing it all my life.'

It was a shortcoming that had mattered very little in the cottages or the tenements. For the most part his solecisms went unnoticed there. But political opponents could seize on them and present him as a clown and a fool by making public mockery of them. It was just as damaging when it came to making written representations. Getting someone he could trust to vet them for him took up a great deal of time and involved much humiliation.

'I know you had your work cut out correcting those articles of mine when you were publishing them in the *Bulletin*,' he acknowledged.

Frank, feeling pity for him, said on impulse, 'If you have difficulty in the future finding someone to cast an eye over anything for you, bring it to me and I'll do what may be necessary.'

Ballcock reflected on the situation for a moment. 'Ever since I was any age,' he added, 'it's been the scourge of my life. I get the meaning of a word right. Then I go and pronounce it wrong. And I can find no way to prevent it.' He contemplated his plight in misery and silence.

Chapter 21

Dear Mother,

I write to you once again this time to let you know that at last Stella is back home, so you won't be receiving any more complaints of loneliness from me. If anybody had told me before she went off to hospital that I would be dreadfully upset – indeed, that I would be upset at all – it would have amused me greatly. For a long time our affection for one another, which stretched away back to childhood, seemed to have died. Worse than that. Had turned to deep dislike and, occasionally, to outright hatred. But separation, plus the knowledge that death hovered invisible but as close as might be, has chastened both of us. We talked of that the other night and had no difficulty agreeing that it was so. And we wondered together at the pattern of events which has left the two of us so isolated. Only we two remain; the rest are all gone: you, dear, dear mother who went first. Then the relentless decimation: Godwin and Jonathan and Father and Uncle Crispin and (yes, she consented to talk about him for the first time in many years) Johnny O'Grady, though I knew he visited her in her thoughts constantly. And she allowed that Margot Penrose should be numbered among them also and that she had been no figment of my imagination but her own good and most agreeable friend. And then we wondered at the thought – and sorrowed together about it too – that when she and I go the Cox line we represent will have disappeared off the face of the earth. Which, taken together with the fact that you gave birth to five of us, is a very odd state of affairs.

Stella seems to be comfortable and even to be making a little progress. Her left leg and left hand are affected, but she is adjusting to it. Of course she can't knit as she used to, which is hard on her and I sympathize most sincerely. But it does mean I can play the

piano in the evenings without the persistent clickety-clack of the
needles which, I must own, is a blessed relief.

    With all my love,
    Lem

When he had left the letter to lie among its fellows in the dark cavity of the tree, he made his way in the dusk that was beginning to shroud the driveway, to join Stella who was reading by the sitting-room fire.

'Is it raining outside?' she asked.

'No. A bit of a wind,' he reported, 'but no rain. Not yet anyway.'

'I thought I heard rain,' she explained. 'I thought I heard it pattering on the windowpane.'

'No,' he answered again. 'It may have been leaves. The wind is stirring them around a bit.'

'When I was a girl,' she remembered, 'I used to love to sit and watch the leaves spinning in a circle, usually where two walls of the yard met and formed an angle. We believed then it wasn't the wind but the fairies whirling around in their invisible dancing. Are you going to play the piano? If you are would you do something to please me?'

'Of course.'

'Include a quadrille or one or two of the old waltzes you used to play for me long ago. While you were out I was remembering. I'd love to hear them again.'

'Certainly.'

He crossed to the corner of the room where the cabinet stood. The loose floorboard creaked under his feet as it always did, setting the vase and the photograph frames on the table behind her quivering softly. Her eyes followed him as usual but now without animosity, although he knew she could never bring herself to approve his nightly tippling. He took out the whiskey bottle and his glass and sat in his chair. He poured for himself.

'Are Frank and Margaret likely to visit us soon?' she asked.

'I could phone and ask them.'

'I'd love to be taken again to visit the old church. It's been much in my thoughts. The village, too. Before it changes beyond recognition.'

'I'll phone them and ask,' he promised. 'I'm sure they'll be delighted.'

When he had finished his drink he searched the music shelves for the old-time pieces. He was impeccably ordered about most things, but with music most of all. He located what he wanted without difficulty and sat to play for her. The tunes were old, unforgettable, overpoweringly evocative. When he had finished and turned around to her she was weeping silently.

'Beautiful,' she said when he went over to put a hand on her shoulder. He was much moved himself. He smiled at her.

'I'll phone Frank,' he said.

On his return he was able to tell her that Frank and Margaret would call very soon. The trip to the church and the village would be part of their purpose. She nodded her head and said 'Lovely', and went on to repeat the word three or four times. He refilled his glass and lent her his attention while she spoke from time to time of the thoughts that passed like lost and questing pilgrims through her mind.

The letter from Con Andrews asked Frank to indicate if he would be free to attend a very special meeting in the office of the *Review*. The date suggested, he said, was tentative and subject to change: he was anxious to secure a full attendance and would shift it around to suit as many of those concerned as possible. How many of them there were and who they might be, the letter forebore to reveal. It offered no hint whatever as to the nature of the business. Morrissey, who had received one which was similar in every detail, was puzzled that Andrews should write a letter at all. His established practice was to use the telephone whenever practicable. He disliked committing himself to paper.

'He's up to something,' he remarked to Frank as they made their way to the meeting together.

There were four or five there when they arrived, and about a dozen in all by the time Con Andrews decided to start. He had handed them an attendance sheet to be passed around among them for their signatures. Don Maguire, the radio producer, was the only one who was known to Frank but Morrissey recognized most of the others either as occasional contributors to the *Review*, or as prominent figures in the city's cultural and intellectual life. Among them were the veteran journalist Daragh McDowell, a man of dogged republican and working-class convictions, and Robin Mallinson, a playwright in the old Abbey Theatre who made a modest livelihood as a drama critic and a theatrical commentator and historian. Another was Art McWhinney, the poet and noted anti-cleric who, in spite of that, managed to cling to his weekly newspaper column and to secure occasional late-night poetry recitals on the radio which were listened to by almost no one.

Con Andrews began with a brief reference to the dropping of the "On The Side Of The Angels" series and the notice to that effect which a recent issue of the *Review* had carried. He had promised in that notice that it was only a pause for breath; the *Review* would be back in the arena for freedom of speech in no time at all. The type of action to be taken, he had concluded, should demonstrate not only intellectually but physically as well, that the *Review* would continue to stand for freedom of speech, freedom of thought, freedom of action. It should also emphasise the international nature of its reputation, its role in bringing to the world at large the work of Ireland's writers and artists. With these ambitious goals in mind he had consulted a number of contacts both nationally and internationally. One of these had been VOKS, the Soviet Union's official organisation for establishing cultural links with writers and artists of other countries. In approaching them he had been less than optimistic, but to his surprise they had expressed interest from the start and had now come up with a firm offer.

He paused to convey his sense of triumph to his now fully attentive audience.

'The offer, in general terms, is this,' he announced: 'VOKS are willing to finance a visit to the Soviet Union of representatives of the creative and cultural life of this country to meet writers and artists of the Soviet Union for an exchange of information and views. The visit will also involve extensive travel to see at first hand the Soviet way of life in all its variety. As editor of the *Review*, they've entrusted me with the selection of those who would be suitable and worthy. I am delighted to see that, with perhaps three or four exceptions, all of those I invited have turned up. Let me dispose of two matters which are bound to be raised. One: all expenses arising from the trip will be met totally by the host organization, and two: no strings whatever are attached, either political or ideological or of any other kind. During the coming couple of weeks or so, I intend to find time to meet each of you who may wish to take up the offer to brief you individually and in detail. In the meanwhile I am here to answer any questions you may wish to raise.'

There was a prolonged silence. Then Art McWhinney stood up. He was a small man, by nature disagreeable, half hidden under an enormous black hat and a black overcoat which reached below his knees.

'I rise to my feet,' he began, 'to point out to Con Andrews that it's easy enough for someone like him to talk glibly about free jaunts to forbidden places and to set up as the intrepid champion of progressive thought and attitudes. Con Andrews, as it happens, is the owner as well as the editor of the *Review*. In the end of all, he's his own boss and unlikely to consent to his own dismissal. But Art McWhinney is a stranger to so rare a luxury. If Art McWhinney dares to take a dander in the direction of atheistic Communism he's going to come back to find his weekly column in other hands and the radio studios bolted and barred for ever against any attempted re-entry. In other words, his livelihood will have been taken away from him. So Art McWhinney is now on his feet to let it be universally known that he won't be a candidate for any such excursion.' He sat down. Robin Mallinson rose immediately to indicate sympathy in his soft and cultivated accent.

'I must confess I appreciate Art's predicament very well,' he told the meeting. 'It is much the same as my own. If there were to be widespread public disapproval – and I fear very much that there might well be – then my livelihood as a freelance would be in peril too. Not all editors have the spunk and integrity of Con Andrews here. Most of them, I'm afraid, bend suppliant knees to popular pressure.'

He bowed courteously in Con Andrews' direction and sat down.

Daragh McDowell, his cheeks blazing, was on his feet like a shot. His principles were easily offended and his passions really inflamed. He was also, the meeting soon gathered, slightly pissed.

'By Christ, Con Andrews,' he bawled in a voice explosive with drink and outrage, 'I'm at a loss to understand how a man of courage and principle like yourself can sit at that table there listening without the bat of an eyelid to such abject poltroonery.'

'Now, now,' Con Andrews offered soothingly. 'We are all entitled to express a point of view.'

'We are entitled to a bit more than that,' Daragh McDowell bellowed back. 'We're entitled in a free country to entertain liberal ideas. And we're entitled as citizens of the same free country to travel where we like and come and go as we please. And we're entitled further to fight like bloody tigers if the time-servers and the crawthumpers dare to threaten to deprive us of our right to a livelihood. But what happens in reality? The first two responses we're offered come from this pair of abject cravens who vie with one another in grovelling—'

There were gasps of shock and someone shouted 'For shame' and Con Andrews held both arms aloft in an appeal for moderation. But the tone had been irretrievably set and the meeting staggered its way through a series of eruptions and angry exchanges.

When it was eventually declared adjourned, Maguire pushed his way across to them and said, 'For God's sake someone, suggest we bespeak potions.'

'I was about to do so,' Morrissey answered. 'Will you join us?'

'Whereabouts?' Frank asked. 'Muldowney's?'

'Not Muldowney's,' Maguire begged. 'Muldowney's will be bulging with ageing Thomists, all keeping themselves metaphysically fit. No place for exchanging views on what we have just heard.'

They found a place that was quiet and suitably off the beaten track. Maguire sampled his first drink and replaced it on the table.

'By God,' he exclaimed, expressing their unanimous thought, 'what an unbelievable opportunity.'

'Breathtaking,' Morrissey agreed. 'Imagine Moscow and the Kremlin and Lenin and Stalin embalmed and tarted up and lying side-by-side like stuffed saints in the shrine of all the Soviets. Imagine walking across Red Square and saying to yourself: Here I am in the Forbidden City.'

'I was thinking more of the Bolshoi Theatre,' Maguire said. 'I believe it has seven tiers of boxes all finished in gold. And the unsurpassable ballerinas, escorted exclusively by Five Star Generals.'

They became silent, their enthusiasm leaking away.

'Are you going to take up the offer?' Frank asked Maguire. But Maguire was suddenly deflated.

'I doubt I'd manage to get official approval.'

'Why should you need it? If we go in our own time who can object?'

'That's the first hurdle,' Maguire answered. 'Con Andrews mentioned during the meeting that the trip is likely to be arranged for either January or February. That would be outside the normal annual leave period. I'd have to make a special application for it and give a reason. A second is that for various situations and contingencies the radio staff are classified as being civil servants, with what is defined as permanent temporary status. This piece of Gilbertian town of Titipoo nonsense is designed to deny us the perks of the ordinary civil servant but to ensure that we are subject to all the usual civil service controls which, among other things, lay it down that a civil servant is not entirely free to dabble in politics or wander where he pleases – even in his own time. So, you see, it's by no means straightforward.'

Frank turned to Morrissey. 'How about you, Simon?'

'The truth is I suspect Art McWhinney's forecast of rabble rousing and reprisals may very well prove accurate, so, in all fairness, P.J. would have to be spoken to for a start,' Morrissey answered. 'He'd have the right to be put in the picture and to have his advice listened to. Like Don here, I can see aspects that demand closer exploration.' Then he put the question to Frank. 'And you?'

Frank was beginning to understand Daragh McDowell's sentiments. He hesitated for a moment to make up his mind.

'When you're speaking to P.J.,' he answered eventually, 'would you do me the favour of speaking for me also?'

'Certainly. If you'll let me know what I'm to say.'

'Tell him,' Frank said firmly, 'that I want to go.'

He wondered what Margaret would have to say to it, but she had no reservations other then a genuine anxiety for his safety.

'I don't want you ending up in the salt mines,' she told him, smiling uneasily. In spite of herself some such possibility lurked ineluctably at the back of her mind.

There was a side to the proposal which began to disturb him as he weighed its implications. It was the recollection, hazy and general in its nature, of the existence of some episcopal regulation which declared that dealings with communism in any shape or form were forbidden under pain of grave offence. It even pronounced it to be mortally sinful to keep communist literature in the house, regardless of whether one intended to read it or not. Margaret's recollection of the matter was as hazy as his own, but she agreed that the ruling had been as severe and comprehensive as that. He was considering the idea of going to Father McDermott for clarification, when Margaret thought of a more agreeable course of action. They were to call on the Coxes within a few days and could consult Lemuel about it. He had a comprehensive knowledge of such matters. It meant letting him know of the proposed trip but that could be done without hesitation. His discretion was unimpeachable.

His first reaction, much to Frank's surprise, was one of astonishment and even envy.

'What a wonderful opportunity,' he exclaimed. As for the regulation, he had a recollection of the one Frank referred to. His memory of it was that it applied only in the diocese of Dublin, but he could find out all the details.

These regulations and restrictions were seldom as intractable close up as they appeared to be from a distance. The public press

usually dramatized their severity when reporting them. He undertook to get authoritative advice. It was readily accessible to him.
Another side of the matter attracted comment from him.

'Your concern for such rules and regulations surprises me,' he
said.

'Why should it surprise you?' Frank wondered.

'I had believed young people nowadays were not greatly
influenced by them. Obviously you sincerely are.'

'I try to abide by them,' Frank confessed. 'Needless to say I don't
always succeed.'

'Nor do I,' Lemuel admitted. 'But my father did. Most rigorously.
He accepted unquestionably, down to every last comma and full
stop, the teaching authority of the Church. Even at this distance his
perserverence astonishes me.'

P.J. came very quickly to the conclusion that the idea of Simon
Morrissey participating in the Russian trip was unthinkable. His
position as partner in the firm would ensure considerable damage to
it in the event of public condemnation. In the case of Frank
McDonagh he was not quite so intransigent. Granting him annual
leave in January or February would appear odd and might be
construed as aiding and abetting. But that could be got around by
taking care not to know the specific reason. He had no desire to
claim the right to control what an employee did with his own leisure
time, or to seem to seek to regulate his comings and goings. In fact
to attempt to do so might give rise to resentment and protest. But if
McDonagh chose to go on the trip and ran into serious public
odium on his return, then he might find himself having to look for
employment elsewhere.

Morrissey said nothing. He believed things were unlikely to
become as serious as that. If they did he could consider his own
response when he was in a position to weigh the various rami-
fications.

'Tell him,' P.J. decided finally, 'if he finds it necessary to apply for
early leave, to put it down to unspecified personal business. Tell him
on no account do I wish to be told its nature.'

Lemuel came back around the same time with word of the
response he had got as a result of his consultation with a
representative of exalted episcopal authority. It was remarkably
brief and detached: if the nature of the proposed trip had been
truthfully and accurately presented by the inquirer, then it was
permissable for the inquirer to act in accordance with his
conscience. There need be no compunction, provided the utmost
prudence was observed.

Chapter 22

The trip was fixed for the beginning of January. A brief phone call from Con Andrews transformed it suddenly from figment to fact and set in motion a flurry of preparation. P.J.'s consent to early holiday leave had to be applied for. It was given. His note conveying his consent was devious. The request, it said, appeared to arise out of private and personal reasons which he had no desire to pry into. He was satisfied to accommodate the request on compassionate grounds.

Con Andrews gave him the name of a lady he was required to meet and the hotel and the time of day at which he would find her. She would be wearing a grey costume and navy beret and would be holding a black and white striped handbag on her knee. It sounded sufficiently conspiratorial to cause him unease but she turned out to be elderly and pleasant and, apart from giving him useful information regarding suitable clothing and the amount of money he would be allowed to take with him, the only request she made was for eight to ten passport-type photographs which should be given into her possession at a further meeting for some purpose which she left unspecified.

He told Ernie Jackson what was afoot. He thought it would be unfair to leave him to find out for himself. He also let Milly Downey know. He felt he might as well. She and Jackson had just got engaged and she was bound to be told anyway. The offices of Kenny, Morrissey and Co., Publishing, Editorial and Advertising Services, throbbed at the proximity of international intrigue.

'Jesus, Mary and Joseph,' Miss Downey blurted out in fright, 'have you taken leave of your senses?'

Ernie Jackson spoke soothingly to her before offering solemn advice. He warned Frank that he was being made use of. In the

Soviet Union, by all accounts, there was little regard wasted on such decadent notions as the free exchange of ideas. The visit would be represented as a sign of widespread intellectual and artistic approval for the totalitarian system.

Morrissey pretended total ignorance of the matter but kept secretly in touch with developments. P.J. held genuinely aloof. He attended to the customary courtesies of the Christmas season: compiling the list of those clients who were to get Christmas cards; those other, more influential ones, who were to receive more tangible acknowledgement in the form of boxes of cigarettes or cigars, bottles of whiskey or brandy and, for the few whose tastes were known to lie in that direction, stand tickets for the Christmas week race meetings at Leopardstown.

He departed from the Christmas routine in one matter only. Instead of the usual office get-together he laid on food in addition to the drinks for the annual party, and hired a vocalist and a small musical ensemble which entertained in between times. In his customary speech to the invited clients he explained that these little additions were to mark the descent of the gracious goddess of romance into the sober precinct of Kenny, Morrissey & Company. He was requesting them, he continued, to raise their glasses in honour of the engagement of Miss Downey and Ernest Jackson or, in the more affectionate and informal day-to-day usage of the Kenny Morrissey office, to toast to the happiness of Milly and Ernie, two loyal colleagues and valued friends. When the applause had continued for the requisite length of time, he signalled to the musicians who struck up *For They Are Jolly Good Fellows*. The guests formed a ring about the happy pair and joined hands as they circled and sang. Ernest grinned hideously and looked embarrassed but Milly, hardly realizing she was doing so, shed tears of happiness and gratitude.

Then the twelve days of Christmas were upon them and passed in a dreamlike state: out of focus most of the time and oddly unreal. With Margaret he went through their financial situation closely. It was reasonably adequate. He would not be allowed to take very much with him to Moscow anyway. Margaret insisted he could afford a new suit for the trip. He could do with one, and his good one at the moment was simply not good enough (she decided) for mixing with foreign artists and intellectuals. There were so many more difficult matters to be considered that he bought another to please her.

Hints of the proposed journey began to trickle into the daily papers: speculative and inaccurate, with no names named as yet but intriguing enough to crop up in conversations at the Christmas parties they attended. They sat with poker faces through one such discussion at a party given by Penny to entertain Simon's friends and business associates. There was a more embarrassing occasion at Margaret's own get-together. Maeve and Peter and Teresa and John were among the guests when the subject arose, and the guests began to speculate if it could be true and who were likely to be involved. Margaret had to remember some overlooked business in the kitchen that required Frank's urgent attention.

At Lemuel's specific request they visited Avonmore in the company of Penny and Simon. Here the subject of the trip could be explored openly and dealt with in a realistic and dispassionate way, which was welcome and reassuring.

'One thing is clear,' Lemuel decided. 'They haven't unearthed any names as yet, which is fortunate. Not having names will cripple their ability to stir up a hullabaloo.'

'We can thank the Christmas season for that,' Simon agreed. 'It cuts off the O'Hallorans among us from their sources.'

'Let's hope it continues like that until you're already well on your way,' Lemuel said to Frank.

Simon Morrissey agreed again. He extended two fingers to the surface of the table and pressed firmly.

'Touch wood,' he declared.

Ballcock Brady hinted at knowing something already. He had put a letter together demanding for his constituents extensions and improvements to the government's Free Winter Fuel Scheme for the Poor, and sought Frank's help in eliminating any errors. When it had been attended to and his gratitude expressed, he put the corrected pages in his pocket and assumed a deeply concerned expression.

'Have you been reading the reports of some excursion or other to Russia and the Iron Curtain?' he asked.

'I've seen them – yes,' Frank said.

'Have you any idea who may be going?'

'If I had,' Frank answered, 'I'd decline to discuss it. It's none of my business.'

'I've been given some information myself,' Ballcock confided, looking at him pointedly, 'but I find it difficult to believe—'

'Whatever it may be,' Frank said abruptly, 'I have no wish to be told.'

Late on the eve of his departure, when both he and Margaret were already in bed, the telephone rang. Margaret was jerked back from the threshold of sleep and sat up in fright.

'Ignore it,' she urged. It was loud and menacing. But he took his dressing gown from the wardrobe.

'I don't think that would be wise,' he told her.

It was Simon Morrissey, who apologized for the lateness of the hour.

'I felt it was important to contact you,' he said. 'I've had a call from Bill Keating in traffic control out at the airport. He's the friend I told you I asked to keep eyes and ears open for us.'

'I remember,' Frank said.

'He advises you to switch to an earlier flight tomorrow. For two reasons: one is that there is heavy icing on the runways in London and the weather forecasts for tomorrow are not good. Cancellations are likely to leave full loads for the later flights. The second is that the press seem to have got word that tomorrow is the departure day for the Moscow jaunt and have been pestering them for information. There's an earlier flight at eight o'clock. It can be arranged for you to travel on that. The press won't expect you to do so because it's a freight plane. He can arrange it. What do you think?'

'I'd like him to do so. Very much. How can I contact him?'

'You don't have to. I'll do it for you. Just ask for him when you get out there in the morning. But be there early.'

'I'm very grateful.'

'Now try to get some sleep,' Simon Morrissey advised. He replaced the receiver.

While he was adjusting the bedside alarm clock he told Margaret.

'That was very kind of him. Very kind indeed.' He kissed her and lay back.

'Simon Morrissey,' she said again, her voice low and grateful in the silence and darkness, 'is a true friend.'

'We'll try to sleep a bit,' he suggested gently.

There were only two other passengers on the freight plane; three if he counted the unknown corpse in the coffin which occupied the aisle. Below him the fields of England spread themselves in snowladen misery. London airport was forlorn under its burden of fog and ice. He had a wait of nearly two hours there for the bus which got him eventually to Waterloo with much braking and crawling through a chaos of traffic. When he had checked in at his hotel and the receptionist was handing him over his key, she asked him to wait a moment while she consulted a list that was pinned to the notice-board behind her.

'Mr McDonagh,' she told him when she had done so. 'I have a message here from a Mr Daragh McDowell to pass on and your name is included. He wishes you to telephone him as soon as you arrive. Shall I try his room for you?'

'Please do.' But though she persisted for some time there was no answer.

He unpacked only what was essential, then stretched out on the bed to rest and await developments. He was glad to be there ahead of the others. It allowed him time to compose himself. The room was warm. He removed only his shoes and drew the coverlet about him and soon began to doze. The room and its furnishing melted gradually away and he was looking down once again on mile after mile of snowladen fields. The pounding of engines sounded remotely in his ears. At a distance from him, a solitary coffin manifested itself dimly from time to time in a limbo of its own.

It was the telephone which jerked him back to his surroundings. It shrilled loudly by the bedside and brought his hand groping out in panic to grab it from its cradle. He recognized the voice immediately.

'Have I Francis McDonagh?' it demanded.

'You have.'

'This is Daragh McDowell. Are you long here?'

'I'm not sure. I fell asleep—'

'Then you'd better wake up and get down to me here double quick. I'm in the bar.'

'Hold on a minute. What's the matter, may I ask?'

'I'll tell you what's the matter,' Daragh McDowell said, roaring so hard into the mouthpiece that Frank had to jerk it hastily away from his ear, 'every fucking thing – that's what's the matter. I'm just back from the Soviet Embassy. The trip is off.' The phone was slapped back on its cradle.

Frank splashed his face with cold water to drive away the heaviness that still pressed on his eyes and head, and hastened downstairs. It was nearly three o'clock. He had slept longer than he thought. As he had done so the others had been arriving. At the bar he found they had already retired to McDowell's bedroom to hold a meeting. The message instructed him to follow.

There were six of them, including McDowell who came across to make the curtest of introductions. The room was enveloped already in a haze of cigarette smoke when he stood up to speak. It seemed

McDowell had gone to the Soviety Embassy to collect his tickets and discovered that the free travel arrangement only applied from Prague onwards — they would have to pay their own fares from London to there at a cost of about £60 each. The informant was the First Secretary. McDowell had told him plainly that he was only an impoverished pen pusher who had no means whatever of raising so large a sum at short notice. He had been told in Dublin that they would travel at the expense of VOKS from London. The First Secretary expressed sympathy. He regretted the misunderstanding. It was quite unfortunate. But it was a question of foreign currency and there was nothing he could do. Moscow was adamant that foreign currency was to be expended on nothing that was not strictly essential. From Prague onwards there would be no restrictions. Once in the Soviet Union all expenses would be met. They would be looked after in every respect. More than merely looked after; they would be treated most lavishly.

They listened in silence and horror until he finished, then began a discussion which they soon recognized to be futile. In the end they travelled in a group to Kensington Palace Gardens where the First Secretary consented to see them again. He was courteous but still immovable. There was nothing the Embassy could do. Currency policy was outside its powers. But he yielded to the extent of agreeing to telephone Moscow on the following morning and to contact McDowell at the hotel to convey the result. He would do his best. But he was not hopeful.

They returned and kept the hotel switchboard busy with their telephone calls. Frank managed to contact Margaret who told him that the news of their departure and a list of their names were now public.

'An hour or so ago Teresa and John telephoned,' she said. 'They have the *Sentinel* delivered to them regularly and this week it is all on the front page: your names, what you do for a livelihood, the name of the hotel you're all staying in. Teresa read it out to me. It's Irish Catholic ranting at its inelegant worst. Quite frightening.'

'Did you get a copy? Can you read it over to me?'

'No. I haven't had time yet—'

'Never mind. I'll get it later. There's bound to be a newsagent somewhere in London that stocks it. How did Teresa take it? Her own religious views are pretty hidebound, aren't they?'

'She took it very well. John too. He was on the phone after her and spoke in the kindest way to me. I was very relieved.'

'Good. I'll phone again tomorrow to let you know how things are.'

'Be careful,' she begged him. 'Don't get angry. Keep a cool head.'

'Don't worry,' he assured her. 'I'll be a rock of sense.'

Throughout the following day, and despite his promise, there was no word at all from the First Secretary, nor was he contactable at the Embassy although they attempted it almost hourly. But the next day, around noon, he redeemed himself. There was a ship – The Beloostrov – which was kept in commission mainly for the convenience of diplomatic staff travelling back to the homeland with their household effects, and took a few paying passengers from time to time. It would be leaving on its last trip before the ice closed. The single third-class fare would be around £14. He could arrange to have a courier from the Consulate bring their passports direct to the ship, and furnished the name of the shipping agency where their passage could be booked. The ship, he informed them, could be boarded via the Swedish Entrance, No. 9 shed, Surrey Dock. He hoped this would resolve the difficulty.

They held yet another meeting. The fare would make a hole in their spending money but it was more realistic. Stephen Barlow, who was from Northern Ireland and had his British cheque book with him, offered to withdraw the necessary cash to lend the fare to anyone who was short until they were able to repay it on their return.

Frank managed to phone Margaret briefly with the news. She said it was great that things had worked out after all. But he caught little hint of delight in the voice that came to him over the line. It was small, tremulous, anxious.

'I'll write at the earliest,' he promised. 'Try not to worry. There isn't any need.'

The others had assembled in the foyer. He could see them through the glass panel of the kiosk.

'The rest are waiting,' he told her, 'and I must go. Goodbye, my darling. All my love.'

'Me, too,' she answered and he knew from the pitch of her voice that she was in tears. 'Be terribly careful.'

He joined with the rest in a chase to the bank, then to the shipping agent's office, then a wild drive along the India Dock Road – or what he guessed to be the India Dock Road. They joined the ship around five o'clock. The Soviet Consul had come personally to see them off and their passports were there in readiness as he had promised. It was already dark. He was waiting for them in the large and draughty loading shed which was cold, ill lit, depressing. But when the preliminaries had been attended to and he led them aboard the ship, a small, 3,000 ton carrier of both cargo and passengers, it was pleasantly warm and comfortable. They found their cabins and settled in quickly. Frank, before going to sleep, fulfilled his promise to write. How he would post the letter he had no notion.

SS Beloostrov
Friday 7th

Dear Margaret,

I can't even start to tell you of the confusion which has finally resolved itself, ranging from taxi rushes across London to a comfortable cabin on the above from which I write. We boarded about half five, and around eight o'clock, as we moved off, we gathered on deck to watch the lights of London port gliding past us in the wintry darkness. After that we were served dinner, which was very good indeed although after the happenings of the last few days I wasn't really in shape to do it justice. It is now after ten and we are still moving down the Thames. The ship has taken on the purposeful movement of a thing that is certain of its direction, and I feel at last we are really and truly on our way. I hope it won't be too rough when we reach open sea. Our final destination is still uncertain and depends on what routes the closing ice continues to leave – Riga and Leningrad seem to be among the most favoured.

I'm sharing this cabin with Stephen Barlow, who is still above on deck but is likely to come below pretty soon. It is small enough but very cosy: two neat tubular beds, a small desk (I'm using it now), hot and cold water for handbasin and shower and a very clever rack arrangement for one's clothes. There is a notice for its inmates on the back of the door which amuses me. It reads:

Passenger No. 56/57
Your lifeboat is No. 4 on the portside
Your lifejacket is keeping in the case.

It's very quiet in here, with the throb of the engines a mere ghost of a sound and the muted slapping of water against the portholes soothing and companionable. Later, when I'm lying in my bunk in the darkness, it will be a lullaby to woo me to sleep. The lid of the porthole has not yet been clamped down for the night, and whenever I look out through it there's a light from somewhere above on the deck which is reflected in the heaving water and paces us mile by mile, a sort of maritime will-o'-the-wisp intent on leading poor sailors astray. I am unconcerned about it. Isn't my lifeboat *number four on the portside, all in readiness and my lifejacket keeping in the case!*

Stephen has just come in and I will close because he'll be waiting to go to bed and, indeed, my own weary eyes are telling me that the sandman is on his way. Give my regards and compliments to dear Mrs Cleary. My love to Paul and Aoife and your dearest self. I'll write soon again, and I may also keep a diary of events if I can find the paper and the time. Peace on thine eyes, sleep on thy breast; would I were sleep and peace

> *So sweet to rest—*
> *Love,*
> *Frank*

Lemuel became aware of the *Sentinel* story a couple of days later than Margaret when his weekly copy came in the post. The banner caption leaped out at him from its front page. Never before had he known it to carry so large a headline. He read the text beneath it with mounting horror.

The Sentinel
This Moscow Jaunt – Your Duty

Well, it has happened and it's not much consolation that we were first with the news. Already the daily press has announced – and practically *acclaimed* – the departure of an Irish 'delegation' to Russia. We can now reveal the names:

Daragh McDowell: journalist and part-time poet, well noted for entertaining rabid republican and socialist views.

Terence Trimble: composer and performer of music.

Frances McDonagh: a cartoonist with Kenny, Morrisey & Co. and a recent contributor of controversial material to the *Review*. The editor of the *Review* is the well-known Cornelius Andrews.

Aengus Lovatt: described as a sculptor.

Stephen Barlow: playwright and drama critic from Northern Ireland.

James Scully: occasional short-story writer. Better known as an official of the Irish Union of Clerical Workers and Shop Assistants.

And one *Oliver Grendall*: whose grounds for claim to artistic and/or intellectual eminence remain obscure at present.

Our duty henceforward will be to follow this deplorable business closely. And you? What Can *You* Do?

See your Urban Councillor, your County Councillor, your local representative of whatever party. Have resolutions passed. Make it clear that this self-styled 'delegation' does not represent you and that you do not wish to be associated with it. If Ireland's voice be loud enough, it will be heard. Even behind the Iron Curtain.

He showed it to Stella who was concerned immediately about Margaret and suggested he should telephone her. He found her deeply upset.

'What horrifies me,' she confessed, 'is that they should publish his place of employment. I can't see what that can possibly have to do with it.'

'It is a time honoured trick in the art of intimidation,' he told her, 'which often enough misfires and does greater harm to the aggressor than to its intended victim.'

'What can we do?'

'For the moment, nothing. Keep silent and let it expend itself. It may not develop.' But it did.

The Country Gives Its Verdict

So numerous were the resolutions of protest which reached us from every corner of the country regarding the guests in Moscow that it would be impossible to give a complete list of them, but here are a few quotations which are not meant to be comprehensive, but rather illustrative:

The Defender: 'If there was any evidence of a change of heart towards Christianity in the Soviet Union we might be able to ponder a little further over the question. But the prison gates have not yet been thrown open. The same anti-God, anti-social, anti-liberty line is followed, a pattern which is so repulsive to our way of living.'

The Illuminator: 'What will the Chinese and the Koreans, who have known only the sublime heroism of Irish missionaries in the face of Communist terror in their countries think of the only Ireland they ever knew? Some of them will not be duped, but thousands, indeed millions of them may.'

The Ballymahon Herald: 'Our corporation registers the opinion that this Christian nation repudiates the idea that the Irish delegation visiting unrepenting persecutors is representative of Irish opinion.'

Councillor Patrick O'Grohan: 'The heads of the Soviet States this delegation proposes to visit have their hands dripping with the blood of the Hierarchy and clergy of their own country . . .'

Councillor Peter Mahone: 'They will only see what is prepared for them by the Communists . . .'
Councillor Nora Creenagh: 'The latest manoeuvre in Soviet propaganda is the indirect method of organised tours of selected persons into the Communist "paradise". The selected persons usually fall under three types: the 'arty' type, whose emotions are unrestrained by reason; the woolly-headed politician; and the broad, tolerant "litterateur"; who can tolerate anything except Christian principles . . .'

SS Beloostrov
Tuesday 11th

Dear Margaret,

When I wrote to you a couple of days ago we had entered the Kiel Canal and encountered our first patches of ice floating on the water. The country on either side was very flat with drains and landlocked water areas frozen solid, but it became hilly later with belts of fir trees to break the monotony. At one a solitary German soldier was pacing up and down, miles from nowhere it seemed, guarding something or other and looking lost and lonely but very soldierly in his fur hat and long, bright green greatcoat. Up to now it has been a risky business to walk on the open deck because of the ice which forms so thickly on it with nightfall. Snow fell in sudden squalls throughout the past couple of days and the world of water about us was bleak and dismal.

Now we are within an hour or so of docking at Stockholm (at twelve noon) and we have been steaming past a series of inlets which present a picture-postcard Sweden at what must be its loveliest – calm water with the sun shining on it and the sky brilliantly blue, and on either side snow-covered hillocks which run down steeply into the water. Fir trees cover every inch of ground except where clearings have been made for houses. It seems the well-to-do classes of Sweden use these as summer houses. If so, there must be a plentiful supply of the well-to-do because there are hundreds of these villas all nestling in among the trees.

Last night it was very rough with the ship plunging and bucking up all over the place. One bad sideslip broke about six glasses in the bar, including one belonging to me with a precious measure of whiskey in it that I hadn't yet touched.

When we ventured outside it was wild and cold. The snow was powdery and came in gusts (it put me in mind of scenes from that marvellous film we saw – Scott of the Antarctic, you remember?).

There's a little boy aboard, younger than Paul, who is called Mischa. He was in the lounge last night and Stephen Barlow and I played that game with him that we play with our own kids at home – the one where the child puts his hand on the table and Stephen puts his on top and I put mine on top of that and the kid puts his on top and so on and the game gets quicker and quicker all the time. The youngster had never played it before and didn't want to stop. But then he brought his toy motors up and started running them on the table. They were like Paul's and made a whining noise when you scrubbed the wheels against a surface. As I listened to the familiar racket I became very sad indeed. Then Terry Trimble – he's the young composer and pianist who reminds me of what Percy Granger is reported to have been like, all high spirits and high jinks – Terry began doing his tricks: putting pennies in his mouth and taking them out again through his ears and so on. The youngster was enchanted. Terry goes in a bit for hypnotism as well. While we were hanging around doing nothing yesterday I offered myself as a subject and it actually worked. These are the little sideshows that help to pass the time.

I'm wondering did you get my earlier letter, the one I wrote to you on our first night abroad? At the time I'd no idea how it was to be posted but two days later, as we were passing through the canal, word went around that there would be a stop for some formalities that night at the city of Kiel and I could post it if I looked snappy about it. When we docked in due course I looked among my things for the letter but couldn't find it. It wasn't in my pocket, it wasn't in my cabin, it wasn't in my case. I thought I might have let it fall in the bar and searched there – but no. Then I began to turn the lounge upside down without success when a thought sent me over to the piano. I'd been doodling at it on and off. The lid was closed on the keys and I lifted it open and there, sitting neatly at the treble end of the keyboard, was the bloody letter. I had only picked it up when I became aware of a throbbing and a faint sense of movement and looked out to see the lights of the city sliding silently past.

Daragh McDowell joined me when I stepped out on deck so I told him my tale of woe. He was making sympathetic noises when a thought struck him. We were still in the harbour, but beating steadily for the open sea. The thought was that we might still have a pilot abroad. It turned out that we had. We found him on the bridge with the captain and other crew members. It was very dark and they were very busy and there was this feeling of mystery and unreality In a broad sweep on either side of us were the lights of Kiel. A sharp seawind was raking the bridge and the ridges of the waves were showing white in the sweeping arc of a lighthouse. The pilot was huge, middle-aged and German, a mysterious figure outlined in the darkness and surrounded by equally mysterious Russian forms. When we had managed to communicate our request and I held out the letter to him with a coin to cover the postage, he accepted it but waved the coin aside. He undertook to post it that night when the pilot tender returned him. He was polite, gentlemanly and kind. It struck me as a good omen for what might be ahead and I cheered up in response to it.

And now an important piece of information: I understand you can write to me in Moscow by addressing the letter like this:

> Francis McDonagh
> c/o Moscow – VOKS
> USSR

If you don't care to write because of possible repercussions, I will quite understand. You may decide it would be wiser to avoid drawing more attention than the matter is already receiving. Meanwhile, if the newspapers start to badger you for information about me tell them you know nothing except that I am on my way. Also Daragh McDowell advises against talking to friends about it on the telephone because our phone is likely to be tapped – the excuse being national security! However crazy that may sound he was serious about it and I'd pay attention to him. He's a veteran journalist who knows what he is talking about.

I will write soon again. The deepest love of my heart goes with this to the children and your dear self.

> God bless you all,
> Frank

To: The Editor
The Sentinel
Sir,

What is going wrong with the decent Godfearing people of this country? A year or two ago it was our fashion to hunt the suspected communist in whatever field he operated. In the field of entertainment alone we prevented Gregory Peck from visiting our Catholic stage guild, bidding him to stay where he was, or else. . . ! We went after Danny Kaye and Larry Adler. We mobbed the Gate Theatre for harbouring Orson Welles. We distributed leaflets outside the Gaiety Theatre warning patrons that Arthur Miller's Death of a

Salesman *was cunningly concealed communist propaganda. We fought the suspected communist wherever we found him.*

But what is the situation today? Already we have a so-called 'delegation' gallivanting behind the Iron Curtain spreading God knows what lies and misrepresentation in our name. Who let them go? Why were they not prevented? Who stamped their passports for them? The Minister for External Affairs must be made to answer. He has evaded the matter so far.

Now we are being told that another real-life, self-confessed, dyed-in-the-wool communist is about to be allowed to come among us to use our Gaiety Theatre to stage the first production of his new play. I refer to the infamous Sean O'Casey, vilifier of this, his native country, and the faith of its people. Who is responsible for allowing this loud-mouthed defamer the hospitality of our leading theatre? The very title of the play, The Bishop's Bonfire, *is ominous. Is this, one must ask, to be more of his blasphemy?*

Outraged

P.J. phoned Simon to ask him if he had seen it. Simon had.

'Perhaps it will switch some of the heat away from the travellers and on to O'Casey,' Simon suggested. 'If it does there won't be an empty seat in the theatre for weeks.'

'By Christ,' P.J. swore, 'but there's plenty of heat and to spare. Every bloody county council in the country has passed resolutions calling for vengeance.'

Simon maintained a prudent silence. P.J. reflected briefly.

'What gets to me,' he added, 'is those other bastards who identified Kenny, Morrissey and Co. as McDonagh's workplace. That's not calculated to earn us the nation's applause.'

'People forget very quickly,' Simon soothed.

'In my arse they do,' P.J. answered. He slammed down the phone. Con Andrews took a hand and tried to put the record straight with the press:

Dear Sir,

In last Monday's issue under the heading 'Irish Delegates to Visit Russia' you state that five members of the Irish-Soviet Friendship Society are leaving on the visit. This is incorrect. As the one who arranged the visit I know that there are seven people going, none of whom has any connection whatsoever with the Irish-Soviet Society. Neither is the group in any sense a 'delegation'.

Although I wrote to you in correction of a similar report which had appeared a week ago, you have repeated the mis-statement, and I must ask you to be good enough to make a prominent correction now. In its published form the report is misleading and misrepresents the situation to the public mind.

Yours etc,
Con Andrews
Editor: The Review.

He was generally ignored.

Diary: Thursday January 13th
Around six o'clock this evening we docked at Riga and left SS Beloostrov behind, presumably forever. It will remain always a memory of long, carpeted corridors so silent and empty most of the time, with a line of small electric bulbs running down the centre of each and the cabin doors in numbered sequence on either side; a small, sturdy, protective seafarer.

At Riga the ice had closed, but not so inhospitably that it was beyond the powers of the icebreaker to put matters right. Through broken blocks of ice which clumped alarmingly against her bow and sides, we pushed resolutely towards our berthing place. The sky was dismal beyond description, a multitude of chimneys belched smoke into a leaden sky, the land on either side lay flat and snowbound, here and there a small craft lay locked in the ice as though someone had decided in a moment of sudden melancholy that it was not worth shifting to safety. It took us almost an hour at a dead slow pace to reach the quayside, where a loudspeaker was blaring away in Russian at no one in particular, and a fur-hatted sentry with fixed bayonet paced up and down in front of the custom sheds. Although the scene disappeared at times behind sudden flurries of snow, we could make out the small group of figures beside three parked cars and guessed rightly that here at last was VOKS. Behind them a line of warehouses and the lighted clock in its centre were being slowly obliterated by the gathering dusk.

From the cars the streets looked equally cheerless. They were crowded with people, black-coated, hurrying figures against the white snow, presumably on their way from work. The public lighting was poor; there were long and not very orderly queues for public transport. We passed a courtyard on our left with a huge poster of Stalin adorning its centre wall and smaller ones of him filling every available inch of the others.

Later, in a quite beautiful house we met the Deputy Minister for Culture and other dignitaries and sat down to a meal which banished the wintry gloom of the streets and turned into a gay and most hospitable affair; the superb food being accompanied by liberal measures of wine and cognac to add to its magnificence.

Then to the train at nine o'clock. A busy station with activity everywhere, which included peasants sitting about and guarding their bundles with practised patience, and a knot of drunken soldiery having what sounded like angry words with some station officials. Here we board the night train to Moscow and are allocated our sleepers. They are ornate and old-fashioned with odd patterns incised on every available inch of their glass panelling, and a Heath Robinson device for operating a handbasin. The aristocracy they were designed to serve passed away with the revolution. Meanwhile we have learned that Moscow is still twenty-seven hours away. Tomorrow will be another lost day.

Diary: January 14th
Last night we lay awake for much of the time, rolling and bumping through the first stages of our twenty-seven-hour journey while the old-fashioned sleeper creaked and groaned and the train travelled at about twenty-five miles an hour. Throughout the darkness it stopped several times while one was aware, as in a prolonged dream, of lanterns swinging past the windows and people tapping the wheels and clearing the snow. There was no dining car. In the morning we breakfasted on mineral water, cum cognac, caviar and bread, which our guides had brought. It is not ideal fare on which to face the newborn day. Outside, the countryside rolled past; the flat, snowbound plains of a vast country in which little settlements of wooden houses appeared for a moment and were succeeded by more and even flatter snow. At times the monotony was broken by a stretch of forest, or by a passing trapper with snowshoes and knapsack. We were elated by the sight of our first droshky, and then forgot our elation in the renewed, endless terrain of snow and flatness. At occasional stations women in padded jackets and thick gloves came along with oil cans and hammers to minister to the wheels. We alighted only once to stand for a while gulping air which although freezing was at least fresh, but the ordeal of remounting by way of iron steps which were treacherous with solid ice discouraged any repetition of an ambush of the healthy out-of-doors. So it went on, hour after hour of it, until at last, around twelve midnight, the lights of Moscow began to slide in procession past our windows and in due course we were being greeted by a party of officials all identical in fur hats and long, black coats.

Another excellent meal in Hotel National and we were shown to our rooms. After nine days in cabins and carriages it is nice to have a bedroom once again, not only a bedroom but a substantial sitting-room and toilet and bathroom ensuite. A while ago I put out the light for some moments while I went over to stare through the large, double-glazed windows at Revolution Square, silent and snow-bound below me. Through a narrow street at the far side I could see Red Square and the Church of Saint Basil. Lights were still burning in some of the windows of the Kremlin opposite. On one of its towers high above the lights of the square and the snow which was once again silently falling, a Red Star blazed.

Diary: *January 15th*
This morning we were conducted around the sights of Moscow, but again snow came down heavily and it was very difficult to see anything at all. However, this afternoon we had a long conference at VOKS HQ at which we were asked to select our preferences for things to see and do from a list of organisations and activities. We made our choice and, whatever else, we are certainly going to be kept busy. Tomorrow – Sunday – some of us who requested it are to be brought to Mass in the Roman Catholic Church of Saint Ludovic, mainly an immigrant Polish community (we are told) but with some Russians. It also seems that we will travel to Georgia and stay for a few days in Tbilisi, and also visit towns near at hand. Leningrad is to be included as well so we will be traipsing far and wide indeed. To my surprise, some post from home was waiting for us when we arrived last night, including a very welcome letter from Margaret. She doesn't say so specifically, but I can guess from what it does not say that there's a bit of a hullabaloo going on in the fair isle of Erin; a bridge to cross when we come to it.

Thursday 13th

Dear Frank,
   It was heavenly to get your two letters this morning. The cards from Stockholm were beautiful – the children are very pleased with them. You know, I had visions of you battling in a blizzard up the Baltic in an old tub of a boat (and you in your new suit!) so it was lovely to know all about it. I am glad you went by boat. It's much nicer touching all the different places, and Stockholm must have been exciting to see.
   I wish you could waft some of that vodka to here – I need it. Everything goes on as usual humdrum, except that it's miserable

without you. And to make it worse the last few days have been desperately cold – frost and ice everywhere. There have been some repercussions about the trip, but I don't worry about anything. Lemuel Cox has been very caring, phoning me every other day to know if there is any news from you and conveying Stella's concern also. Teresa and John called to see me and brought their welcome in a couple of bottles to cheer me up. She's expecting again, their fifth. But though she and John are struggling most of the time to make ends meet they have their simple and sincere faith in God's Providence which, however simple-minded it seems to be, you have to admire. Maeve and Peter are calling for a confab tomorrow night. I'm dying to see (and hear!) her reaction to the news about Teresa.

Paul, I think, has grasped the situation but Aoife doesn't seem to understand you being away because every night she says, 'Let me stay up until Daddy comes home'. A long wait!

You mention your boat is the last before it freezes so I hope that means you'll return by plane, because it would be dreadful if another week was added on at the end. I don't want to write too much in case this letter never gets to you, but if you do get a chance to phone, do so be it midnight or a.m. or anything. I love you, darling, take care of yourself.

    Margaret

Diary: *January 16th*
Today we were brought to Mass in the Church of Saint Ludovic, a Roman Catholic one as we had requested. It is in the Malaya-Lubianka area, in the middle of a mainly Polish quarter, with Father Butovorich, a Polish priest, in charge. Roman Catholic churches are not so easy to find: since the eleventh century the prevailing religion has been Eastern Orthodox, at least up to the post-revolutionary years. The ritual of the Mass was exactly the same as at home and I recognized the Gospel right away and could follow the Latin with ease: 'In illo tempore: Nuptiae factae sunt in Cana Galilaeae: et erat mater Jesu ibi. Vocatus est autem et Jesus, et discipuli ejus, ad nuptias . . . (At that time: There was a marriage in Cana of Galilee: and the mother of Jesus was there. And Jesus also was invited, and his disciples, to the marriage). Daragh McDowell was kneeling beside me and I asked him if he recognized the gospel and he said of course he did.

Then I remarked to him, 'I find it a relief to understand what is being said. It makes a welcome change.'

'Yes indeed,' he agreed. A moment later he touched me on the sleeve to draw my closer attention.

'Do you know what,' he said very softly, 'you've just given me an idea.'

I wondered what it could be, then directed my attention back to where it should have been – on the Mass.

It was a pleasantly appointed church in the main, with the exception of the music gallery where a harmonium substituted for a church organ. The choir consisted of four or five middle-aged ladies. At the treble end of the harmonium the lady playing it had placed a quite conventional alarm clock, complete with alarm bell and striker. She probably used it to ensure that the musical interludes were kept within reasonable limits. As it was, the proceedings occupied one whole hour and a half, but mainly because Father Butovorich gave a long sermon in Polish and then went on to repeat it in Russian.

Afterwards we were brought in to the vestry to meet him. The interview was, of course, conducted through the interpreters: Father Butovorich speaking in Russian and they translating into English. He told us that the name of the area, when translated, meant 'The little district of the makers of the wooden shoes', which I found amusing but also oddly moving. He told us he had no contact with Rome because there are no diplomatic relations, but his bishop is Peteris Strods of Latvia who attended the Peace Convention of Religions in the Soviet Union. When we congratulated him on his packed church he told us there was an earlier Mass and communion that morning at eight o'clock for the children.

At this point Daragh McDowell threw the interpreters into a spin by suddenly addressing the priest in Latin. I knew then the nature of the idea I had inspired when I spoke to him of understanding all that went on during the celebration of the Mass. After some initial surprise and a questioning glance at the interpreters, who obviously had no Latin and had not yet worked out how they should cope, he began to answer in Latin. However, no great secrets were revealed. To Daragh's first question he said no, he had no grant or aid of any kind from the Government. They had complete freedom to practise their faith. There were indeed some difficulties such as the unavailability of missals and books of religious instruction, and devotional items such as prayer books and rosary beads. Daragh attempted a joke. He said that he hoped that soon he would have Malenkov among those sitting in the front row. But Father Butovorich was not prepared to be facetious. He shrugged and said with unaffected seriousness, 'He has given us our freedom. That of very great importance to us.'

On the way to lunch we visited the Pushkin Gallery and viewe some paintings by European Masters, including an early Picass called, I think, The Kiss. But strangely, there was no moder Russian work. We were told they were not on view becau preparations were in hand for an exhibition. After lunch we visite another gallery but I forgot to note the name and at the moment am unable to recall it. We are now just back from the Bolshoi and dull performance of Carmen with a stout heroine sans passion, sar grace. This was a disappointment because last night we attended a absolutely electrifying performance of Moussorgsky's Hovar shchina. It was set at the time of Peter the Great and was full gusto and vitality, with a very large orchestra and a chorus of Go knows how many. There were wonderful stage effects, includin the burning of a house in a most spectacular way that would hai won the plaudits of Dion Boucicault and his Victorian audience But then to be actually in the Bolshoi Theatre at all was enough set the pulse running amok. It is draped magnificently in red, an the seven tiers of boxes are finished in gold. We occupied two box and could look down at the vast audience in the stalls; seriou attentive, all of them dressed in black, some of them studious. making notes on what was happening. These, presumably, wei students, the rest were ordinary, everyday people. I remarked Terry Trimble that it was wonderful to see working-class peop thronging to the opera and ballet. He looked for some moments o the hushed and soberly clad rows below.

'My dear Frank,' he said at last, 'I must confess that my middl class heart longs for the glint of a tiara or two.'

I saw his point.

It is time to go down for a late-night meal. Two more days Moscow. Then the second act of our adventure will begin when u are driven to Moscow airport and board our plane for Tbilisi Georgia. There will be sunshine and warmth there, at least. I sha be glad to bid adieu to snow and ice.

Chapter 23

The foul weather throughout January, and Stella's growing dependence on Lemuel's attention were an added burden to the normal restrictions of the season. Day after day he rose and rubbed the frost rime from the inside of the window pane to peer out on a paralysed world. The grass in the fields that spread out on all sides was buried under a thick blanket of frost; the puddles on the driveway had frozen solid, the garden paths were iron hard. When it all possible he avoided the driveway, which was icy and treacherous to walk on.

Keeping warm inside the house demanded management, too. Fuel had to be drawn in quantity; keeping the fires built up required a boy taken on almost exclusively for that alone. Water bottles were necessary nightly for the beds. Stella's had to be renewed half way through the night hours to keep her from sleepless misery. That, and her need for attention throughout the daytime made the services of an extra young girl essential. He himself paid her additional visits during the day to keep her interested and occupied. Because of Frank's involvement, they both followed the public debate over the Russian trip and waited each morning to see what the extra papers they had specially ordered might bring. When they came he left them with her to note any relevant report or letters to the editor. She would mark them but was unable to use the scissors herself to cut them out and had to await his return. She was then able to file them away in the album she was compiling.

They were plentiful. When one struck her as especially silly she might read it aloud to him:

Visitors to Russia are Criticized
'We have had an Irish delegation which went to Moscow, its

members making speeches on what the Soviet government said to them and what they said to the Soviet government. What this delegation said will go to every communist prison behind the iron curtain.'

So spoke the Rev. Kieran Martin, who was a communist prisoner in China in 1951–1952 when he gave an address last night on communism in Rochfort Town Hall. Fr. Martin, a native of Co. Limerick, returned to Ireland about a year ago after his release from captivity. In a further reference to the Irish visitors to Russia he added: 'We have Irish priests suffering for their religion while those who are on this delegation are praising the Communists.'

Alderman Bloomer, who presided, said they were honoured to welcome Fr. Martin who was one of the great soldiers in the great army of Christ.

Lemuel took the paper from her to see for himself.

'If Father Martin had followed the controversy with even the minimum of attention,' he remarked as he handed it back, 'he would know they had several times denied that they travel as a delegation. They have insisted they are a group of individuals representing only themselves. And how can he know they were praising the communists, as he puts it? He hasn't been travelling with them. In fact you and I know more about them than the glib-tongued Father Martin.'

'Shall we keep it?'

'Why not. Put it by for the record,' he decided.

As he was reaching for the scissors to cut it out she interrupted to pass him the current copy of the *Sentinel*.

'There's a piece in this which puzzles me,' she told him. 'You'll find it on page three.'

It was boxed to give it extra prominence:

The rumour has been spread that His Grace the Archbishop, or one of his secretaries, gave approval for the visit to Moscow. On inquiry at Archbishop House I have received authoritative information that the Moscow visit was never in any way referred to the Archbishop or to any of his secretaries and, further, if any form of approval had been sought, it would never have been granted . . .

He left the *Sentinel* down on top of the small bundle already awaiting the attention of his scissors.

'Didn't you consult a qualified person on Frank's behalf?'

'I certainly did. And got a perfectly clear answer.'

'Then what can have happened?'

'Someone is either misinformed or is seeking to mislead us.'

'Who was it you consulted?'

'I am not a liberty to tell you. It was most strictly confidential.'

The report troubled him as time went by. It could cause complications. He worried that, inadvertently, he may have misdirected Frank.

The Cyrillic script on the postage stamp and beneath the scenic photograph on the front of the card conveyed nothing to her, but on the back – as he tended to do when in high good spirits – he had scribbled a limerick:

> *Dear Margaret attend, if it plaze yeh*
> *I've breached the far borders of Asia*
> *Doesn't that take some beating*
> *And this jubilant greeting*
> *Astonish, astound and amazia!*

Only have time to despatch this at the moment. Letter follows.
Love Frank

It came a few days later:

Dear Margaret,
    Hope you got my card. Here's the letter I promised. Am writing from Tbilisi, capital city of the Republic of Georgia, which lies between the Black Sea and the Caspian Sea. On Tuesday (18th) last we were brought to Moscow Airport by quite hazardous roads and sat in a waiting room there from two in the morning until the plane arrived which was to take us the 1,200 miles of our journey. Outside, the darkness was impenetrable, the wind freezing and the runway obliterated by the inescapable snow. When we had been airborne for an hour or so, something went haywire with the temperature control system. The cabin lights had been put out and we had eased our seats back in the hope of snatching some sleep when the nightmare began. The cabin started getting warmer and warmer. We had kept our overcoats on because, before, the interior had been quite chilly. These were the first and obvious things to discard, but then followed jackets, pullovers, shirts – even shoes and socks. It was no use. The night became a purgatory of suffocating heat, a nightmare of nausea, tossing and turning, feverish dreams. When at last the temperature became bearable

again, dawn was breaking and through the tiny porthole one could see the whole sky filling with crimson light. Far down below, winding with wintry blackness across a plain of snow and sprawling shadows, was the Don. We landed at Rostov for breakfast and for some other reason at Sukhumi. Shortly after midday we were here in Tbilisi, being greeted with smiles and some floral bouquets. Blue skies and warm sunshine after the snow and gloom of Moscow, deep valleys and towering mountains instead of monotony and flatness. We've been up in the hills to view a new hydro-electric scheme and explored the ancient Persian part of the town, where an old woman piloting two hogs on the end of a chain joined us and held a one-sided and incomprehensible conversation with us for five or six minutes, then went off satisfied.

We have been to the Church of the Archimandrate of Georgia away up in the mountains also, among a rather battered collection of wooden houses which constitute the town (or village). I can't spell it but it was built in the fourth century and has battlements surrounding it and contains a tomb where, so legend says, the Coat Without Seam is buried.

Tonight we go to an opera, Daici, by a Georgian composer named Paliachvili who died in 1933. A striking thing here is their feverish regard for their twelfth century National Poet, Rostovelli. There are statues to him round every corner.

There have been graver (and duller) topics to report about, but these can wait until I get back. With all my love as ever. Tell Paul and Aoife Daddy sends his love to them also.

God bless.
Frank

Diary: January 23rd

A few nights ago at the opera Daici there were some moments of almost disastrous misunderstanding. The curtain fell on the first act amid a prolonged storm of loud boos. Our confused reaction puzzled our interpreters at first, but then they tumbled to what was wrong and explained that this was the Georgian way of expressing enthusiastic approval. Excellence of performance, it seems, is greeted with slow hand-clapping!

Tonight we are staying in Sukhumi in the Republic of Abkazia and I am sharing a bedroom with Daragh McDowell. He is sitting up in his bed across the room with his portable typewriter balanced on his belly. His shirt is draped over the bottom rail of the bed to dry. It is a drip-dry but he has never time to leave it to dry completely so he only washes the collar. This means the collar looks all right but the rest of it is becoming progressively maggoty. However, when we had discussed the matter in more detail we discovered that, while he had two fresh pairs of socks but no clean shirt, I had two clean shirts but had run out of pairs of socks. We made the obvious swap around and decided to demand as a matter of urgency that time must be set aside to attend to the needs of decency and hygiene.

Tomorrow we are to visit a Collective Farm where an aged expert has earned three Orders of Lenin and been named a Hero of Socialist Labour for increasing the yield from the vineyard by 200 per cent.

Inspiration seems to have struck at the other side of the room. McDowell's typewriter is clacking away confidently. Not for long, I hope. I want to sleep.

The denial that Archbishop House knew anything about the trip in advance shocked Margaret. It was to have been their ultimate response to public reaction should it prove threatening enough to warrant it. It looked as though it would. The correspondence columns of several of the newspapers were growing fat on the letters it was generating. The spate of condemnations from local councils continued unabated.

She consulted others. Teresa was very upset herself. She wondered that people who professed to follow precepts of charity and forbearance could behave with such blithe disregard for others. Maeve said a lot of it was being drummed up by zealots of one kind or another and would drain away again very quickly. Nevertheless, she could very well understand Margaret's anxiety. One had to be worried by it. Simon Morrissey and Penny called to insist on taking her out for something to eat and to a pub after it.

'Didn't Lemuel Cox make inquiries in some quarter?' Simon asked.

'In what quarter I don't know,' Margaret answered, 'but it was someone with authority.'

'And what was the response?'

'He said there was no moral compunction. Whatever that means.'

'If I know anything about episcopal pronouncements,' Simon said, 'it will mean whatever turns out to be expedient.'

'That's why I worry,' she confessed.

'You should phone Lemuel Cox,' he advised.

Some days later she overcame her reluctance and did so. She asked if anything had gone wrong.

'My feeling about it at present,' Lemuel told her, 'is that the response from the laity has taken them by surprise. It's much more vehement than they had anticipated, mainly because it was deliberately implanted at first and then pumped up and plentifully fed. They're probably trying to determine how they should handle it. I know it's hard, my dear, but try for the moment to keep it from your mind. I'll make what inquiries suggest themselves and phone you within a few days.'

His voice was deeply concerned and she trusted him totally. But she wished Frank were near at hand and longed for the days to be past until he was home with her again.

Dear Margaret,

Since my last we have seen what was to be shown to us both in Georgia and in the small neighbouring Republic of Abkazia where the Collective Farm was located. Now we are back again in the snow and ice of Moscow and I have bought myself a true-as-God black Russian fur hat (they are quite cheap) to keep out the cold. I look like a high-ranking member of VOKS. To be fair about it, though, I am enjoying the centrally heated Edwardian splendour of Hotel National once again. We are kept busy visiting all sorts and shapes of things: the HQ of the Council of Trade Unions, Moscow Radio, etc., etc. The highlight, naturally, was the Kremlin itself. We gaped at the Czar's cannon, a huge monster of a thing which was probably regarded with more uneasiness by its own gun crew than by the troops of Napoleon, and the Czar's bell, the biggest in the world, so they claim, which sits on a concrete pedestal with a gaping lump ripped out of its side by a fall it sustained when a fire consumed the rafters which supported it. The churches of the Assumption and the Annunciation, no longer used for worship, are still overpoweringly beautiful shrines; rich and breathtaking. In the Armoury we glimpsed examples of the wealth of the former nobility: the ornate goblets and royal treasures of Peter, the sumptuous coaches in which the aristocracy travelled when the horse and the sailing ship symbolized hazardous journeys. Then, as a fitting climax we were conducted to the tomb. Early on in this trip I had looked from my bedroom window in Hotel National at the black-coated queue winding from its entrance back across the white snow until hidden from sight. Whenever I looked, day or night, it was there and it replenished itself as fast as it was being depleted.

Being privileged as visitors we were not required to join the queue and were brought straight in. We went at a snail-like pace down flights of dimly lit steps and then began to climb. On the left, under glass covers with concealed lighting showing up the features already familiar from a thousand portraits and a multitude of statues, were the two bodies. Lenin seemed surprisingly small, as though death had uniformly contracted him. Stalin's face was as in the portrait: the hair grey at the temples, the deeply lined forehead, the strong nose and full moustache, the grim mouth. The strange thing was that these mummified effigies meant, to me anyway, nothing at all. Nothing whatever lingered of the personalities that had once inhabited them. All melted away into the interstellar spaces, or into nowhere at all. It was a relief to get out once more into the land of the quick, the living streets and the patient children of the revolution.

So, after a late meal later tonight we leave Moscow for the last time and go by Red Arrow (a luxury train by all accounts) to Leningrad, leaving after midnight (twelve-thirty) and arriving there at ten a.m. We spend a few days in Leningrad, then by Helsinki and Stockholm to London and so home – I reckon about five or six days. You will probably just about have received this, but I intend in any case to telephone you either from Stockholm or London. I look forward very much to being home again – my wanderlust is sated. I hope our reception will not be too unpleasant, but can only wait and see.

    All my love,
    Frank

He sat with Stella by the fire as was usual in the wintry nights, listening to the wind soughing about the house and wondering if there was snow on its way once again. She sat as usual in the fireside chair opposite his, the sidetable with its framed photographs at her back, her hands tremulous for much of the time. But she had managed to find the clipping with the statement on the trip alleged to have come from Archbishop House, which he had asked her for earlier. He had been in contact with his authoritative source, as he called it, and the opinion expressed coincided with his own. The campaign from more extreme quarters to fuel public reaction for all it was worth, was causing deep unease in official quarters in case it grew beyond the prudent controls they might at some stage deem it desirable to impose. Looking over the statement again and more closely, he saw that it could be understood to mean that it was the matter of the visit that had never been referred for official approval. It had not. There was never the slightest possibility of approval. What had been sought was simply clarification of the moral implications and the answer had been given: there was no moral compunction. This could be meant to convey that, while the visit was disapproved of, it fell short of being sinful.

Stella found it all extremely devious.

'Such statements,' he agreed, 'invariably are. It leaves room for manoeuvre.'

'I hope it doesn't spell trouble for poor Frank.'

'If it does, much of the responsibility will be mine.'

'You only meant to help.'

'That doesn't alter it.'

'You must wait and see.'

She brooded over it.

'If you were to make representation in person,' she suggested, 'it might bear fruit. After all, Father was very deeply involved in church affairs. As a family we are well known to them and much respected.'

'We are still the laity,' he said with resignation. 'And in these matters the laity don't count. Ultimately we are mere ornaments.'

Diary: *January 30th*
Writing on board SAS DC6 en route London via Copenhagen. We left Stockholm at eight-thirty a.m. and are dropping in altitude preparatory to landing at Copenhagen. We have just finished breakfast. A beautiful morning. The sun streams through the window. Below us wooded country with occasional houses and the trees very black against the perpetual background of snow. Except for Georgia I've been seeing snow daily for almost four weeks now, and even in Georgia the higher peaks of the Caucasus were white with it.

After lunch in Leningrad yesterday, when we left for Stockholm via Helsinki, the snow was thick everywhere and still falling steadily. At Stockholm airport we found we had only about four pounds between us and tried to exchange our first-class tickets for third-class in order to cash-in on the difference, but no go. A pilot who was passing the information desk overheard our request, discussed our difficulty and asked us to wait. He went off and returned with forty kronor which he gave to us. He said we could return it to him care of Prestwick airport and wrote down his name. He didn't bother to ask for ours or for an address. Then he got the girl on the desk to book us into Hotel Christenberg. So, we had a roof over our heads for the night. The hotel was a series of corridors all on the same level. Our good Samaritan had referred to it as the horizontal skyscraper, which we agreed was very apt.

With me are Daragh McDowell and Aengus Lovatt, the sculptor. There were two return bookings and the others got away the day before us. Daragh is staying over in London in order to see his British newspaper editor, for whom he has been doing three commissioned reports on the trip. (That's what all the midnight typing was about. He's going to put up Aengus for the night and lend him some money to book his fare back tomorrow, which he can get from his publisher.) His title for the trio of articles is 'Here Be Dragons'. He's ridiculously smug about it and believes the editor will be quite bowled over.

Wondering will I be able to connect the two-twenty p.m. London to Dublin flight, and if so have I enough money for the ticket. I don't know exactly what it will cost. If not, I could contact Margaret's Uncle Fred in Chingford. But how long would it take me to get out there?

I had a marvellous lunch complete with lovely wine and cognac to follow, so I'll leave the worrying until we've touched down. Daragh McDowell has polished off his and is dozing beside me. Aengus Lovatt, on the other side of the aisle, is nodding over a magazine. He was telling me earlier of a statue of the Virgin he had completed just before he left. It had been commissioned from him by the Institute of Advanced Lay and Religious Pedagogy to mark the declaration of the dogma of the Assumption in 1950, but for one reason or another had to be delayed. It is all ready now: the site for it has been laid down in the grounds of the Institute, with the ornamental chains for marking it off in place about it and the plinth set up in the centre awaiting it. Now he's worrying in case his Russian sojourn has given rise to some unpleasantness and antagonism. I think it probably has and advised him to have it delivered the moment he gets back. He agreed with me that that would be the sensible thing to do.

Flying at 10,000 feet, the tannoy has just announced. Below us the North Sea. We are told to fasten our seat belts. Bumpy . . .

It was around four o'clock when the telephone rang. She had cleared away after a very late Sunday dinner and was sitting by the fire with Paul and Aoife. The ringing of the telephone had become quite a frequent occurrence over the past few weeks and she took her time about answering. It would, she guessed, be Penny or Simon Morrissey checking about the latest developments, or Ernest Jackson perhaps, or Teresa or Maeve, Lemuel Cox who was very attentive, or Con Andrews who constantly sought information and passed on what few morsels he had gathered himself. Or even Joe Dunne of the Union who kept constantly and sympathetically in contact.

The sound of his voice struck her dumb, so that he had to repeat his hello three or four times and then ask 'Is there anybody at that end?'

'Frank—' she managed at last.

'Margaret, my darling. Is something wrong with the line?'

'Not with the line, love, with me. I couldn't believe it. Are you speaking from Moscow?'

'No. London airport.'

'Thank God. So you're on your way. How soon?'

'There's a flight at twenty to eight. I'll be on that. There was an earlier one at twenty past two but I found I hadn't enough for the ticket. I phoned your Uncle Fred in Chingford and he drove all the way in to lend me the necessary. We had a drink together and he's just left.'

'I'll be at Collinstown to meet you.'

'Don't do that. If the weather is anything like here you'll freeze to death.'

'I don't care. I'll be waiting.'

She was adamant. He decided not to argue.

'How are things over there?' he asked instead.

'The children and everyone else are fine. But things are not very pleasant elsewhere.'

'You mean the press?'

'A section of the press. And the usual pressure groups. I only say it because I don't want you to bump straight into it without some kind of forewarning.'

'Is it that bad?'

'Darling, don't ask me about it now. We'll talk when you're here at home and safe and sitting at the fire once more. I can't wait for that.'

He decided not to press that either. Her tone told him that the situation was far from good. As he left the booth the reflection in the glass panelling reminded him that he was wearing his recently acquired fur hat. He thought for a moment of removing it. He decided he would not.

Margaret spent over an hour making telephone calls. She informed Lemuel Cox who asked if they would both try to call out to him as soon as possible. Simon and Penny offered to mind the children; Ernie Jackson knew she was unable to drive herself and offered to come over and drive the car for her and bring her to the airport. Milly came with him to offer her help if it were needed and stayed in the house to prepare sandwiches and savouries for later on. Then it was time to set off. She found the car keys for Ernie Jackson and they travelled by roads that were treacherous with ice. Beyond the city's limits the fields on either side were heavily rimed with frost. They had tea in the waiting room and spoke very little. From time to time they went out on the viewing platform to look down at the runways. A light but freezing wind chilled them. Icy droplets hung in the air and settled on face and hair. The plane was late.

The decision to wear or not to wear his Russian hat arose again when the plane came to a stop and it was time to gather together his luggage and disembark. He took it up from the seat where he had left it and stuck it back on his head. He was the last down the gangway of the very few passengers on the flight. Crossing the tarmac to customs he could discern faintly the knot of people waiting on the viewing platform. Some of them were waving down to him. Voices drifted thinly on the freezing air.

The customs officer stared for a moment at the fur hat. Then he addressed himself to his duty.

'Anything to declare?' he asked.

'Have you an hour or so to spare?' Frank answered.

'I have all bloody night to spare,' the customs officer said. He was elderly. He was already very tired. He stared again at the fur hat.

'I could probably confiscate that for a start,' he said.

'My crown of thorns,' Frank said, smiling, 'surely not?'

'What have you in the paper parcel?'

'It's a cheap, quarter-size violin,' Frank said. 'It's for my little daughter. She's just of an age now to start learning it.'

'I thought violins came complete with properly made cases?'

'Not in Leningrad,' Frank said. 'They just wrap them like this. The customer can like it or lump it.'

'So you're just back from Uncle Joe,' the customs man remarked.

'Back to the land of the free,' Frank acknowledged. He lifted his case and placed it on the counter.

The customs man said in a friendly tone, 'Conserve the bravado, oul' son. You'll need plenty of it later on.'

Frank fumbled for the keys but the customs man waved him aside and marked the parcel and the case with chalk.

'And hold on to your energy too,' he advised. 'You'll need that as well.'

'Thank you,' Frank said. 'I understand I've made an enemy or two.'

'You have,' the man confirmed. 'The nastiest kind. Holy ones. So go ahead.'

Frank collected his things together. 'And good luck,' the man added, 'that's something else you'll need.' They smiled. 'Thanks,' Frank repeated.

Ernie Jackson stood aside while Margaret came forward to embrace him. He held her to him and kissed her. Then he stood back. Her face was lined and tired. He could see that she had had a hard time. Ernie Jackson came forward.

'Let's get going,' he said, 'it's too cold for hanging about.'

Milly had prepared the food for them. Simon Morrissey had gone out and returned to stack the sitting-room with drink. The children had been allowed to stay up to greet him. Simon Morrissey busied himself distributing the drinks. They talked until after midnight, advising him not to start going through clippings and such things until he was completely rested.

'Take the coming week off as well,' Simon Morrissey told him. 'I'll explain to P.J. that I've suggested you should do so.'

But on his way home he said to Penny, 'I know P.J. won't want him next or near the office until he has had a chance to assess public reaction. Frank will be better off keeping out of the way.'

The next day the daily press headlined the news of their return. After that everything seemed quiet enough until the Friday afternoon. When Margaret was approaching the school to collect Paul and Aoife, she could hear children's voices alternately singing hymns or raised in prayer. The sounds were coming not from the school itself, but from the convent grounds. It was the first Friday of the month, she remembered, and thought it possibly had something to do with that. In the grounds she found the children of the school walking in a circle about the statue of Our Lady, Refuge of Sinners. A nun was leading them, punctuating the successive decades of the rosary with hymns. Margaret asked another nun who was watching what the purpose might be.

'When Reverend Mother read the news of the return of the travellers to Russia earlier this week, she instructed that the children be freed from class half an hour early on this First Friday to recite the rosary and to petition God to give them the grace to recognize their error and to have repentence for their sin.'

Margaret nodded dumbly. She could see Aoife and Paul among the walking children. The sight stabbed at her heart. But later, as she watched their behaviour at home she realized that they had made no connection whatever between the sinful men they had been praying for and their own father. She felt she had to tell Frank. He shrugged it aside. He had been reading the clippings.

Part Four

Chapter 24

Lemuel Cox, with brotherly solicitude, occupied his chair night after night opposite his sister Stella and worried increasingly about her health. She was failing. He had kept watch on her under the pretence of struggling with the daily crossword puzzle, and was convinced of it. The most alarming moments were when she dozed off asleep. With her mouth sagging open, her breathing laboured and irregular, her skin wrinkled and slack from neck to forehead, she had the look of death.

What had she done with her life? What had either of them done, for that matter. These were questions he frequently brooded over. He himself had at least continued his studies of monasticism in an easygoing, but nevertheless reasonably fruitful fashion, sufficiently to find ready publication in the more esoteric of the scholarly magazines when he thought well of doing so. Scholars in related fields more learned than he were prepared to correspond occasionally with him. As did others in response to his more leisurely but useful researches into the records of local history and customs. These were labours that bestowed some modicum of dignity.

But Stella had distanced herself. When in the mood she had occupied herself for brief spells with humdrum things: with the organization of flower shows or sales-of-work and similar parish activities of a not very demanding nature. But she engaged only superficially. She had been twenty-four when Johnny O'Grady was killed, and thirty-nine when the outbreak of the First World War brought back again, this time in fearsome measure, the sufferings and tragedies of wartime. Perhaps those years in between had not been propitious for the kind of adjustment that needed to be attempted. She had not succeeded in putting her loss to rest, and by the time she had entered her thirties the desire to seek elsewhere for hope and companionship had leaked away. The deaths of Godwin and young Jonathan, and the heartbreak of those war years, had in themselves put the seal on the matter. As, indeed, they had done, though not quite so thoroughly and inescapably, in his own case. For him there had been a few close friends to tempt him to open a window at times to cast a glance beyond his immediate surroundings. Not so with Stella.

However, he was glad to concede that she had become altogether more agreeable. She no longer pretended blank amnesia if he mentioned Margot. If she continued to reject his belief that there were at least strong elements of reincarnation between Margot and Margaret, she now had the grace to keep it to herself. And, while she could never be wholly able to accept his habitual nightly tipple, she no longer attempted to maintain that their father had totally disapproved of alcohol.

She had also begun to take closer note of his interests and activities. She remarked that for a time he had ceased to go near the piano.

'You used to be so keen,' she observed, 'especially on Bach. You don't seem to turn to him so frequently nowadays. In fact you don't seem to play so frequently at all.'

'It's my hands,' he evaded. 'I think it may well be a touch of arthritis.' But then he decided to be forthright. 'To tell the truth,' he amended, 'I am becoming more and more distressed over the situation of Frank McDonagh. I find it hard to settle down to many things. The piano is only one of them.'

'Have you had bad news about him?'

'For some weeks now I have hesitated to talk directly to either Frank or Margaret because I felt it only served to increase their anxiety. So I telephoned Simon Morrissey. He tells me Frank is not yet back at work. The senior partner – they refer to him habitually as P.J. – felt it would be damaging for the present to have him around the office. So he has agreed to continue payment of his salary for two months, after which the situation will be reviewed. I'm worried because five or six weeks of that period have gone already and there is no hint of a change.'

She thought it a great shame and wondered if there was anything they could do.

'Should he lose his job,' Lemuel answered, 'I'd feel morally bound to offer some kind of financial assistance. But there's a limit to what I could raise.'

'If it should come to that,' she suggested, 'I would be willing to bear some share of it.'

'That would relieve me greatly,' he confessed.

Meanwhile, the customary outlets for pious fervour were being availed of. The Left Book Shop had its much afflicted windows shattered and had to send the hat around yet again among its down-at-heel members to have them replaced. The insurance companies had long ago pronounced the premises to be an unacceptable risk. A fresh handful of missionaries, returned recently from China, lectured on the tortures they had endured at the hands of the communists and went on to condemn the visitors to the Soviet Union trenchantly and usually (Lemuel once again noted) for things they had not, in fact, done.

Daragh McDowell told Frank he had lost one column worth about ten pounds weekly to him as a result of the trip, but he didn't really care. The three articles he had written were already gaining a foothold in the English market for him and it paid a great deal more. There was also a much more liberal attitude editorially as to what you were allowed to express. The Irish papers, he regretted to admit, because it fitted in badly with his republican pride to have to do so, had become completely craven. But then it was well known everywhere that something similar had occurred in that great bastion of free expression, the United States. Even their cinema idols were being hounded.

Terry Trimble, Frank discovered, was back teaching in the John Field Academy of Music. There had been no comment whatever from the board of governors and no public reaction from the parents. But the director had asked him to avoid any discussion with the students about the affair, and to be generally discreet. Left to itself, he predicted, the whole thing would die away and everyone would be able to get on in peace with thinning out the high incidence in the community of individuals who, musically speaking, went through life with wooden ears. The director was an easygoing, unflappable man. For him music alone was worth getting steamed-up about.

Aengus Lovatt reported to Frank that he had acted on his advice and despatched the statue of the Virgin to the Institute of Advanced Lay and Religious Pedagogy immediately on his return. He had been unable to establish subsequently whether it had actually got as far as the grounds or had been intercepted at the gates, but it had come back to him like a shot off a shovel. The lorry driver was tight-lipped about it. All he would say was that he had been advised that the delivery was unacceptable and he had a wife and family and wanted neither hand, nor act nor part in any further developments.

The authorities claimed that the contract had been broken when Lovatt had failed to complete the statue on time. The students who had subscribed by monthly instalments for its erection had their money refunded to them but got no official explanation. They decided to throw a party in their club at the Institute and invited Lovatt as their guest. He brought Frank along. Three or four students were waiting to welcome them at the gates and led them ceremoniously to inspect the plot which had been laid down in readiness for the statue. A plinth stood in the centre of a slab of concrete which was marked off by black-painted, decorative chains supported by carved pillars at each of its four corners. Dusk was falling and the air felt damp. It threatened rain. Indicating the now pointless structure, one of the students remarked, 'We have no statue but we have a name for it. Everybody is using it.'

'And what is that?' Lovatt asked.

The student smiled and said, 'The Red Madonna.'

They were led companionably to the clubhouse.

While the students roistered with the proceeds of their un-expected windfall, the decorative chains marked the empty site and the plinth waited patiently under a dull sky and the waning of the light. All looked forlorn and served no purpose. The rain began.

Chapter 25

It was the first time ever in their long acquaintanceship that Ballcock had telephoned him at home. He was conspiratorial, low spoken.

'Is that Frank McDonagh?'

'Speaking.'

'It's Peter Brady here, Frank. I'm sorry to disturb you at home. I phoned your office but they told me you had taken some leave?'

'P.J. offered it to me,' said Frank. 'He reckoned I could do with some time off to weather all the hullabaloo.'

'That's what I'm calling you about – the hullabaloo. Could I see you? It's very urgent.'

'I'll drop down to your office—'

'Jesus, no,' Ballcock said, horrified. 'That's where the trouble is. Could I meet you somewhere that's well out of the way. Gilmartins maybe? Tonight, if possible.'

'Gilmartins. What time?'

'Half-past eight?'

'Half-eight. Fine', Frank agreed.

Ballcock was there before him, his bowler pushed back from his forehead as usual, the legs of his pinstriped trousers carefully creased, the twin strands of his silver watch chain decorating the waistcoat which bulged a little under his dark jacket. He fetched the drinks himself and glanced quickly around to check the area immediately about them.

'We'll skip the preliminaries,' he suggested in a low-pitched voice. 'I always prefer to keep the preliminaries for afterwards. There's a hell of a move brewing on the Co-op Committee and it concerns you.'

'What in God's name can I have to do with the Co-op Committee?'

'What in God's name have you to do with any of the committees and councils that are queuing up in their hundreds to condemn yourself and the others you travelled with. Every crawthumper in the country is fulmigating against you.'

'Fulminating,' Frank corrected, doing so now from sheer habit.

'That's right – fulmigating – it's become a national pastime. And now there's a few upright Christians in the Co-operative Society who think the committee should join the queue by passing a resolution of its own condemning you. They've succeeded in having one put forward. As secretary I've no option but to list it for discussion at the next monthly meeting. That's on Friday week.'

'Will they pass it?'

'I've been using every bit of influence I can muster to stop it,' Ballcock assured him, 'and I'll fight my hardest on Friday. The stumbling block is they know of your close connection with the Union *Bulletin*. They want you removed from editorship.'

'I'm not the editor,' Frank pointed out. 'Joe Dunne is.'

'Joe leaves most of it to you,' Ballcock said, 'and they know that very well.'

'So what am I supposed to do?' Frank demanded. He was angry. The set-up puzzled him. The avalanche of condemnations from county councillors and committees suggested that the country was in a fever of revulsion, yet so far not a single individual he had spoken to appeared to care a damn one way or the other.

'Do nothing,' Ballcock urged.

'Doing nothing is very difficult,' Frank protested. 'Haven't you anything at all to suggest?'

'There's a trick or two up my sleeve still,' Ballcock assured him, 'and I'll keep on canvassing on the quiet to have it either withdrawn or rejected.' He lifted his glass and emptied it. 'I suppose you could buy me a pint,' he suggested, returning the empty glass to the table. Deep gloom enveloped him.

Simon Morrissey was appalled. A resolution of protest from such a source would almost certainly set Frank's future beyond rescue. The Co-op was an indivisible part of the Union's structure and the Union *Bulletin* was handled by Kenny Morrissey and Co. and attended to almost exclusively by Frank McDonagh. That was how P.J. would see the matter, and for P.J. that would be the last straw.

Morrissey had little faith in Ballcock's championship if it looked like ending in damage to Ballcock himself. He tried to sound out P.J.'s mind by drawing it to his attention that the period of Frank's two month's leave of absence on full salary was coming to its end.

'The rumpus has almost died away,' he pointed out. 'I feel we should have Frank back in harness as soon as possible. Apart from being fair to him there's the day-to-day workload to be coped with. His absence is causing problems.'

'That's been in my mind,' P.J. conceded, 'and I agree that the rumpus, as you call it, seems to have shot its bolt. I'll give it a few more days and then I'll probably talk to him.'

That sounded as hopeful as he could expect. He warned Frank to keep a vigilant eye on Ballcock.

'Use every ounce of influence you can muster when you're dealing with him,' he urged. 'A great deal is going to depend on him.'

'He's already promised to do everything in his power,' Frank said.

'But can you believe him?'

'I think so. He acknowledges that I've helped him from time to time in a variety of ways. Others who are his enemies know that, too. They could use a vote disapproving of me to involve him as well. It would be a dangerous weapon when he comes up for re-election in a couple of months and they're trying to have him dumped.'

'That may be so,' Simon acknowledged. 'Nevertheless, I want a few words with Brady.'

Ballcock talked freely. There had been many acts of assistance from Frank which commanded his appreciation. Among his enemies were at least three anti-Communist fanatics who would stick at nothing in their determination to get rid of himself as well as Frank.

'I'm going to conduct a bit of a canvass,' he confided 'to convince as many of the Co-op members as I can that Frank is an honest young man who does his job impartially and has no axe to grind. In fact, I was wondering should he come around with me himself. He's done so before.'

'It sounds a bit extreme,' Simon thought. Then he changed his mind. 'Nevertheless,' he remarked, 'it could prove a wise move. I'll have a word with him.'

So it was that Frank found himself, for the third or fourth occasion, ferrying Ballcock around his constituency to the artisan's cottages and the blocks of corporation flats and the dilapidated rows of tenements; sitting patiently in the driving seat while Ballcock called at door after door or being summoned from it to be presented in person to a Committee Member or someone of equal eminence and influence. It was embarrassing at first. But then it became almost entertaining. The people they talked to proved genial enough. After the third or fourth round Ballcock showed faint signs of optimism.

'I think we might be getting somewhere,' he conceded. 'I think I detect a tiny twitter of common sense.'

On the Friday of the meeting Simon and Penny joined Frank and Margaret to await news from Ballcock on the outcome. It was a long drawn-out wait, as they knew it most likely would be. Ballcock's main plea would be for withdrawal of the motion on the grounds that it would do harm to the Co-op, instead of good by drawing the situation to the attention of a public which so far knew nothing about it. His canvass around his constituency had resulted in promises of support, some of it from committee members themselves. After three hours of repetitive argument and much complicated manoeuvring, Ballcock left the smoke-filled room to find a telephone he could use in privacy. His voice was hoarse, his eyes red and streaming, his mind barely functioning any longer. But his mood was triumphant. He had carried the argument. The resolution had been withdrawn. He had won.

Frank shouted the news from the hallway to the rest. They rushed out to join him. He sealed off the mouthpiece with his hand and said, 'I think I should ask him for a drink.' They approved wholeheartedly.

He said to Ballcock, 'The pubs are closed by now but I'm sure you could do with a drink. Why don't you call in here for one? I'll drop you home after it.'

Ballcock was more than willing. 'I've to phone Joe Dunne first to let him know the outcome. He's anxious about it and I promised to do so. Then I'll get to you right away.'

He was treated like a hero and driven to his doorway when all was over. He felt he deserved it. He had done them a valuable service. Joe Dunne would appreciate his achievement also. If the resolution had been passed it could have led to the kind of press reaction that the union could well do without.

Ballcock went late to his bed and was still in it long after his usual rising hour when the ringing of the telephone in the hallway wakened him. His wife answered it and after a while came up to the bedroom.

'That was Joe Dunne,' she told him. 'He'd like you to get down to the office as soon as possible.'

'Did he say what for?'

'No, only that he'd like to see you as soon as you can.'

If it was to find out the details about the committee meeting and to congratulate him on his success, Ballcock felt, Joe Dunne might have let him enjoy his hard-earned rest first. But he dressed and despatched his breakfast without delay and set off. The streets were quieter than usual. The morning rush-hour had passed but the day's activities were not as yet in full flood. Joe Dunne was standing in the porchway scanning the street for his arrival. His face bore no signs of the pleasure and congratulation Ballcock had anticipated. It was thunderous.

'Come with me, Peter,' he said grimly. 'I want to show you something.'

Ballcock followed. He found he was being led, not to Joe Dunne's office, but to his own. When they came to a halt at its door he saw, with unbelieving shock and horror, why. Somebody had scrawled on it, in large letters in white paint which had dribbled here and there while it was being applied, a slogan which caused his heart to jump:

Red Brady Or The Pope!

'Jesus Christ,' he moaned.

'Whoever did it,' Joe Dunne told him, 'made sure it was not going to go unnoticed. There were reporters and photographers already gathered about it when I got in this morning. Somebody had tipped them off.'

'Some poisonous bastard,' Ballcock began. He was unable to continue.

'Come upstairs with me,' Joe Dunne invited. 'We'll talk about it.'

But both knew talking about it would not affect the matter in the slightest. Things would now take their predictable course. There would be the photographs in the papers of the defaced door with its scrawled message. The battle over the resolution and its subsequent withdrawal would be reported on and combed over and over for the forces and the ideologies that were likely to have been at the bottom of it all. Claims that hidden and undesirable influences were at work within the Union would come from the more fervent and persistent among the religious activists. The Co-op could expect opportunist attacks from the element among the city traders who deplored the co-operative movement in any shape or form. Joe Dunne would take it in his low-key, almost phlegmatic fashion. He had weathered such assaults with success times out of number. Ballcock was painfully aware of having blundered into creating a perilous threat to his own political security. The job now was to wriggle his way out of it.

P.J. was firm and unequivocal. Frank would have to go. He called Simon in to tell him so. The summons was not unexpected.

'I don't want him a day longer,' P.J. announced. 'This business of ours is cut-throat enough. It can't drag any extra weight.'

'I don't agree Frank should go,' Simon answered quietly. 'I'm your partner for a long time now and I feel I have some moral right to a say in his future. He's a friend of mine.'

'I hate to overrule you,' P.J. said, his voice matching Simon's in its moderation, 'but the agency comes first.'

'And Frank? He has his wife and two kids.'

'I've given thought to that. I'm prepared to extend his salary payments to cover three more months. That will give him a reasonable period to look around.'

Simon, who had made up his mind already what he would have to say should the situation arise, announced in the same quiet voice as before, 'If Frank goes, I go too.'

'We have a partnership agreement,' P.J. pointed out. 'You can't walk out just like that.'

'It isn't indissoluble. I'll meet all my legal obligations meticulously.'

P.J. rose to come around from behind his desk. 'Simon, I want you to think very carefully about this.'

'I've done so already, P.J. Your decision is no surprise. I know your style.'

'If you withdraw from partnership and take your financial interest with you it will do no harm from my point of view. I've already made plans about replacing it. But the cash you take with you won't be sufficient to set you up on your own. I know you have friends in high places – your huntin', shootin', fishin' relations among them – but I wouldn't put too much faith in them. You'll end up shopping around the agencies for employment and, as things stand, your chances will not be good.'

'As things stand,' Simon said, 'I'm left with no alternative.'

'Let it rest at that for the present,' P.J. suggested, avoiding confrontation. 'We'll talk together again later.'

But there were no further talks, no harsh exchanges between them, no actual falling-out. P.J., of his nature, remained immovable; Simon, his mind firmly made up to it, was equally unwilling to budge. The process that had begun proceeded of its own volition. The partnership contract required him to give six months' notice. He put his intention in writing to P.J. and proceeded to work through it month by month with no idea what lay at the end of it. P.J. replaced Frank by sending to London for Patricia Lennon. While over there she had exercised her remarkable charms to captivate her fashionable and influential boss and, greatly to her advantage, to marry him. She had then, to even greater advantage, managed to divorce him. In her possession there now reposed enough of his money to buy herself a partnership. Simon, watching P.J. and herself as he worked through his notice, reckoned that that was precisely what P.J. intended to persuade her to do: when his notice period had been served she would be ready to replace him. He mentioned the idea to Frank who thought it sounded a highly likely outcome.

'P.J. can look after Number One,' he remarked. 'I wish I had a little of his flair.'

He himself was already doing some part-time editorial work on the *Review* for Con Andrews. What Con could afford was little enough, but it helped to stretch out P.J.'s ex-gratia offerings.

Chapter 26

On the day of Stella's second collapse, Lemuel had spent most of the afternoon in his father's study, his mind for much of the time brooding on the situation in which Frank McDonagh found himself. He must do something about it he knew, but what form should it take? The advice he had given to Frank had been passed on in good faith. Now there seemed to be a change of stance in exalted places, calling for their use of the strategy of silent revision which, it seemed, it was their usual habit to keep prudently in reserve. What the outcome of their recourse to it might be for Frank was of lesser importance to them than retaining their own room for manoeuvre.

Lemuel found that consideration of Frank's situation oppressed him. So, too, did the crowded bookshelves and their volumes that were ponderous with the labours and texts and glosses of the Early Fathers; men who, as his father had never tired of pointing out, had presided over the triumph of the Christian Church as the new, all-powerful influence in the western world. Some of them, Lemuel was well aware, had been just as cruel, just as autocratic, just as merciless as the forces they were determined to overthrow. The thought made him wish his father was at hand to approach for advice. But he was not. It was solely up to himself. He decided to put it to Stella once more. If she again offered to help with financial assistance it would prove that she had fully meant what she had said and had not been carried away by sentiment.

When he joined her she wondered at not having seen him.

'Have you been out?' she asked.

'I've been sitting in Father's study for quite a long time,' he told her, 'brooding about things.'

'About Father?'

'About Father, yes. But mostly about Frank McDonagh's situation.'

'I've thought quite a lot about that myself,' she confessed. 'Have you made up your mind what we should do?'

'I think I should offer financial assistance, either as a long-term loan, or simply as a present. Something that would help him to buy into a job, perhaps as a partner or as a working investor. You thought you might be able to help?'

'I intend to do so,' Stella confirmed.

'I've reckoned I can offer around a thousand pounds. Perhaps even fifteen hundred. What had you yourself in mind?'

'About the same. When you're in touch with Stopford making your own financial arrangements, I'd like you to tell him I, too, would wish to see him.'

'You are very generous, Stella,' he said.

'They are a young couple who are in difficulties and I am deeply fond of both of them,' she said. 'Also, I think it should be a straightforward gift. At our time of life to talk of long-term loans seems somewhat unrealistic.'

Rosie, their new young maid, brought in the beginning of their evening meal, Stella having decided earlier that they should take it by the fire. Rosie withdrew.

'While I was in there,' Lemuel said, 'I remembered something very vividly and I have no idea why. It was of the two of us sitting together with Father – not here, but in our Lansdowne Road house – when he suddenly asked me to play a piece by Schumann. What it was I was unable to recollect – a little piece, perhaps a simple arrangement of his *Traümerei* for the young pupil. It was certainly dreamy enough to be that. I was just nine at the time, and when I had finished he was much moved and said: "Ah! Schumann. I was six years of age when Schumann died. But then of course he had been quite mad for some years." The belief stayed with me, for a long time, that composers were all doomed to end up either deaf or blind or mad. Do you too remember the occasion, by any chance?'

'No,' Stella confessed. 'Nor can I remember what year Schumann died in.'

'In 1856,' Lemuel answered.

Stella, who had always been admired for her detailed retention of historical events, pondered the matter in silence, then said, 'In that year the allied troops were withdrawn from the Crimea. I'm sure there would have been more attention being paid by the public to talk of Florence Nightingale than to the death of poor Robert Schumann.'

'I also recollected another odd thing he said to me. He told me it is quite true that there are ghosts, and that they are only poor, tormented souls who had been unable to take all of themselves with them.'

'Yes. I remember that he used to say that,' Stella said, nodding her head and giving a sad smile of recollection.

When they had finished their meal and all had been cleared away, she asked him to play *Traumerei* for her. The gentle introspection of the melody filled the room with a melancholy which was healing and charming, rather than sad. When it had finished, she thought, although it was earlier than usual, she would like to go to her room. She felt tired and wished to rest. He protested, though with only the slightest hint of his irritation, that she ought to have mentioned this before he had sat down to play.

'You know that it is best to turn the lights on at least half an hour before you intend to use them. I have told you so several times.'

'You have, Lemuel, but I think you are misled,' she answered. 'The lights are quite as efficient in the beginning as they are at any time later.'

'I have told you repeatedly that this is not so,' he said patiently, 'and I shall explain again. The walls of a room absorb light when lights are turned on and lose their reserves throughout the darkness when lights are turned off. When the lights come on again it takes them some time to replenish their supply. When they have re-acquired the correct amount they begin to exude from this supply once more.'

'You picked that nonsense up from Uncle Crispin,' she countered, 'but never mind – just please yourself.'

'Uncle Crispin proved it. He took exhaustive readings on an instrument he had himself invented for that specific purpose. It could register the number of lumens per square metre of wall. He found time and again that the variations were constant.'

'Well, my dear, do as you wish, but don't delay too long. I feel I should rest quite soon.'

He went to her room and switched on the centre light and then the one standing on her bedside locker, checking his watch as he did so. To fill in time he wandered out on to the driveway. It was an April evening, not by any means warm, but with signs of better things to come. The trees were bursting into abundant leaf, the gorse was ablaze once more and Whitethorn blossom decked the hedges. In the distance, worried sheep called out intermittently to their lambs and were answered in bleating chorus. He walked and enjoyed the air until his watch had measured off the thirty minutes he considered adequate for the walls to woo their maximum performance from the lights.

At first, when he opened the sitting-room door he thought Stella had been helped from her chair because she was not to be seen. But when he entered he found she had slumped down and had been hidden from his view by the back of her chair. Only her safety belt kept her from falling to the floor.

For some seconds he feared she was dead. There was no evidence of breathing. But her pulse under his investigating fingers fluttered weakly and her eyes opened momentarily. He straightened her into a sitting posture and was rewarded after a few moments by signs that her breathing had become easier.

Some hours later he found himself once again a passenger in Doctor Slattery's car, trailing for a second time the ambulance that was taking her to hospital. When they got there he felt it necessary to keep vigil and remain throughout the night. In the morning he phoned Frank and Margaret because he knew they would wish it, but when they offered him accommodation he had to decline. Should Stella's condition improve sufficiently to allow him to leave the hospital, he would hurry back to put the domestic affairs of Avonmore on some kind of emergency footing.

'If that should happen,' Frank offered, 'let me know and I'll take you down in the car.'

'Can you spare so much time?'

'Time,' Frank explained, making light of the matter, 'is a commodity I find in plentiful supply at present.'

'It would be a great convenience,' Lemuel admitted. 'In addition, there is something I am very anxious to speak to you about.'

In the afternoon he telephoned to say that Stella's condition was considered stable and it should be safe to make the trip to Avonmore. They would telephone him should there be any sudden change. On the way down he confined his thoughts to his anxiety about Stella's attack. Not only was it her second, but it came at a time when he had already begun to notice a process of general deterioration in her health. But when they were seated over a drink after their arrival, he came directly to the point about Frank's situation.

'I have been told that, in fact, your position in Kenny Morrissey is simply not being restored to you. Is this true?'

'I've been replaced already,' Frank admitted.

'But Margaret and the children – how are you to manage financially?'

'I was given an ex-gratia payment of three months' salary in lieu of notice. I've about two months of that left to find work elsewhere.'

'Is it possible to buy into a job, either as a working investor or a partner?'

'It usually is,' Frank said, 'but not on the remnants of three months' salary.'

'Would three thousand pounds make it possible?'

'Certainly. If one could lay hands on it.'

'Stella and I have spoken about this. Between us we can raise approximately that amount. I am to see Mr Stopford, our solicitor. I am to have him call on Stella also to have her share arranged on her behalf. It will take the form of a long-term loan, with no repayments to commence until the lapse of two years.

Frank hesitated.

'The offer is far too generous, I shouldn't accept,' he said at last. 'But with that kind of money, and with the money Simon Morrissey will get to buy out his partnership interest, the two of us could set up an agency of our own, which I believe would thrive. Simon is well-liked and highly experienced.'

'Then that's settled,' Lemuel announced, glad to have spoken out his wish at last and have his peace of mind restored. 'I have held myself very much responsible for your difficulties. Stella will be as pleased as I am that you have agreed. You and Margaret are both very dear friends.'

On the road home Frank stopped to telephone the news to Margaret and to ask her, if possible, to have Simon and Penny present to meet him and talk about it when he got back. It occupied their thoughts and kept them on edge until a cheque for the money and a covering letter from Stopford & Baggotrath arrived after an interlude of some weeks. They phoned Lemuel and called to see Stella with him to express their gratitude. The change in her shocked them. She was set to slip quietly and irreversibly downhill.

In due course, as had been suspected, the door behind which Miss Downey used to hold court had its Kenny, Morrissey nameplate removed and replaced by a new one:

Kenny Lennon & Co. Ltd
Publishing, Editing and Advertising Agents

Within a few days a door in an office block a few streets away had a new nameplate affixed to it also. It read:

Morrissey, McDonagh & Co.
Publishing, Editing and Advertising Agents.

Chapter 27

Lemuel left down the telephone and stood pondering in the hallway over what the hospital had to say. The word was still the same. Stella was weak but in no immediate danger; that moment, although it was making its slow but sure way, had not yet arrived. They were confident of being well equipped to track its course and alert him in good time, and had spoken to him kindly in their understanding of his deep anxiety. But they had left no room for ambiguity. She would not go home alive.

In the hallway, distant voices from the kitchen and the muffled sounds of crockery only emphasized the stillness elsewhere. He moved into the unlit sitting-room where the silence was total and stood to stare through the window at the approach of night. The fields were all silver and shade, the mountains great black masses. About them shafts of pale yellow light were merging into grey. Across them small black clouds moved steadily and endlessly in marshalled line on line, like a great army bent on the super-terrestrial business of some all-powerful Someone or Something. The window framed it all and the wind, though unheard within the house, was tossing the trees and the hedges. He knew the roads winding high into the mountains above him would be flanked by tormented heather and bracken.

Like people, the seasons came and went. Unlike people, the seasons, in due course, returned. He thought of himself as a youth descending with his companions from those hills on such an evening long years ago; a boy with calf muscles grown stiff from effort, with the sweat on his back grown cold and the chill smell of damp canvas and rubber rising from his cape and haversack. Stella and Margot had been there to greet them then with food and warmth and comfort. A lifetime ago. Several lifetimes ago. If such were possible.

The world was very beautiful: cruel – undeniably; comfortless – certainly; uncaring – yes. But beautiful. Nature put on an unending display of sublime virtuosity in which shape and movement and colour in everchanging combination echoed at times his occasional intimations of immortality, and at others scorned them. It was an immortality, he often felt, far above and beyond the soul of Lemuel Cox. Nevertheless, the soul of Lemuel Cox found it hard not to pine for it.

O my poor soul, he asked, why do you grieve? Why do you look with such longing and heartbreak on these casual and unregarding glories? Because (he answered to himself, and not for the first time) in the end of it all they are the only symbols we have that are fit to stand for the comical aspirations, the laughter, the kindliness and the heartbreak that we lowly clods can, in our rare moments of nobility, encompass. Perhaps, after all, they were not the mere antics of a mindless accident. Perhaps they were indeed manifestations proclaiming the majesty of a creator, which was his usual view of the matter. It puzzled him that he could not only vacillate between the one view and the other: as often as not he could entertain both views at one and the same time.

He sighed and drew the curtains. He left the window. He turned on the lights and then busied himself elsewhere for the required thirty minutes.

Morrissey, McDonagh and Company found from the beginning that they were able to pick up occasional orders here and there with unexpected ease, but only acquired their first regular commission when Joe Dunne transferred responsibility for his Union's monthly *Bulletin* to their care. It expressed his disapproval of P.J.'s treatment of Frank. It also brought Ballcock back on the scene once more. He invited both Frank and Simon to join him for a congratulatory drink.

'For a while,' he told them, 'it looked as though the transfer might not come off. When Joe's decision to bring Frank back into the picture became known there was a move to have the motion about his Russian jaunt put back on the agenda. However, I worked out a way to stymie that one.'

'And what way was that?' Simon asked. He found it difficult to take Ballcock seriously.

'First of all, I advised Joe Dunne to threaten to close down the Co-op and Benevolent Society if the committee persisted in putting the resolution forward. However, he told me he didn't need my advice because that was exactly what he had intended to do. So then I asked his permission to start spreading the word of his intention immediately, and he told me to fire ahead.'

'If he closed them down,' Frank said, 'wouldn't you be left without your post as secretary?'

'I had that one well worked out,' Ballcock explained. 'It was a time to use what I call 'women power'. So I told one of the wives – her name is Lizzie Armstrong – of Joe's intention. I impressed on her that it was in confidence and to keep the information strictly to herself, knowing the oul' bitch couldn't wait to leave my office to announce it to all and sundry. I knew the wives would be up in arms. They couldn't get along without the loans section of the Benevolent. It's their port of call for loans at Christmas and Easter, or when there's a wedding coming up, or when they've to tog out one of the kids making their first Holy Communion or Confirmation, or when the Sunday suit is beginning to fall off himself from age and wear. In two or three days Lizzie had rows raging between husband and wife in every other home where our members lived. The result was the holy willies couldn't wait for the next committee meeting to withdraw the resolution. They came to me beforehand in a blind panic to beg me to tear it up. I told them I would, but with great reluctance.'

'And what was it you said you called that?' Simon asked.

'Women power,' Ballcock repeated. 'I'm a long time on the road now and I've learned most of the rules for survival. One of the most important is to be shrewd and watchful all the time. Make sure you keep your finger on the tempo of the people.'

Simon Morrissey nodded his head in grave and solemn approval. The admiration Frank expressed was quite genuine. Whatever his other activities, Ballcock was a practised politician. Later, when he resumed responsibility for the *Bulletin* it brought a feeling of security which he found welcome. He resumed also, and without resentment, responsibility for correcting the prose in Ballcock's occasional public pronouncements.

Stella died near the end of June. She went quietly. He was present at her bedside but she was unconscious and would not have known. Frank and Margaret were his only company when they took her the long journey from the hospital to the small church outside the village of Edmundscourt. There she lay at rest overnight. In the morning, when her requiem mass had been followed by the last prayers and the burning of incense and the sprinkling of holy water, they took her to the little church and laid her to rest in the grave of her father and mother. A few neighbours joined Frank and Margaret in paying their last respects. None of her blood, except Lemuel, remained to do so. As he watched the graveside ceremony he recalled the little boy who had observed a similar one at the same grave from beneath the rowan tree that grew at the top of the hill and wondered if it could really have been he. When all had been concluded some of the neighbours came back to the house and stayed for a little refreshment and some subdued conversation, and after a polite interval, left.

He took it quietly for a few days afterwards and then set about attending to the tasks before him. He spent some hours on two occasions with Mr Stopford in the offices of Stopford & Baggotrath, and when all had been sifted through and re-arranged he wrote to Frank and Margaret:

Dear Frank and Margaret,

I write first and foremost to thank you both most sincerely for all your kindness to me, and the support you gave unstintingly and at all times during dear Stella's final illness. It made the inevitability of it all easier to bear. She was the last of my line and a sister loved so deeply by me from childhood. When I go myself that will put an end on this earth to the clan that bore me, and to its kith and kin.

I have been to see my solicitors to re-arrange my affairs in the wake of Stella's death. Half the lump sum which my father invested to supply the income that supported Stella and myself will now, in accordance with my father's instructions, be withdrawn and donated to the Church: half of it to the Dominican Order and half of it to the Holy Ghost Fathers for the furtherance of their great missionary work. (When I die myself the other half will be distributed in like fashion).

There remains a capital sum which I have instructed shall, on my demise, be distributed in various proportions to servants of one kind or another. Also remaining is our family house, Avonmore. This is to become the property jointly of Francis and Margaret McDonagh, with my gratitude and blessing.

The debt due in the form of the recent long-term loan has been forgiven in its entirety, as from the signing of the will which took place and was completed yesterday.

I look forward to a visit from you both when I have come to terms with the worst effect of my loss which, I hope, with the grace of God, will not be too long delayed. I will write again soon to invite you so to come.

With my deepest affection.
Sincerely,
Lemuel Cox

A week or so later he saw – or thought he saw – Norris Curtis again. The first time was near the grouping of trees in which the old beech that sheltered his letters stood, but before he could make contact he disappeared among the greenery and, though he searched diligently, was nowhere to be found. The second appearance was also on the river bank, this time on the other side of the Pooka's Pool. It was in the twilight and the figure faded away before he could focus the distance.

Then for days he was on his own. It was lonely enough during the daylight hours; it could be almost unbearable when night came and the hour arrived for sitting alone at the fire which, despite the warm weather, he insisted on having lit. It gave companionship. It lent a modicum of comfort when some common and once unremarked occurrence released the floodgates; simple things such as the creaking of the defective floorboard when he walked past the empty chair to fetch his bottle and glass. He increased his nightly ration a little and found it helped him to sleep. He played the piano hardly at all. It was no longer sufficient to do so for his own ears only. He left a note of his dejection in the tree for his mother. She would understand and her sympathy would somehow reach him.

Dear Mother,
I have been reflecting on the pattern of my life and what I have made of it. I find that, in essence, I have hidden it in the bole of a tree, a refuge I found for it in a secret place amid wilderness and isolation. In the silence of the night, for year after year, moons and stars have hung in the skies above it. Frost has rimed the grass about it a thousand times. The river in spate in winter has thundered, tormented and foam-laced, past it. In seasons of drought it has become a trickle in a bare, stone-strewn bed about it. Its ink has faded.
I am seventy-seven years of age. I am beginning to think that the double seven may make it a propitious year in which to die.
Your loving son,
Lemuel

One evening, after a brief doze, he woke to find the chair on the other side of the fireplace no longer empty.

He exclaimed in surprise,

'Uncle Crispin I do believe!'

'So, you're awake, Lemuel. I thought I'd make a call.'

'That was kind.'

'I applied for leave of absence,' Uncle Crispin explained. 'To tell the truth, I can't bear to see you moping and grieving the way you are.'

'Have you come from heaven?'

'I have. And I don't wish to be kept away from it for too long. It's quite pleasant.'

'And what of hell. And purgatory?'

'It has never been acknowledged officially,' Uncle Crispin answered, lowering his voice, 'but the general belief up above is that hell no longer exists. And in all my time up there I have met only one individual who came via purgatory – a conman who travelled from village to village in the fifteenth century selling sacred relics manufactured by himself. He claimed he had a phial which contained Our Lord's tears. That put the tin hat on the matter and booked him for purgatory.'

Uncle Crispin stood up.

'I want you to take a little stroll with me. The evening is mild. You won't need your coat.'

They walked down the driveway and later along the riverside path. The heat of the early August evening lingered pleasantly.

'I saw you paying one of your visits to that tree of yours the other day,' Uncle Crispin remarked.

'You know about it, then?' Lemuel asked.

'An old beech tree,' Uncle Crispin confirmed. 'Did you know there was a beech in Norbury Park in Surrey at one time which was 160 feet in height. The leaves of the beech are extremely delicate and tender. Evelyn, a friend of Pepys, recommended them as a stuffing for beds instead of straw. They use them for that in Switzerland.'

He led the way past the Pooka's Pool until the valley widened out and sloped down gently to scattered thickets and broad, well-fenced fields, where the marshalled ricks shone golden in the light of the evening sun. The sky beyond was aflame with green and crimson light. They gazed in admiration for some time, then turned and retraced their steps until they were approaching the Pooka's Pool again.

'We must be careful where we walk,' Lemuel warned. 'The recent storm did a lot of damage and there are fallen branches hidden among the grass.'

'You forget I am a pure spirit,' Uncle Crispin said. 'I simply walk through such obstructions.'

They sat down on a fallen tree.

'It was around here,' Lemuel said 'that I lost the watch you gave me. The dress watch you bought in the States.'

'I have a confession to make about that,' Uncle Crispin said. 'I pretended I had bought it in the States because your dear mother might not have cared for the truth. In fact I won it from a professional card sharper in a game of poker while I was attending the Inventions Exhibition in London in 1885. It was one of my rare ventures into a professional gambling den.'

Lemuel appeared not to hear. He was staring out across the pool. The sky had lost most of its light by now and the reeds bordering the river were shadowy silhouettes stirring gently in the light breeze. He remained lost in thought until Uncle Crispin rose to his feet at last and began to move away.

'I know where your thoughts are heading,' he said quietly as he did so.

'Is Stella above with you?' Lemuel asked.

'She is,' Uncle Crispin replied.

'And Margot?'

'Margot, too.'

'Then I wish I could join them.'

'But you can,' Uncle Crispin said.

'How?'

'You know very well how. In fact you are already contemplating it.'

His image faded slowly into the dusk and disappeared. But what Uncle Crispin had meant was very clear to Lemuel. The next day he wrote a note telling Frank how to find the beech tree, and requesting him to remove and burn all that had been hidden there. He propped the note against the face of the clock on the mantelpiece in the evening and, beneath a sky filled once again with greens and crimsons, he went down to the Pooka's Pool and sat for some time in silent thought. The air about him was warm, the silence complete. When he stirred again it was to remove his shoes and stockings and leave them aside. He slid into the water and disappeared beneath the surface. If he was to join her as Uncle Crispin had clearly been hinting, he would start the eager journey from the spot at which their parting had taken place.

When some local children came on him some days later, he was seated on the underwater shelf, his feet jammed into the lower crevices, his hands clamped firmly to the ledge he was sitting on. There were no signs of any last-moment struggle. All was neat, orderly, decorous.

Frank and Margaret got down to the house in late September. Mrs O'Halloran and the other servants had already left, so Simon and Penny came with them for company. The rowan trees were bright with their clusters of red berries, the heather was in bloom along the little mountain pathways. The weather was pleasant. After a hike up to see the shooting lodge which was also a part of the property, and a picnic in the woods on the second day, they dropped Penny and Simon at the station and returned to spend the night on their own. They talked the matter over at some length and decided that, no, to live in the house would not be practicable, if only because of the problem it would pose regarding the children's schooling. It was an obstacle which had been obvious enough from the start. But Margaret had other reservations as well. In the first place, it was spooky.

'There were noises in our bedroom all night through — strange noises,' she complained.

'I didn't hear anything,' said Frank.

'You, my dear, once you settle your head on the pillow, go out like a light. Besides, it's September and the leaves will soon be lying all around the railings of Mount Pleasant Square once again. I want the delight of shuffling through them. Do you remember doing so on our very first meeting? They were nearly knee deep at the time and it's something which has recurred again and again ever since. There are other little things like that which I prize very highly.'

'Of course,' he agreed, 'there are many small but very precious things like that.'

And that night as they lay together in their bedroom, all alone in the largeness and strangeness of the old house, she said:

'Also, I think we should now consider adding to the family. I believe another child would be a good thing for both of us.'

'I think it would too,' he answered, in complete agreement again.

'So that's that,' she said, contented. But a while later she asked:

'Are you asleep?'

'No.'

'There's that noise I spoke of. Can you hear it?'

He levered himself up on his elbow to listen. Then he lay back again.

'Mice,' he concluded.

'I hope so,' she answered.

Some moments later he heard her chuckle softly to herself.

'What's that for?' he questioned.

It was a scrap of verse that had crept into her head from long ago. She said it aloud:

> All dressed in grey a little mouse
> Has made his home within my house . . .

He turned to her.

'Where did that come from, Peggy?' he asked.

'God knows,' she answered, 'from childhood, I suppose. Mother Splendiferous, perhaps—'

When they listened again together, the sound had ceased.

The House For Sale notice went up sometime in November. It was the wrong time of year to expect much interest. But it would be there in place when spring returned and with it the cowslips and the primroses and all the wild and unpretending flowers that would deck in simple loveliness the ditches and the lanes.